Studies in Theology and Sexuality, 7

D1557299

Gospel
and
Gender

A Trinitarian Engagement with
being Male and Female in Christ

Edited by Douglas A. Campbell

Consulting editor: **Alan J. Torrance**

T&T CLARK INTERNATIONAL
A Continuum imprint
LONDON • NEW YORK

British Library Cataloguing-in-Publication Data
A catalogue record for this book is available from the British Library

Library of Congress Cataloging-in-Publication Data
A catalogue record for this book is available from the Library of Congress

Typeset by TMW Typesetting, Sheffield
Printed on acid-free paper in Great Britain by The Cromwell Press, Trowbridge.

ISBN   0-567-08350-0

CONTENTS

PREFACE

This volume of studies was made possible by the Otago Theological Foundation (OTF), whose regular practice is to organize and to undergird financially symposia at the University of Otago, Dunedin, New Zealand, although in 1996 the symposium on gender was also held in collaboration with the Department of Religious Studies. Special gratitude in particular in relation to the publicity and organization of this event is also due to Ms Jenny Beck and Ms Rachel Campbell. It was in large measure thanks to them that an international slate of speakers and a national slate of respondents was so smoothly co-ordinated (Jenny and Andrew Beck were also inordinately generous financially). The OTF itself also depended heavily at this time on the commitment of the indefatigable Hilary Regan, and is deeply grateful to him for his sacrifices of time, energy, and resources. In addition, the discussions at the conference were facilitated by national respondents; however, not all of them were able to contribute self-standing chapters subsequently to this volume—neither were they able to attend the further conference in London in late 1997, as many of the main speakers were. The conference organizers and editors nevertheless remain deeply grateful to Bishop Penny Jamieson, Revd Dr Murray Rae, Caroline Kelly-Johnston, Revd Dr Bruce Hamill, Manuka Henare, and Professor Elizabeth Isichei, for their outstanding contributions. Finally, the OTF and the editors are profoundly grateful to Sheffield Academic Press, who have been so encouraging, diligent and patient.

Douglas A. Campbell

ABBREVIATIONS

AJA	*American Journal of Archaeology*
BA	*Biblical Archaeologist*
BAGD	Walter Bauer, William F. Arndt, F. William Gingrich and Frederick W. Danker, *A Greek–English Lexicon of the New Testament and Other Early Christian Literature* (Chicago: University of Chicago Press, 2nd edn, 1958)
BDF	Friedrich Blass, A. Debrunner and Robert W. Funk, *A Greek Grammar of the New Testament and Other Early Christian Literature* (Cambridge: Cambridge University Press, 1961)
BETL	Bibliotheca ephemeridum theologicarum lovaniensium
BNTC	Black's New Testament Commentaries
BZ	*Biblische Zeitschrift*
BZNW	Beihefte zur *ZNW*
CBQ	*Catholic Biblical Quarterly*
EWNT	H. Balz and G. Schneider (eds.), *Exegetisches Wörterbuch zum Neuen Testament* (3 vols.; Stuttgart: W. Kohlhammer, 1980–83)
HNT	Handbuch zum Neuen Testament
HTKNT	Herders theologischer Kommentar zum Neuen Testament
ICC	International Critical Commentary
JAAR	*Journal of the American Academy of Religion*
JBL	*Journal of Biblical Literature*
JR	*Journal of Religion*
JRE	*Journal of Religious Ethics*
JSNT	*Journal for the Study of the New Testament*
JSNTSup	*Journal for the Study of the New Testament*, Supplement Series
KD	*Kerygma und Dogma*
KEK	Kritisch-exegetischer Kommentar
LSJ	H.G. Liddell, Robert Scott and H. Stuart Jones, *Greek–English Lexicon* (Oxford: Clarendon Press, 9th edn, 1968)
LXX	The Septuagint, i.e. the Greek translation of the Hebrew Old Testament
MR	Mythes et religions
NHC	*Nag Hammadi Codices*
NRSV	New Revised Standard Version

NTS	*New Testament Studies*
RTL	*Revue théologique de Louvain*
SBL	Society of Biblical Literature
SBLDS	SBL Dissertation Series
SBT	Studies in Biblical Theology
SIGC	Studien zur interkulturellen Geschichte des Christentums
SJT	*Scottish Journal of Theology*
SNTSMS	Society for New Testament Studies Monograph Series
SR	*Studies in Religion*
TDNT	Gerhard Kittel and Gerhard Friedrich (eds.), *Theological Dictionary of the New Testament* (trans. Geoffrey W. Bromiley; 10 vols.; Grand Rapids: Eerdmans, 1964–76)
ThHK	Theologischer Handkommentar
TynBul	*Tyndale Bulletin*
WBC	Word Biblical Commentary
WUNT	Wissenschaftliche Untersuchungen zum Neuen Testament
ZNW	*Zeitschrift für die neutestamentliche Wissenschaft*
ZTK	*Zeitschrift für Theologie und Kirche*

CONTRIBUTORS

Veronica Brady, Department of English, Communications and Cultural Studies, University of Western Australia

Douglas A. Campbell, Department of Theology and Religious Studies, King's College London

Judith M. Gundry-Volf, Yale Divinity School

Elaine Storkey, Department of Theology and Religious Studies, King's College London

Joan E. Taylor, Department of Religious Studies, University of Waikato and Department of History, University College London

Alan J. Torrance, Department of Theology, University of St Andrews

Miroslav Volf, Yale Divinity School

Linda Woodhead, Department of Religious Studies, Lancaster University

Douglas A. Campbell

The collection of essays in this volume are the culmination of a long process of research, discussion and reflection, by a select group of biblical, theological and literary scholars, on a central set of problems for the church in its modern context.

The process began in 1996 under the auspices of the Otago Theological Foundation (OTF). As is its regular practice, that organization invited a group of international scholars to a symposium at the University of Otago, Dunedin, New Zealand, to present their views on a particular question or set of questions, in this case organizing the symposium in July 1996 to address the broader issue of gender. The OTF was convinced that previous engagements from Christian perspectives with the question of gender had tended to focus primarily on female problems and viewpoints in isolation or, alternatively, to concentrate in a similarly isolated fashion on male issues (the latter perhaps most often unconsciously in a fundamentally andro-centric church, many feminist theologians would contend). It seemed par-ticularly important then to try to unite reflections on both genders within one discussion on the assumption that such a consideration, by introducing a directly relational and interactional element between the genders into that consideration, might result in more than the mere sum of the two tradition-ally opposed parts. Furthermore, the engagement was to be attempted in specific dialogue with trinitarianism, another rather neglected area within the gender debates, although the latter part of the twentieth century wit-nessed a widespread revival of interest in the resources of trinitarian theology on the part of systematicians. This second commitment created in turn, however, a further—third—set of correlative questions, namely, those provoked by a consideration of the relationship between current construc-tions of gender and trinitarian reflection itself. That is, any theological reflections would now have to proceed in two directions. Not only was it to be asked how the Trinity might impact upon current constructions of gender, both male and female, but it had to be asked simultaneously how those constructions could impact in turn on perceptions of the Trinity; a question necessarily devolving into a careful consideration of language.[1]

This was the agenda, then, for the July 1996 symposium at the University of Otago as arranged by the OTF.[2] The symposium turned out to be a powerful and thought-provoking event. But even as views were being articulated and scrutinized it was becoming apparent that the questions were far from being resolved. Instead, a process of theological inquiry was being pushed through to another stage. Almost all the main speakers decided to reshape their positions significantly in the light of the symposium.

Shortly after this, the Research Institute in Systematic Theology at King's College London (KCL), chaired at this point by one of the Symposium's main speakers (and a founding member of the OTF), Professor Alan Torrance,[3] offered to give the process additional impetus. A further one-day conference was arranged at KCL for November 1997. Two of the Otago Symposium's main speakers were again involved, namely, Professor Torrance himself and Dr Linda Woodhead, but they were joined additionally by Dr Douglas Campbell and Elaine Storkey. Professor Francis Watson[4] also responded to these four speakers and their major presentations. Following this second event, the number of scholars involved in the central group of international invitees and its engagement with the OTF Symposium's important, if difficult, set of issues had expanded effectively to eight figures. But again—and perhaps hardly surprisingly—the speakers wanted time to reconsider their positions in the light of the criticisms offered at the public presentation.

1.   The OTF also wished to arrange the programme in such a way that dialogue was fostered between the group of visiting international scholars and local New Zealand views. So all the main presentations were subjected to critical responses by a representative spectrum of local scholars and churchpeople: Bishop Penny Jamieson, Revd Dr Murray Rae, Caroline Kelly-Johnston, Revd Dr Bruce Hamill, Manuka Henare, Dr Joan Taylor, and Professor Elizabeth Isichei. The OTF remains grateful for the excellent quality of those responses, and the discussions and reformulations that they provoked; something several of the main speakers remarked upon.

2.   An event promoted, coordinated, and run, largely by Jenny Beck, and Douglas and Rachel Campbell, with the assistance of the Department of Religious Studies.

3.   Then a senior lecturer in Systematic Theology at KCL; now a Professor at the University of St Andrews.

4.   Then a Reader in New Testament at KCL; now Professor of New Testament at the University of Aberdeen.

That process is now complete and the resulting essays are collected together in this volume.

Both the OTF, associated with the University of Otago, and the Research Institute in Systematic Theology, based at King's College London, are also interested in the biblical witness to theological reflection, while being aware of the complexity of that relationship. In accordance with this additional foundational methodological commitment, both the Otago Symposium and the shorter London conference involved a considerable amount of reflection on certain key biblical texts; in this debate characteristically drawn from the writings of the Apostle Paul, who tends to table theological information more programmatically than most authors in the New Testament, but who was also forced to confront just the issue of gender at Corinth (prompting immediately the further question as to whether he has been consistent in his own terms). Moreover, Paul has provided the scriptural *leitmotiv* for the entire modern discussion in Gal. 3.28 where precisely the issues of gender, alongside ethnic and social divisions, are brought into some sort of christological correlation, although in pithy and hence somewhat ambiguous formulations (as well as, perhaps somewhat surprisingly, in the original context of a crisis over Jewish law-observance at Galatia). So this crucial but difficult text predictably receives extended treatment here; in fact, both from the hands of Professor Judith Gundry-Volf[5] and Dr Douglas Campbell (KCL). Their essays reflect the differing perspectives circulating in current scholarly debate concerning both this text and the shape of Paul's Gospel as a whole, as well as—probably more importantly—adumbrating important common interpretative ground. Professor Gundry-Volf's analysis also includes the currently important debate concerning the function of this text and its theological implications at Corinth, where both sides of the *ancient* debate seem to be appealing to it. Dr Joan Taylor (Waikato and UCL) also focuses on Paul's practical contingent advice in its Corinthian context, and again assesses this situation from a slightly different vantage point in the current scholarly debate. The result is a fascinating set of reconstructions of this ancient situation, and also a fascinating interplay of scholarly methods and perspectives.

Following this sustained engagement with the programmatic Pauline texts, embracing, somewhat characteristically, both liberational and (to modern eyes) oppressive claims, the essays begin to address the Symposium's central problematic, namely, 'being male and female in Christ'

5. Then at Fuller Theological Seminary; now at Yale Divinity School.

(cf. Gal. 3.28). However, at this point, although committed to the inherent unity of the broad discussion, it proved impossible to address the question of both genders simultaneously, and in trinitarian perspective, before detailed preparatory discussions of one or other gender and their customary scholarly treatment and cultural construction. The first theological essays consequently focus overtly on one gender, and primarily the female, since women have been the main preoccupation of recent gender debates. These essays also evidence, however, a dimension strongly critical of non-christological approaches to such construction that nevertheless claim Christian warrant (see especially the contributions by Dr Woodhead [Lancaster] and Elaine Storkey [KCL]). That is, the criteria whereby critical analyses lay claim nevertheless to represent a Christian perspective on the fundamental matter of gender construction and identity, here primarily female, must themselves be subjected to careful scrutiny otherwise one risks merely displacing one cultural stereotype with another. But the obverse side of this initial feminist criticism, namely, the experience of genuine marginalization and false construction on the part of women, and that often within the church, is also present in the more literary reflections of Professor Veronica Brady (Western Australia). Taken together these studies suggest that the problem of false gender construction and marginalization is genuine and painful, but merely antithetical and hostile responses are an inadequate response to such a situation. The way is thereby prepared for the more constructive and integrated studies that follow.

Professor Torrance then offers a pointed analysis of the dangerous implications of the current presuppositions of the gender debate concerning women for men, at which point the inherently relational nature of the gender issues begins to emerge, as well as the need to ask more searching methodological questions of such analyses.

With these more focused and often critically charged essays complete, the overarching objective of the symposium and its subsequent discussion could be approached more clearly, namely, a consideration of the two genders in relation to one another, and a consideration of trinitarianism itself. So Professor Miroslav Volf[6] argues powerfully and persuasively for the reconciliation of the two genders within their differences in Christ. And Alan Torrance addresses the need for the correct controls on the reconfiguration of our language (which is the central point at issue in our

---

6.   Then at Fuller Theological Seminary; now Professor of Theology at Yale Divinity School.

gendered trinitarian reflection), which is to make recourse to the Trinity itself to control speech about it. In this way the methodological problematic tabled initially by the OTF in 1996 reaches both a methodologically consistent, self-aware, and theologically plausible conclusion, and also offers a practical vision for reconciliation between the genders that is grounded simultaneously in this fundamental divine self-disclosure. In a sense then, these two essays are the climax to our long process of deliberation. All of which is not to say, however, that any of these essays are either an exhaustive analysis or a definitive set of conclusions. Rather, they represent an important and more definitive point within a long process of reflection on a distinctive set of questions from a particular, and arguably fundamental, methodological perspective. And as such they offer considered arguments for certain distinctive future directions and judgments, without claiming to end debate. Indeed, it is to be hoped that as such these recommendations will move the broader discussion of this vital set of issues in both church and society forwards into greater clarity as well as into more effective reconciliation.

Part I

BIBLICAL PERSPECTIVES

BEYOND DIFFERENCE?
PAUL'S VISION OF A NEW HUMANITY IN GALATIANS 3.28

Judith M. Gundry-Volf

Introduction

Galatians 3.28 is clearly Paul's most radical statement about gender identity and roles: 'There is neither Jew nor Greek, there is neither slave nor free, there is no male and female, for you all are one in Christ Jesus.' What precisely does the statement, 'there is no male and female', mean? That sex difference itself is erased in Christ—not literally, but as an eschatological ideal already 'experienced' in baptism, so that believers receive a new identity that is no longer male or female? Does Gal. 3.28 articulate a vision of a humanity beyond sex difference? Or are the religious and social disadvantages and divisions traceable to sex difference thought to be overcome, while the difference itself continues to be significant in some sense, and if so, in what sense? Second, what is the relationship of Christ to gender? How does Paul reflect from his christological 'center' on the 'periphery' of gender identity and relations?

In this chapter I will mount an exegetical argument[1] for the view that Paul does not intend his declaration in Gal. 3.28 as an abolition of sex difference in a new creation of a unified, sexually undifferentiated humanity; rather it refers to the adiaphorization of sex difference in a new creation where being male or female is no advantage or disadvantage in relation to God and others, and where man and woman are reconciled and united as equals. I will try to show that Christ is not portrayed as amalgamating Christians into a new 'one' above fleshly distinctions by virtue of being himself genderless or androgynous; rather he equalizes and unites opposites by his death for them, by their coming to belong to him in the same way—through faith—and by indwelling their (differentiated) flesh

---

1. My argument here goes into considerably more exegetical detail than others which take the same position on this text. Cf., e.g., Snodgrass 1986.

through the Spirit. Within this new humanity of equals created in Christ the creaturely differences remain and play a role in the formation of Christians' new identity and interrelations.

I will develop my argument in dialogue with two recent major discussions of gender identity in early Christianity that reflect the 'abolition of differences' interpretation of Gal. 3.28: Antoinette Clark Wire's *The Corinthian Women Prophets: A Reconstruction through Paul's Rhetoric* (1990), and Daniel Boyarin's *A Radical Jew: Paul and the Politics of Identity* (1994). In many respects these two influential studies—Wire's more in the tradition of modern thought and Boyarin's more in the tradition of postmodern thought—are representative of a dominant trend in reading Paul on the cluster of interrelated questions surrounding the topic of 'Christ and gender', namely, the questions of difference, sameness, equality, hierarchy, and unity as these relate to the character of Christ and salvation. In the course of their wide-ranging discussions, both Wire and Boyarin make many controversial exegetical moves. I will eschew discussion of many of these and present only their construction of gender difference and the relation between Christ and gender as a backdrop for my investigation. Although Wire and Boyarin uncover and highlight important issues concerning this topic, I will argue that both fundamentally misconstrue the way Christ is related to gender in Gal. 3.26-29 and the tradition that lies behind it.

Part 1

Christ and Gender in Antoinette Clark Wire's Interpretation of Galatians 3.28

Adopting the common view that Gal. 3.28 is a piece of early Christian baptismal liturgy,[2] Wire claims that the tradition as it stands in Gal. 3.28, and also Col. 3.10-11, refers to the creation in Christ of *a new humanity no longer characterized by the distinctions 'male' and 'female'*. It is a 're-working of the Genesis story' which declares the original creation 'in the image of God' as 'male and female' to be supplanted by a new creation in Christ, the image of God who is 'not male and female'. The argument rests on (1) the allusion to Gen. 1.27 in Gal. 3.28, 'there is no "male and female"', as well as Col. 3.10-11, 'having put on the new person, being remade for knowledge in the image of the one who created him', and (2)

2.　See below, n. 11.

the understanding of the image of God in Gen. 1.27 as entailing sexual differentiation, *in contrast to* the understanding of Christ as the genderless image of God as presupposed in the baptismal tradition. By virtue of being neither male nor female, Wire argues, Christ bestows on Christians a new, sexually undifferentiated identity.[3] 'All who put on Christ, God's image, are no longer male and female' (1990: 184); they have a 'single common identity' (p. 126). The result of this erasure of differences is the *cancelling of male privilege and the attainment of social gains by women* (p. 126).

Though Paul quotes the baptismal tradition entailing equality through the erasure of differences in Galatians, Wire argues that in 1 Corinthians he 'reverses' it (p. 126)—against the Corinthian women, who affirm it.[4] In 1 Cor. 11.2-16 he argues for the creational *difference* between male and female, and *hierarchy* based on this difference. Here Christ does not ground a new, sexually undifferentiated identity of Christians but grounds the difference and hierarchy between man and woman, as seen especially in 11.3: 'the head of every man is Christ, and the head of woman is man' (pp. 120-21). Tellingly, in 12.12-13 Paul uses the baptismal tradition to support the 'integration of parts with different degrees of honor into a functioning whole "whether Jews or Greeks, slaves or free"' (pp. 185-86). Even 11.11-12, which affirms the interdependence of man and woman 'in the Lord'—'but there is neither woman without man nor man without woman in the Lord, for just as the woman is from the man, so also the man is through the woman'—presupposes that 'in the Lord' the difference between male and female remains. Finally, Wire sees in the statement in 11.12 'that woman's power is through birth' a 'shift away from the identity in Christ that is "not male and female"', particularly for any woman in Corinth practising this identity through sexual abstinence' (p. 128).[5]

---

3.   Wire (1990: 125) rejects the view that the tradition presupposes an androgynous Christ; contrast Betz (1979: 197).

4.   Wire attempts to reconstruct the Corinthian women's views through Paul's rhetoric, a methodology that is open to the charge of 'mirror reading'. But here is not the place to engage in a methodological discussion with her.

5.   The idea of a new creation in the image of a genderless Christ, of course, can easily presuppose a devaluation of the body and of sexuality, which Wire seems eager to avoid attributing to the Corinthian women. On the basis of her reconstruction of their theology as affirming freedom and authority over the body and as stressing 'physical demonstrations of the spirit' (1990: 172), she denies that they would have thought of 'Christ as an *ideal* image rather than a *sense-perceptible, sexual body*' (emphasis mine), or that 'when putting on Christ as God's image according to the baptismal tradition, they would see themselves as heavenly humans, made before

What then is the fate of Paul's assertion of a new genderless humanity through Christ in Gal. 3.28? Wire answers that in 1 Corinthians he is still in basic agreement with the Corinthian women about this, for in the process of defending the status quo he does not outright deny either the idea of a 'genderless Christ' or the correlation between a 'genderless Christ' and the equality of the sexes that the Corinthian women assert on the basis of the tradition. Yet he relegates a genderless humanity to the future, whereas they claim it for the present. In their view already now 'male and female are related in the same way to Christ as God's image' (p. 125), but Paul 'delays human identification with Christ until the future in his defense of the resurrection of the dead, distinguishing the earthly Adam or first human being whose image of dirt they have borne from the last, life-giving Adam or second human being whose heavenly image they will bear (15.45-49)' (p. 123).[6]

Adam's time and directed to spiritual wisdom rather than physical desire', along the lines of a Platonizing exegesis of Genesis (pp. 171-72). She even remarks in passing that the Corinthian women prophets viewed Christ as the *female* wisdom of God who was present in their own hearing and speaking (pp. 53, 187). Yet these claims appear incompatible with Wire's view that they saw Christ as the image of God 'not male and female' and themselves as 'no longer male and female'. It is clear why both assertions concerning Christ in relation to Christian identity are important: one grounds equality between the sexes and the overcoming of social divisions, and the other preserves a positive view of the body and of woman. The tension between the two contrasting claims, however, goes unrecognized in Wire's discussion and raises questions about her account of the relation between Christ and gender in the baptismal tradition as both the Corinthian women and Paul interpreted it (the difference between them being Paul's relegating the new creation to the future instead of the present, as noted above).

6.   Wire's overarching thesis is that both the Corinthian women's and Paul's theologies of gender and their christological bases are rooted in their social experience (1990: 188-95). The 'women prophets achieve a rising social status in the church', which fosters their theology of new creation in the Christ-image not male and female. They experience Christ as the risen One, the 'life-bringer', who sets them free, endows them unreservedly with knowledge and speech, replaces their shame with honor, and makes them mediators of God to others. Paul's social status, on the other hand, is falling, which corresponds to his theology of suffering, shame and subordination. For Paul, Christ is the crucified one who leads this free, educated, male Roman citizen down a cruciform path of suffering and shame. Paul's experience of suffering and social loss thus leads him to reject the idea of present oneness without difference in Christ which elevates those who have a low status to full equality. He proposes instead leaving everyone in their place and not upsetting the social hierarchy, lest others rise as he falls. The social conflict between Paul and the Corinthian women prophets is directly related to this conflict between their theologies, in Wire's reading.

Is the normative construction of the relation between Christ and gender that Wire attributes both to the Corinthian women and to Paul plausible? Does Christ, ideally, erase gender differences? Before I explore this question further, I will look at Daniel Boyarin's interpretation of Gal. 3.28 and note both agreements and disagreements with Wire.

Christ and Gender in Daniel Boyarin's Interpretation of Galatians 3.28

According to Boyarin, 'Paul was impelled by a vision of human unity born of two parents: Hebrew monotheism and Greek longing for universals' (1994: 228). The dominant influence, 'a Hellenistic desire for the One', produced among other things 'an ideal of a universal human essence, beyond difference and hierarchy' (p. 7). 'This universal humanity, however, was predicated…on a dualism of the flesh and the spirit, such that while the body is particular, marked through practice as Jew or Greek, and through anatomy as male or female, the spirit is universal' (p. 7). Universal oneness is attained 'beyond and outside of the body' (p. 24) at the level of the spirit. Boyarin takes Gal. 3.28 as the key expression of Paul's ideal of a spiritual oneness beyond difference and hierarchy, and elevates the last verses of this chapter through ch. 4 to the hermeneutical key to Paul's thought as a whole. Here 'Paul makes most explicitly and passionately clear his stake in Christ, namely the erasure of human differences, primarily the difference between Jew and gentile but also that between man and woman, freeman and slave' (p. 22).

Paul's Christology, according to Boyarin, is characterized by the same flesh/spirit dualism (in which the flesh is subordinate to the spirit) as Paul's anthropology, which is crucial for Paul's ideal of universal oneness. Boyarin writes:

> The coming of Christ is, in fact, the perfect model for Paul's ontology, for just as Christ had a physical nature and a spiritual nature (Romans 9.5), and both are valuable, though the former is subordinate to the latter, so also the physical observances of the Torah and the people of Israel. On the present reading, the fundamental insight of Paul's apocalypse was the realization that the dual nature of Jesus provided a hermeneutic key to the resolution of that enormous tension that he experienced between the universalism of the Torah's content and the particular ethnicity of its form. Paul understood both the dual nature of Christ's person as well as the crucifixion in the light of the familiar platonic dichotomy of the outer and the inner, the material and the spiritual, or in Paul's own terminology, the flesh and the spirit. Jesus was explicitly of a dual ontology, having an outer aspect of the flesh and an inner aspect of the spirit, or in more properly hermeneutic terms:

There was a Christ according to the flesh (ὁ Χριστὸς τὸ κατὰ σάρκα [Romans 9.5])—which corresponds to the literal, historical Jesus—and a Christ according to the spirit—the allegorical, risen Christ... [Romans 1.3-4] (1994: 29).

Presupposing this split between the 'fleshly' and the 'spiritual' Christ, Boyarin argues that 'putting on Christ' in baptism (Gal. 3.27) refers to incorporation into the *risen Christ, the Christ according to the spirit*. In baptism believers put off the individual body, which is male or female, and 'put on Christ', or 'the non-corporeal body of the risen Christ', which is neither male nor female (pp. 24-25). Christ is here essentially spirit, devoid of any corporeality through which particularity subsists. Through incorporation into this Christ 'all the differences that mark off one body from another as Jew or Greek...male or female, slave or free, are effaced, for in the Spirit such marks do not exist' (p. 23). Christ, the one and the Spirit, overplays the particularities of the body and hence unites all in one 'universal human essence beyond difference and hierarchy'. Although at the level of the flesh differences continue to subsist—for Paul is no simple dualist, denying the body and affirming the spirit, as 1 Corinthians amply demonstrates with its thematization of the body and 'fleshly concerns'—at the higher level of the spirit differences disappear, and this undifferentiated *spiritual* oneness is what Paul is claiming in Gal. 3.26-29.[7]

To make plausible Paul's ideal of a universal, undifferentiated, spiritual oneness Boyarin compares Philo's ideal of spiritual androgyny (pp. 19-22, 187-91). For Philo the original Adam made in the image of God according to Genesis 1 was an unbodied, singular creature whose male-and-female-ness must be understood spiritually. Or in Philo's words, 'he' was 'neither male nor female'. Genesis 2 introduces an entirely different creation, a carnal Adam who is male and from whom the female is constructed. Bodily gender was thus not part of the original creation of 'Man'. More-over, Philo thinks of embodiment and the division into two sexes which results from it as highly problematic. The paradisiac notion of the man leaving his father and mother and cleaving to his wife and becoming one flesh with her is thus interpreted allegorically by Philo to refer to the mind abandoning God the Father of the universe, and God's excellence

---

7.　Boyarin does not see a contradiction between Galatians and 1 Corinthians on gender. Rather Galatians emphasizes oneness at the level of the spirit over against too much stress on the flesh, while 1 Corinthians emphasizes differences at the level of the body over against those who have gone too far in the pneumatic direction (1994: 190, 195).

and wisdom, the Mother of all things, and cleaving to sense-perception and resolving itself into the inferior order of flesh. Embodiment and the division into male and female is thus something to be overcome through denial of passion and return to the original, undifferentiated, androgynous, spiritual Adam. Boyarin proposes that 'Paul, no less than Philo, sought to overcome that embodiment' (p. 22) which was the source of the fateful division into genders, and that Paul's ideal too is a spiritual androgyny, which correlates with Christ's 'spirituality'.

This ideal is found both in Gal. 3.28 and in 1 Cor. 11.11, according to Boyarin. 'In the Lord' in 1 Cor. 11.11 corresponds to 'in Christ' of Gal. 3.28. And if, he continues, we translate (with Josef Kürzinger) the Corinthian text as 'woman is not different from man nor man from woman', this 'perhaps speculative interpretation [of 1 Cor. 11.11 as referring to spiritual androgyny]' would be dramatically strengthened (pp. 194-95). Thus, Boyarin concludes, we can read 'both passages as a representation of an androgyny that exists on the level of the spirit' (p. 194).

To summarize, in Boyarin's reading of Gal. 3.26-29 Christ *the Spirit* erases gender difference *at the level of the spirit* and restores the ideal of a universal *disembodied* humanity beyond difference and hierarchy. Thus Boyarin, unlike Wire, portrays Paul as 'a passionate striver for human liberation and equality' (p. 9) whose driving vision expressed in Gal. 3.28 was that of a 'non-differentiated, non-hierarchical humanity' (p. 8), a 'new humanity in which indeed all difference would be effaced in the new creation in Christ' (p. 187). Like Wire, however, Boyarin thinks that Paul (by and large) postpones the new creation beyond difference until the future. It could not 'be entirely achieved on the social level *yet*' (p. 187). Paul was 'realistic' enough (p. 200) both about social conditions in the first century and about the passions of the flesh to know that, though 'in the life of the spirit…there may be no male and female', in 'the life of the body there certainly is' (p. 185). His vision of universal undifferentiated oneness, however, still had 'social meaning' (p. 187) and was even also historically powerfully effective (cf. pp. 228-60).

Boyarin, the postmodern cultural critic, goes on to offer a radically different evaluation than Wire of the erasure of differences which, in both of their views, is implied in Gal. 3.28. The erasure of differences is not unambiguously good! Though Paul's stress on universality, equality and tolerance is important, Boyarin also calls them into question from a postmodern perspective. The very passion for equality, he argues, made Paul's thought 'deeply flawed' because it led him 'for various cultural reasons, to

equate equality with sameness' (p. 9). For it was 'only in a social acting out of a disembodied spiritual existence [presupposing sameness],
that gender parity ever existed' in early Christianity (p. 196, citing Clark
1986). To be equal to men, women had to adopt celibacy—that is, re-
nounce female sexuality and maternity. As proof, Boyarin points to 1 Cor.
7.32-35 and much of the immediate post-Pauline tradition (pp. 196-97; cf.
Clement of Alexandria, *Gospel of Thomas* and other literature of early
Christianity) and also to the celibate Therapeutrides in Philo's *Vita Contemplativa*. Virgins, however, are no longer really women but 'andro-
gynes, a representation, in the appearance of flesh, of the purely spiritual
nongendered, presocial essence of human being' (p. 196). Furthermore,
'the erasure of gender seems always to have ended up positing maleness as
the norm to which women can "aspire"' (p. 8). There are thus fundamental
problems with the universalizing and spiritualizing impulse leading to
'equality' that emanated from Paul.

The important differences between Wire and Boyarin (on the intention
of Paul and on the valorization of the erasure of differences) notwithstanding, notice four significant commonalities. First, both Wire and Boyarin
presuppose that in Paul's mind the erasure of differences is needed to
achieve equality, and inversely, the affirmation of differences is construed
to entail hierarchy. (Wire implicitly affirms this thought whereas Boyarin
highlights its flaws.) Second, according to both, Paul (and for Wire, the
Corinthian women too) understands the ideal state which is to be realized
eschatologically as a state of such equality with all differences erased.
When Paul insists on gender differences this side of the eschaton it is either
to exercise social control over women (Wire) or because he has to make
concessions to the stubborn realities of social and bodily life (Boyarin).
Third, they agree on the 'mechanism', so to speak, by which equality is
achieved. Men and women must become *like* Christ—either like the image
of God 'beyond gender' (Wire) or like the resurrected Christ 'beyond the
particularizing body' (Boyarin). Christ unites and equalizes those who are
different by erasing their differences in the act of bestowing upon them his
own identity. Fourth, and most generally, both Wire and Boyarin construe
the problem Paul is dealing with, and therefore the solution he is offering,
along the categorical axis of 'sameness' and 'difference'. Difference is the
problem Paul is combating because it entails hierarchy; sameness is the
solution Paul is offering (or, in Wire's reading, considers to be appropriately implemented only in the eschaton) because it entails equality. In
the remainder of this essay I want to challenge all four of these opinions

that Wire and Boyarin share; my discussion will center, however, on the second and third commonalities.

Part 2

Wire and Boyarin make the methodological decision to interpret Gal. 3.28 primarily in the light of parallels outside Galatians, and in Boyarin's case, within the cultural context of the hellenistic world broadly speaking. In so doing they fall within a major methodological trend in the study of this text. Wayne Meeks first substantially developed this approach in his influential article, 'The Image of the Androgyne: Some Uses of a Symbol in Earliest Christianity'(1973–74), where he uses comparative material to locate Gal. 3.28 within the widespread hellenistic tradition of 'reunification' through the erasure of differences. He notes the similarity between Gal. 3.28 and statements in later Christian writings that express eschatological expectation in terms of the abolition of differences, including the difference between 'male' and 'female'. For example, in *Gospel of Thomas* 22 Jesus says: 'When you make the two one...and when you make the male and the female one and the same, so that the male not be male nor the female female...then will you enter [the kingdom]'.[8] Meeks goes on to argue that 'no male and female' in Gal. 3.28 reverses the fateful division of Gen. 2.21-22 and declares the original masculofeminine divine image—'male and female', Gen. 1.27—restored in a new creation of an androgynous humanity without the gender dimorphism of the original creation.[9] Henning Paulsen (1979–80) argues similarly for the hellenistic notion of reunification in Gal. 3.28 and even expressly rejects the view that it denies only the religious significance of difference. Hans Dieter Betz also favors this interpretation and suggests that an androgynous Christ image stands behind the baptismal formula (Betz 1979: 197; also MacDonald 1987). Boyarin, as already noted, agrees that androgyny is in view and draws on Paul's contemporary Philo for support, while Wire argues for genderlessness rather than androgyny and appeals chiefly to the baptismal tradition in Col. 3.10-11.

8.   *NHC* II 2.37, 25-35. The dominical saying is also found in the Tractatus Tripartitus of the Nag Hammadi Library, *NHC* I 5.132.16-28; *2 Clement* 12.2-6; the *Gospel of the Egyptians* as quoted by Clement of Alexandria, *Strom.* III 13.92.2; see also *Gos. Phil.* 70; see Paulsen 1979–80: 82 n. 35 for other references.

9.   Meeks 1973–74: 185. The probable allusion to Gen. 1.27 LXX in Gal. 3.28 is commonly noted. Litke (1995) has recently argued for a citation. On the ancient ideal of androgyny, cf. Baumann 1955; Delcourt 1958; and Eliade 1965.

But is this methodological starting point plausible (regardless of whether one ends up—in the process of exegesis—affirming that Paul agrees with the 'hellenistic one' or not)? Yes, if one is interested in interpreting Gal. 3.28 as a free-floating tradition. But is it plausible if one is interested in deciphering the meaning it had *for Paul in Galatians* as I am trying to do here rather than what it could have meant outside its present literary context and as a baptismal tradition in a hellenistic setting? The question I am posing is, insofar as Gal. 3.28 is a piece of *Pauline theologizing*, does it express the ancient ideal of an undifferentiated humanity, and do the hellenistic parallels about the erasure of differences rooted in the body and in fleshly existence unlock the meaning of Paul's statement? On the one hand, the basic assumption is correct that the cultural context can shed light on Paul's claim, and it is also true that the results of this methodology seem to correspond to the 'plain meaning' of 'there is no male and female'. Moreover, given the absence of any thematization of *gender* difference and unity in Galatians, this approach seems to win by default. On the other hand, it is essential that the statement be compatible with Paul's argument in Galatians and find support from his thought elsewhere. To interpret adequately the claim, 'there is no male and female', I propose that we need to proceed along the following two routes. First, we need to examine the larger argumentative context in which the phrase is embedded and at whose culmination it appears (Gal. 3.6-29), and do so within the broader framework of Paul's reflection on similar issues elsewhere.[10] Second, we need to explore whether the theological grounding Paul gives the phrase—being 'in Christ', 'baptized into Christ', 'put on Christ', 'one in Christ', or 'belonging to Christ'—in any way entails the erasure of differences, and if so, in what sense. These two routes form the basic outline of the second part of this essay.

'There is neither Jew nor Greek'

The context in which the statement 'there is no male and female' is embedded does not make immediately clear what those words mean. Interpreters have often commented on the lack even of discussion of sexuality or gender issues in Galatians, and this lack is one of the main supports for the view that the statement is part of a baptismal formula inserted into the argument here, though not relevant in all particulars.[11] Even if we accept

10. Cf. the similar approach by Thyen 1978 and Witherington 1980–81.

11. Arguing that the statements about slave and free, and male and female, do not appear relevant to Paul's argument in Galatians, many scholars have detected a

Brigitte Kahl's (2000) argument that Galatians is indeed concerned with sexuality and gender issues, since the central point of debate is circumcision, we will still have to conclude that Paul nowhere in this letter explains what he means by 'there is no male and female'. Since he does, however, speak amply to the issue of Jew and Gentile in Galatians, we can proceed to determine the sense of the parallel assertion, 'there is neither Jew nor Greek', and then extrapolate from the clear to the obscure ('there is no male and female').[12]

The baptismal formula is found in the concluding part of Paul's argument in 3.6-29. Significantly, interpreters have understood the closing verses (3.26-29) of this section as 'the goal which Paul has been driving at all along' (Betz 1979: 81) and 'the presupposition for Paul's argumentation all along' (Hays 1983: 232; see also Paulsen 1979–80: 75). This is indicated by the concentration of key terms from 3.6-25 in 3.26-29 (υἱοί, πίστις, Ἀβραάμ, σπέρμα, ἐπαγγελία, κληρονομία, κληρονομοί), the allusion to the crucial event of baptism in 3.27 (εἰς Χριστὸν ἐβαπτίσθητε, Χριστὸν ἐνεδύσασθε), and the concluding δέ clause in 3.29, which extends and caps the argument of this section. We are then to interpret 3.26-29 in the light of 3.6-25.

In this main section Paul argues that faith in Christ is the distinguishing mark of God's eschatological people—as seen with Abraham himself, the original recipient of the promises, who was reckoned righteous as a believer apart from being a Jew under the Law—over against the intruders' teaching that Jewish identity markers (circumcision and other key works of the Law) were essential to membership in God's eschatological people. In this light the statement 'there is neither Jew nor Greek' in 3.28 should be taken as *denying the presumed significance of fundamental Jewish and*

---

traditional formula in 3.28 (Betz 1979: 181; Meeks 1973–74: 180-81; Paulsen 1979–80: 77-78; Schüssler Fiorenza 1983: 208, and others). The arguments for the view that 3.28a-c is taken from early Christian baptismal liturgy are (1) the complex structure; (2) the occurrence of similar statements with pairs of opposites in 1 Cor. 12.13 and Col. 3.11; (3) the occurrence of baptismal motifs in the contexts; and (4) the use of motifs that are foreign to the context or merely loosely related (male and female, slave and free in Gal. 3, as well as in 1 Cor. 12, and Col. 3). Schüssler Fiorenza also sees traditional material in 3.26 and 3.27 (1983: 208), but this view is contested (see Paulsen 1979–80: 87-88). Some also contest that the baptismal formula is pre-Pauline (Eckstein 1996: 223 n. 225).

12. For this interpretative strategy, see also W.S. Campbell (1991: 110), and Thyen (1978: 111-12). On the middle pair, slave and free, see Thyen (1978: 156-68), and Lührmann (1975).

Gentile identity markers for inheritance of the eschatological blessings and membership in the people of God. What made a Jew a Jew or a Greek a Greek was irrelevant in this respect. Or, to borrow Paul's own terminology, the traditional marks of religio-ethnic identity are *adiaphora*.

It is important to note here that Paul nowhere in 3.6-25 argues that Jews should stop being Jews, or Gentiles should stop being Gentiles in the new age inaugurated in Christ. He makes no attempt to abolish the differences between the two themselves as a way of integrating both Jew and Greek into the eschatological people of God. Instead he opposes the imposition of a particular identity according to the flesh upon anyone. The rest of Galatians provides further confirmation for this conclusion.

I will focus on two texts in particular from the later chapters of Galatians that provide especially strong support for my view.[13] In 5.6 Paul writes: 'In Christ Jesus neither circumcision counts for anything (τι ἰσχύει) nor uncircumcision counts for anything, but faith working through love'. And in 6.15, similarly: 'neither circumcision is anything (τί ἐστιν) nor uncircumcision is anything, but new creation' (6.15).[14] Here we have a saying that explicitly states the adiaphoral character of circumcision, in Paul's view. The saying plays an important role in Galatians, as seen by its double appearance, the emphatic position of its second appearance at the very close of the letter, and the description of it as a κανών, 'rule', in 6.16. H.D. Betz describes the circumcision saying as 'the cutting edge of the whole letter' (Betz 1979: 263 n. 93).

Building on these observations, I would like to argue that Paul uses the circumcision saying to indicate the meaning of the traditional saying in 3.28, 'there is neither Jew nor Greek' (cf. Betz 1979: 262). In favor of such a direct link between the two it should be noted that: (1) The sayings have corresponding pairs of opposites: circumcision/uncircumcision and Jew/Greek; indeed, περιτομή and ἀκροβυστία may be used metonymously for Ἰουδαῖοι and Ἕλλην (cf. Gal. 2.7-9; Rom. 3.30; 4.9; Col. 3.11), in which case the referents are the same in both sayings.[15] (2) The

---

13. Further arguments are Paul's noting that his Greek companion Titus was not compelled to be circumcised in Jerusalem (2.3); his circumcision-free gospel was not supplemented in any way by the Jerusalem pillars (2.1-10); those who are by nature Jewish (φύσει Ἰουδαῖοι) and have 'works of Law' have nevertheless believed in Christ for justification (2.16); the Gentiles have received the Spirit by hearing with faith, even though they have no works of Law (3.1-5). See further below.

14. Similarly, 1 Cor. 7.19: 'circumcision is nothing [οὐδέν ἐστιν] and uncircumcision is nothing, but keeping the commandments of God'.

15. D.A. Campbell (1996) has argued persuasively that the baptismal formula in

sayings follow the same basic structure: a double negation (οὐκ ἔνι...
οὐκ ἔνι, 3.28a; οὔτε...οὔτε, 5.6; 6.15) followed by a contrasting positive
assertion ('for [γάρ] you are all one in Christ Jesus', 3.28d; 'but [ἀλλά]
faith working through love', 5.6; 'but [ἀλλά] new creation', 6.15). (3)
They are embedded in contexts with similar argumentation: justification
by law versus justification by faith in Christ (2.16-17, 22; 5.4-5), reception
of the Spirit (3.2-5; 5.5), and death/crucifixion with Christ and new
creation (2.19-20; 6.14-15). (4) The ἐν Χριστῷ formula appears in 5.6[16]
and in 3.26, 28. (5) They appear at key junctures of Paul's argument in
Galatians: 3.28 is part of the culmination of the argument in 3.6-29, and
6.15 forms a climactic close to the letter. Thus I conclude that the Pauline
'rule' stating unambiguously that circumcision/uncircumcision 'counts for
nothing' (οὔτε...τι ἰσχύει) and 'is nothing' (οὔτε...τί ἐστιν) explicates
the somewhat enigmatic assertion, 'there is neither (οὐκ ἔνι) Jew nor
Greek', of the earlier baptismal formula. In that formula, therefore, Paul is
also referring to the adiaphorization of traditional religio-ethnic identity
markers. Possibly Paul intended in this way to rule out interpretations of
the baptismal formula that he regarded as illegitimate.[17]

Daniel Boyarin has raised the objection that Paul's adiaphorization of
circumcision/works of the Law amounts precisely to the *erasure* of the
difference between Jew and Greek. As Boyarin points out, part and parcel
of the religious Jew's self-understanding is that circumcision is *not* a
matter of indifference. Paul's flexibility on the keeping of Jewish food
laws 'thoroughly undermines any argument that Paul intended Jews to remain Jewish' (Boyarin 1994: 9-10). By adiaphorizing circumcision and food
laws, Boyarin concludes, Paul is 'inimical to Jewish difference' (p. 156).

Yet one has to make room for the evidence that Paul expected Jews to
continue to circumcise their males; that he himself retained a Jewish

---

Col. 3.11 is structured chiastically, so that 'Jew' corresponds to 'circumcision' and
'Greek' to 'uncircumcision', which indicates that 'circumcision' and 'uncircumcision'
are used metonymously for 'Jew' and 'Greek' there.

16. In some textual tradition ἐν Χριστῷ Ἰησοῦ (a A C D F G M) also appears in
6.15.

17. Cf. 1 Cor. 12.13, 'for we all by one Spirit have been baptized into one body,
whether Jews or Greeks...', which appears to be a reformulation of the baptismal
tradition avoiding the implication of erasure possible in Gal. 3.28. There is no such
attempt in Col. 3.11: 'there is no Greek and Jew, no circumcision and uncircumcision...'. The tension between this statement and the Pauline rule about circumcision/
uncircumcision in Galatians may suggest that Col. 3.11 is a deutero-Pauline
formulation.

identity as a Christian (cf. 2 Cor. 11.22; Phil. 3.5; cf. Rom. 9.3; 11.14); and that he elsewhere *prohibits* the erasure of both Jewish and Gentile difference ('Was anyone at the time of his call already circumcised? Let him not seek to remove the marks of circumcision. Was anyone at the time of his call uncircumcised? Let him not seek circumcision. Circumcision is nothing and uncircumcision is nothing, but keeping the commandments of God', 1 Cor. 7.18-19).[18] He accepts, and even insists on retaining, the differences as ethnic-identity markers at the same time as he strips them of soteriological relevance. So, then, we cannot conclude that Paul is inimical to *all* Jewish difference. Rather we ought to conclude that for Paul circumcision/works of the Law have mutated from a religio-ethnic identity-marker to an ethnic identity-marker. This may not satisfy from a Jewish perspective, but clearly no total erasure of differences is entailed.

In conclusion, the immediate context of Gal. 3.28 suggests that the assertion 'there is neither Jew nor Greek' is not about erasure of differences but revalorization of differences. The point is not that fleshly differences do not persist in the eschatological community, but that they do not and should not 'count'. Jewishness is not essential; Greekness is no disadvantage. Thus within the single people of God neither should Jews become like Gentiles[19] nor Gentiles like Jews, nor both become 'one new humanity which is neither' (with W.S. Campbell 1991: ch. 4). For the new unity and equality of the community is attained not through the elimination of differences but through their revalorization.[20]

By analogy, we can conclude, the assertion 'there is *no male and female*' does not refer to the erasure of differences, either through return to (spiritual) androgyny (Boyarin)[21] or through attainment of a new genderless identity in Christ (Wire). Interpreters who reject that view are correct,

18. Paul does this for reasons rooted in his soteriology: erasing the marks of being Jew or Gentile would, just as much as insisting on Gentile law-keeping, imply the soteriological relevance of these marks, with unacceptable consequences for Paul's understanding of Christ and his saving death. 1 Cor. 7.17-24 with its prohibition of erasure of differences is all the more significant for our reflections on Gal. 3.28 in that 1 Cor. 7.17-24 can be seen as an extended commentary on Gal. 3.28 (see Scroggs 1972: 293; and Gundry-Volf 1994a).

19. Eckstein (1996: 119) has rightly argued that Gal. 3.8-9 does not suggest that Jews have to see themselves first as 'Gentiles' in order to have a part in the blessing promised to Abraham (Gen. 12.1-3).

20. See also Stauffer 1964 and Dunn 1993a: 93.

21. Against the interpretation of Gal. 3.28 in terms of androgyny, see Trible 1978: 18; Schrage and Gerstenberger 1981: 150; Snodgrass, 1986: 171; and Wire 1991: 125.

The Gospel and Gender

as my exegesis supports.[22] Instead the possibility presents itself that the reference to 'no male and female' refers to the *adiaphorization of sexual difference* in the new creation in Christ. That would mean that maleness or femaleness is irrelevant for membership in the people of God (as made tangible by the fact that the Christian rite of initiation, baptism, is for women as well as men, by contrast to the Jewish rite of circumcision). Distinct sexual identities would remain significant in some sense, but lose their significance with respect to salvation and participation in the eschatological people of God.[23]

The Christological Basis of Equality in Galatians 3.28
The thesis that sexual and gender differences are erased in Christ, which underlies some of the contemporary egalitarian readings of Gal. 3.28c, is not supported by the larger argument in Galatians. Could it be, however, that the soteriological and christological underpinnings Paul gives to the claims, 'there is neither Jew nor Greek, there is neither slave nor free, there is no male and female', in the immediate context (3.26-29) drive him beyond what his larger argument (especially 3.6-29) suggests and demands, and that the inner logic of these underpinnings implies the erasure of differences? After all, the baptismal unit opens with the words, 'you *all* (πάντες) are sons of God' (3.26), and closes with, 'you are seed of Abraham and heirs' (3.29). It will be recalled that Boyarin, Wire and others have argued that the equality as 'sons', 'seed', and 'heirs' rests on the erasure of differences as Jew/Greek, or male/female, and on becoming 'the same as Christ'. Those who were once different through the flesh are seen to have

22. Cf. W.S. Campbell (1991: 110): 'despite what our baptismal formula seemed to suggest, sexual differences are not eliminated within the Christian community, even if for a time in the earliest days some Christians attempted to make it their ideal'; Scroggs (1972: 293): Paul himself 'does not...advocate the elimination of the distinctions themselves' (cf. Jewett 1979: 74-75); Schüssler Fiorenza (1983: 211): 'Gal. 3.28c does not assert that there are no longer men and women in Christ.'

23. I leave the question of the implication of socio-ecclesial equality for a different occasion. Many have made Gal. 3.28 the basis of a Pauline/early Christian notion of gender equality (cf. Stendahl 1966: 32-33; Schüssler Fiorenza 1983: 210-13; W.S. Campbell 1991: 109; Scroggs 1972: 288, 293; Betz 1979: 189; Bruce 1982: 190; and Jewett 1979: 65, who comments, 'the authentic Pauline letters move on a progression that leads to a full acknowledgement of equality, while maintaining an insistence on the divinely given quality of sexual difference' [pp. 74-75]). Yet some recent interpreters, despite their own sympathies, have denied that Paul has equality in view (see Martyn 1997a: 377, and Martin 1998).

died to the flesh and risen with Christ. They have 'put on Christ', and are 'in Christ' as 'one [undifferentiated] person'.

The crucial question, however, is whether these soteriological claims imply more than that all Christians, with all their differences in ethnicity, social background, and gender, *share something in common on equal terms which unites them.* In the following I will examine whether the soteriological and christological foundations of the claim, 'there is no male and female', entail such erasure of difference and thereby trump the simple adiaphorization (not erasure) of differences that is implied in Paul's larger argument in Galatians. I will investigate (1) whether the key soteriological terms in 3.26-29 imply a relationship of identity with Christ; (2) how Christ is soteriologically related to existence 'in the flesh' (2.19-20); (3) what 'one' (εἷς) in the claim, 'you all are one', means (3.28d). On the basis of these considerations I will ask (4) whether the fundamental *problem* to which Paul gives an answer in 3.28 is primarily that of differences in the flesh.

(1) *Soteriological Terms.* Do the key soteriological ideas that support and explain the claim, 'there is no male and female'—namely, 'baptism into Christ', 'putting on Christ', 'in Christ', and being 'of Christ'—suggest that Paul conceives of salvation in analogy to the hellenistic abolition of all differences and merging into undifferentiated oneness? Do believers' relationships with Christ replace their difference with sameness?

'You are Christ's'. The concluding inference in 3.29, 'now if you are Christ's' (εἰ δὲ ὑμεῖς Χριστοῦ)—which states a fulfilled condition based on the preceding statements that the readers are (1) 'sons of God through faith, in Christ'[24] (3.26); (2) have been 'baptized unto Christ' (3.27a); and (3) have 'put on Christ' (3.27b) (Burton 1962: 208)—clearly offers no support for the thesis of erasure of differences in Christ. Instead, the idea of belonging to Christ underlines *the abiding difference of the believer and Christ.* It also suggests what kind of relation to Christ—namely, belonging—is the essence of Paul's argument.[25] E.D. Burton captures Paul's

---

24. ἐν Χριστῷ does not modify διὰ τῆς πίστεως—'through faith in Christ Jesus'—'a construction which appears only in the deutero-Pauline letters' (Dunn 1993a: 131 n. 17). Rather it is an adverbial addition and indicates that Christians' 'sonship' (υἱοὶ Θεοῦ ἐστε) is grounded and constituted ἐν Χριστῷ (Oepke 1973: 123).

25. For the concept 'belong to Christ', see also Gal. 5.24; 1 Cor. 1.12; 3.23; 15.23; 2 Cor. 10.7; Rom. 8.9.

logic in 3.29 correctly when he paraphrases: 'If you belong to Christ, who
is the seed of Abraham, you share his standing as such' (Burton 1962:
210). Believers share something with Christ because they belong to him
(rather than become indistinguishable because they are merged into him).
Will, however, what 'belonging to Christ' suggests be born out by closer
examination of the other christological references here—'baptize unto
Christ', 'put on Christ', and 'in Christ'?

Baptism into Christ. The idea conveyed by the words εἰς Χριστὸν
ἐβαπτίσθητε in 3.27,[26] if understood in a local sense ('baptized into
Christ'), might be taken to connote passage into a kind of union with Christ
through baptism that implies the erasure of differences.[27] Otfried Hofius,
however, has cogently argued that a local sense of εἰς in the baptismal
formula can be excluded on the basis of 1 Cor. 10.2, 'they were baptized
εἰς τὸν Μωϋσῆν'. The expression appears to refer to the people's
belonging to Moses as their leader and the one in whom their destiny was
bound up.[28] Hofius also argues against a local sense of εἰς in the baptismal
formula on the basis of 1 Cor. 1.13, 15, which supports the connotation
of belonging through baptism.[29] Here Paul uses what is to be seen as
an unabbreviated version of the baptismal formula, βαπτίζειν εἰς τὸ
ὄνομα followed by a name in the genitive ('baptize in the name [of some-
one]'):[30] 'were you baptized in the name of Paul (εἰς τὸ ὄνομα Παύλον
ἐβαπτίσθητε)?'; '...lest anyone say that you were baptized in my name
(ἵνα μή τις εἴπῃ ὅτι εἰς τὸ ἐμὸν ὄνομα)'.[31] The expression connotes
belonging, as indicated by the Corinthian slogan, 'I am Paul's' (Ἐγὼ μέν
εἰμι Παύλου, 1.12), to which Paul is responding with these rhetorical
questions. The non-local sense of εἰς in the unabbreviated version of the

26. Similarly, Rom. 6.3, ἐβαπτίσθημεν εἰς Χριστὸν Ἰησοῦν.

27. Cf. Best 1955: 69-70, and Paulsen 1979–80: 86, who both explain baptism as
incorporation into the body of Christ resulting in the removal of differences (cf. 1 Cor.
12.13). Contrast Oepke 1973: 124, who denies that the expression means 'in den
Pneuma-Christus mystisch hineintauchen'.

28. Hofius 1994: 143 n. 31, 144 n. 35; cf. Wolff 1982: 41 n. 231, and Eckstein
1996: 221.

29. Hofius 1994: 143-44; so also Eckstein 1996: 221; and Burton 1962: 203.

30. Cf. BAGD, s.v. βαπτίζω 2.b.b.

31. Hofius 1989: 143, Eckstein 1996: 221, Schlier 1965: 173, Burton 1962: 203.
For the longer expression, cf. Acts 8.16; 19.5; Mt. 28.19b. εἰς τὸ ὄνομα may also be
used (Acts 10.48; 2.38 ἐν or ἐπί; BDF § 206.2). For the speaking of the divine name
over the one baptized during the ritual of baptism, cf. Jas 2.7.

formula is determinative for its use in the abbreviated version. Thus, we should take the expression εἰς Χριστὸν ἐβαπτίσθητε in Gal. 3.27 not as having a local sense (as in the translation, 'baptized *into* Christ') but as having the connotation of belonging to Christ.[32] This connotation is perhaps best captured by the translation, 'baptized *so as to belong to* Christ' (cf. Hofius: 'auf Christus';[33] Burton: 'with reference to Christ'[34]). 'As many as[35] are baptized so as to belong to Christ' in 3.27 thus has nothing to do with believers' 'immersion into Christ'[36] but connotes their coming to belong to Christ through baptism, as already suggested by the concluding inference in 3.29, 'If then you are Christ's'. A transmutation into Christ through baptism that erases creaturely differences is not implied.[37]

'Put on Christ'. But does the notion of baptism as 'putting on Christ' (Χριστὸν ἐνεδύσασθε) imply such a transmutation?[38] Wayne Meeks and Daniel Boyarin think so. They argue that 'put on' implies a prior 'taking off', namely, of the 'old person' (Col. 3.9; Eph. 4.22), 'the body of flesh' (Col. 2.11; Meeks 1973–74: 183-85), the 'garment of shame' to be 'trampled on', which is the body (the Dominical Saying from the Gospel of the

32. Cf. Acts 19.3-5, βαπτίζειν εἰς τὸ ὄνομα τοῦ κυρίου Ἰησοῦ, which also implies belonging to Christ and thus being able to receive the Spirit of Christ. Relevant to this discussion is also Rom. 8.9, 'if anyone does not have the Spirit of Christ, that one is not his (αὐτοῦ)'.

33. Hofius 1989: 143 n. 31; so also Eckstein 1996: 221. Eckstein (n. 214) compares the use of εἰς cum accusativum of the thing with consecutive or final sense in Mt. 3.11, βαπτίζειν...εἰς μετάνοιαν; Acts 2.38, βαπτίζειν...εἰς ἄφεσιν τῶν ἁμαρτιῶν; 1 Cor. 12.13, βαπτίζειν...εἰς ἓν σῶμα. On the latter, cf. BAGD, s.v. βαπτίζω 2.b.b: 'The effect of baptism is to bring all those baptized εἰς ἓν σῶμα'.

34. Burton 1962: 203. Cf. BAGD, s.v. βαπτίζω 2.b.b, for the meaning, 'baptize in, or with respect to the name of someone'. Burton appeals to Acts 19.3.

35. ὅσοι is not restrictive—'only as many as'—but comprehensive, with Schlier 1965: 173, *et al.*

36. Against Dunn 1993a: 131. Dunn proposes not only that Gal. 3.27 speaks of believers being transformed into Christ, but that baptism itself is metaphorical here (see also his 1970: 109-10). He appeals to 1 Cor. 12.13 for a parallel metaphorical understanding. But this argument falters since there, as in Gal. 3.26-28, according to most scholars, Paul is drawing on actual baptismal liturgy and thus alluding to the readers' *literal* baptism.

37. In Rom. 6.3 Paul develops the notion of baptism 'into Christ' in terms of baptism 'into his name', which refers to the baptized person's participation with Christ in his death, burial and resurrection. No transmutation into Christ is implied.

38. The metaphor is suggested by the act of re-robing after baptism: see Moule 1961: 52-53, Longenecker 1990: 156, and Meeks 1973–74: 183.

Egyptians in Clement, *Strom.* 3.13.92.2; Boyarin 1994: 23-24). Creaturely differences are thus seen to be erased through the putting on of Christ in baptism.

While the baptismal formula of Gal. 3.28, 'there is neither Jew nor Greek, etc.', might seem to support such a view, the interpretation of this verse is precisely what is at issue here, so we cannot take it as evidence for the view that Meeks and Boyarin propose. The New Testament parallels adduced also do not speak for this view on closer examination. In Col. 3.9 'having put off the old person (ἀπεκδυσάμενοι τὸν παλαιὸν ἄνθρωπον σὺν ταῖς πράξεσιν αὐτοῦ) *with its practices*' refers to casting off the sinful human nature that leads to sinful practices, not to casting off of the body itself.[39] In Col. 3.10 and Eph. 4.24 the corresponding idea of 'putting on[40] the new person' (ἐνδυσάμενοι τὸν νέον/ἐνδύσασθαι τὸν καινὸν ἄνθρωπον)[41] also refers to *ethical behavior in the body*. The closest parallel to Gal. 3.27, which is found in Rom. 13.14, 'put on the Lord Jesus Christ (ἐνδύσασθε τὸν κύριον Ἰησοῦν Χριστόν) and make no provision for the flesh and its desire!', also clearly refers to ethical renewal and not to the erasure of bodily differences.[42] The double metaphor—put off, put

39. On 'the old man [i.e. person]' as denoting not only the condition of the individual but also the old and new order of existence, see O'Brien 1982: 189-90. Cf. Rom. 6.6; Eph. 4.22.

40. For occurrences of the figurative use of ἐνδύσασθαι for the taking on of characteristics, virtues, intentions, etc., see BAGD, s.v. ἐνδύω, 2.b.; Oepke 1964a: 319-21; to denote eschatological transformation, cf. 1 Cor. 15.53, 54; 2 Cor. 5.2, 4; further, Rev. 15.6; 19.14; in connection with baptism in Col. 3.10; Eph. 4.24. For references to and literature on the notion of 'putting on' a redeemer figure in the mystery religions and in gnosticism, see Betz 1979: 188 nn. 60 and 61. Oepke (1964a: 320) correctly rejects as parallels to the Pauline usage the donning of a garment or mask of a god by an initiate. For further reasons against using this material as illuminating the New Testament expression 'put off the old person' and 'put on the new person', see O'Brien 1982: 189.

41. In Col. 3.10 the 'new person' seems to be distinguished from Christ (Paulsen 1980: I, 1104; Bouttier 1976: 9—'he' is being renewed according to the image of the Creator, i.e., Christ—yet an identification with the corporate Christ is not necessarily excluded; see also O'Brien 1982: 191-92).

42. The only other biblical reference to 'putting on' a person is Isa. 49.18, which is not similar to the New Testament occurrences. Outside the Bible the figure of speech occurs in Dionysius of Halicarnassus, *Ant. Rom.* 11.5; Libanius, *Ep.* 968 (350 CE) to denote acting a role. But, as Oepke (1973: 124-25) has correctly observed, to draw a parallel with Gal. 3.27 would result in the completely un-Pauline idea that being 'sons of God' derives from ethical imitation of Christ. For an example of 'putting off the man' illuminating Pauline usage, see van der Horst 1972–73.

on—is thus used to ground the taking on of new behavioral patterns, namely, the patterns of Christ and not of the old sinful self, by the baptized.

Boyarin interprets the metaphor of 'putting on Christ' in the context of Paul's statements about entering the body of Christ on the basis of identification with Christ as 'the seed' of Abraham. In Boyarin's reading of Paul, believers enter 'the body of Christ *in the Spirit*' and 'the individual body itself is replaced by its *allegorical* reference, the body of Christ of which all the baptized are part'.[43] Entrance is based on identification with Christ as 'the seed' which entails 'substituting [one's] literal genealogy for an allegorical one'. It can be objected, however, that since Christ is for Paul the *physical* seed of Abraham with a *literal* genealogy (Rom. 1.3; 9.5), Paul must conceive of those who 'put on Christ' as gaining a place in this *literal* Abrahamic lineage 'by faith', as grafts onto the 'cultivated olive tree' which are supported by its physical 'roots' (Rom. 11.17-24). We cannot therefore speak of the substitution of physical genealogy for 'allegorical genealogy' in Paul.

Even though 'putting on Christ' implies eschatological transformation— cf. Col. 3.10: 'having put on the new person being renewed in insight according to the image of the One who created him'—it does not appear to entail the erasure of bodily differences.[44] Similarly, Paul can speak of being a 'new creation' (καινὴ κτίσις) without implying the erasure of differences, only their revalorization, in Gal. 6.15, as seen above: 'neither is circumcision anything nor is uncircumcision anything, but new creation' (contrast Betz 1979: 189). My conclusion will be further undergirded below by an analysis of Paul's theologically parallel statement, 'I no longer live, but it is Christ who lives in me' (2.20).

What then does 'put on Christ' mean, if not transmutation into Christ that erases differences in the body? Two possibilities emerge on the basis of the observation that v. 27, which opens with γάρ, apparently gives a

43. Boyarin 1994: 22-24. Mussner (1977: 263) argues similarly that Christ is 'der pneumatische Christus' whom Christians 'put on' as an 'Einheitskleid, das die unterscheidenden Zeichen der früheren Existenz wesenlos macht, wie der folgende Vers darlegt'.

44. Paulsen 1980: I, 1104. Contrast Schlier 1965: 174-75: 'die Taufe hat die gesamte Vergangenheit des Menschen getilgt... An den Getauften sind die aus dem alten Äon stammenden metaphysischen, geschichtlichen und natürlichen Unterschiede sakramental, d.h. aber verborgen und real aufgehoben... Sie [sind] nur noch Glieder Christi... natürlich nur als Getaufte, als solche, die "in Christus Jesus" sind. Aber als solche sind sie es und ist das Bestimmende ihrer natürlichen Individualität... erloschen'.

ground for v. 26. 'For as many as have been baptized unto Christ have put on Christ' could be taken to ground the claim in the previous verse, 'you are all sons of God through faith, in Christ', or an aspect of that claim (with Oepke 1973: 124). If 'put on Christ' grounds the claim about being 'sons of God' (3.26; cf. 4.5-7) as Christ is the 'Son of God' (1.16; 2.20; 4.4, 6; Burton 1962: 203-204; Lietzmann 1932: 23), the metaphor clearly has nothing to do with putting off the differentiating body. The contrast with being 'sons of God' is rather being 'minors' and 'slaves' under the law (cf. 4.1, 3, 7). Alternatively, 'put on Christ' has been taken in terms of the final phrase in v. 26, 'in Christ',[45] which also does not imply erasure of bodily difference, as I will argue below. A third alternative is that 'put on Christ' anticipates 3.29, 'you are seed of Abraham (τοῦ Ἀβραὰμ σπέρμα ἐστέ)' and refers to taking on Christ's status as 'the seed' (τὸ σπέρμα) of Abraham (3.16).[46] As I have argued above against Boyarin, however, even this interpretation would not imply the complete replacement of believers' literal genealogy with a spiritual genealogy. In conclusion, 'put on Christ' (in baptism) connotes a kind of eschatological transformation that takes up rather than leaves out the differences in the body.

'In Christ Jesus'. The phrase ἐν Χριστῷ Ἰησοῦ is used twice in 3.26-28: once after the opening christological claim in 3.26, 'you all are sons of God through faith', and the second time after the climactic statement in 3.28, 'you all are one'. Franz Mussner interprets the phrase to entail participation in an existence that completely transcends the former differences, for it is an existence 'in the pneumatic Christ'. The spiritual Christ provides the eschatological model of existence for Christians which transcends ethnic and gender differences (Mussner 1977: 263-64).

Against this line of thought, however, for Paul 'Christ' always 'denotes Jesus of Nazareth' (Wright 1991: 165; see also Best 1955: 7), the possible exception being 2 Cor. 5.16. If that is the case, 'Christ' cannot be a spiritual space devoid of all corporeal reference (similarly, Longenecker 1990: 153), and being 'in Christ' cannot presuppose leaving behind all bodily inscribed differences. As a matter of fact Paul frequently uses the phrase ἐν Χριστῷ Ἰησοῦ to describe the new life of believers in which nevertheless human differences of various kinds are left intact (cf. Rom. 16.7, 10, 13; 1 Cor. 3.1; Gal. 1.22; Phil. 1.1; 1 Thess. 2.14; see, further, Best 1955: 23-27). The phrase is also used in Gal. 5.6, which I have

---

45. Among others, see Oepke 1964a: 320. On ἐν Χριστῷ, see further below.
46. Wright (1991: 165) notes that 3.15-18 anticipates 3.26-29.

argued is an interpretative key to Gal. 3.28, that refers to the adiaphorization of differences rather than their erasure: 'in Christ, neither does circumcision count for anything nor does uncircumcision count for anything'. The equivalent formula, ἐν κυρίῳ, is used in 1 Cor. 11.11 with the clear implication that sexual differences are adiaphorized but remain intact 'in the Lord': 'in the Lord neither is woman independent of man nor man independent of woman'.

Thus neither 'in Christ' nor the similar 'in the Lord' formula implies erasure of differences in the flesh. This conclusion holds true whether or not we understand ἐν Χριστῷ to refer to Christ as a 'corporate personality' (Best 1955: 20-21; Wright 1991: 165; Mussner 1977: 262), 'the body of Christ' (Betz 1979: 186), or 'the sphere of salvation' (cf. Oepke 1964b: 542). Betz is probably correct to infer from the structure of Paul's argument that 'in Christ' conveys the same kind of relationship as the expression 'you are Christ's': 'The conditional protasis [in 3.29] sums up 3.26-28 by now using the genitive construction "to be Christ's" instead of the expression "in Christ Jesus". This shows that the two phrases are not different in meaning' (Betz 1979: 201; similarly, Burton 1962: 208).

(2) *The Death of the Old Self.* It would seem that the strongest argument in favor of the erasure of differences based on the character of believers' relation to Christ comes from Gal. 2.19-20, which, according to Betz, is the main passage to compare with 3.26-28 (1979: 122-23). In this autobiographical—or, rather, autobiographically paradigmatic (Betz 1979: 122)—passage Paul says: 'I have been crucified with Christ; and it is no longer I who live, but Christ who lives in me' (2.19b-20a). The assertions that the self has died and the indwelling Christ has taken its place presuppose an identification between Christ and the self, such that the death of *Christ* is the death of the *self* and the resurrection of *Christ* is 'the raising of the *new person* who is reconciled to God and has passed through judgement to life' (Hofius 1989: 46). The change is not merely ethical but ontological. But does this ontological change entail the erasure of creaturely differences, as such a scenario might suggest?

On the contrary, this passage provides some of the strongest evidence against the thesis of the erasure of differences in Christ. The crucial point is the anthropological distinction Paul makes between the 'I' (ἐγώ), or the 'personal center' of the human being, and the 'flesh' (σάρξ), or the bodily, mortal, transitory environment (cf. Schweizer *et al.* 1971: 125-28), which the 'personal center' indwells. The 'I' has died, been crucified with Christ, and no longer lives. Now there is a new 'I': 'the life that I now live…'. This new 'I' dwells in the flesh: '…the life that *I* now live *in the flesh*…' (ὅ δὲ νῦν ζῶ ἐν σαρκί…). While the 'I' has died and a new 'I' has come, the 'flesh' in the sense of the bodily, mortal, transitory environment of the self[47]—but not the *sinful* 'flesh'—has *remained*. Thus the death and resurrection to new life of the 'I' is clearly not that of the whole human being but of the 'I' *as distinct from* 'the flesh'. Only the *sinful self* has died[48]—the self that stands under the condemnation of the law, as implied in 'I died to the Law'—and been raised to new life (Betz 1979: 123). The self has been raised to live in the same 'bodily environment'—ἐν σαρκί— as before its death. Whatever other continuity there may be between the life that is 'no longer' (οὐκέτι) and the life that is 'now' (νῦν),[49] there is clearly a continuity of the gendered and ethnically or culturally differentiated 'flesh'. That 'flesh', though mortal, is still *not dead*. Christ indwelling 'me' (ἐν ἐμοὶ Χριστός),[50] therefore, does not make the new person indistinguishable from others who are indwelt by Christ. Though believers 'put on' the *one* Christ, he 'puts on' their *differentiated* 'flesh'— to reappropriate Paul's metaphor—and 'lives in me', that is, in each individually differentiated 'me'. The 'new creation' (6.15), therefore, takes place not by simple annihilation of the old creation, but by the death of the enfleshed self and the indwelling of Christ (see Eckstein 1996: 72) in the same flesh, whether Jew or Greek, slave or free, male or female.[51]

47. Cf. Gal. 4.13-14; 6.12-13; 2 Cor. 4.11; 10.3; Phil. 1.22, 24; Phlm. 16.

48. Similarly, in 5.24 and 6.14 the sinful 'flesh' and 'world' have been 'crucified'. Cf. Eckstein 1996: 71: '…infolge des Gekreuzigt-Seins mit Christus ist für Paulus die definitive Vernichtung der *Sündenexistenz* vollzogen' (emphasis added).

49. There must be a continuity also in the self, otherwise the 'I' that was crucified and the 'I' that now lives by Christ indwelling it ('Christ lives in me [ἐν ἐμοί]') would be two numerically different things and therefore not the same human being. The continuity, however, cannot be conceived as 'einer *immanenten* Kontinuität des Lebens', as Käsemann, commenting on Gal. 2.20, has cautioned, but as rooted in the divine 'Wunder' that bridges the gap between the old and the new, death and new life (1969: 20).

50. Cf. Rom. 8.9-11; 1 Cor. 6.13-19.

51. Correctly, Oepke 1973: 96: 'Durch das Christusleben ist nun aber die kreatürliche Persönlichkeit allerdings nicht einfach aufgehoben. Paulus muß zugeben, er lebt auch noch *im Fleische*, wobei hier nicht an die sündliche Natur, sondern einfach an die empirische Seinsweise gedacht ist'. Paul's retention of creaturely differences is also implicit in his affirmation of the body as 'for the Lord' and the Lord as 'for the body' in 1 Cor. 6.13. Käsemann's comment is also appropriate here that 'der Apostel den Menschen ganz und gar von der Leiblichkeit her verstanden wissen will und darum sogar Christologie und Soteriologie darauf bezieht' (1969: 39).

(3) *'You all are one'*. 'For you all are one (εἷς) in Christ Jesus' at the end of 3.28 restates in positive form the opening assertions, 'there is neither Jew nor Greek, etc...' (Burton 1962: 207). When the negations are understood in terms of erasure of creaturely differences, the closing statement appears to express an ideal of undifferentiated oneness. But is this the connotation of εἷς?

εἷς is to be taken in the sense of 'one, in contrast to the parts of which a whole is made up', as indicated by the contrast with πάντες, 'all'.[52] The connotation of εἷς is thus wholeness or unity, not sameness. The masculine singular form (εἷς) is used here,[53] suggesting the idea of unity in one person rather than unity in an abstract sense.[54] 'One (person)' contrasts to the many persons named at the beginning of the verse: Ἰουδαῖος, Ἕλλην, δοῦλος, ἐλεύθερος, ἄρσεν, θῆλυ ('male', for 'man', ἀνήρ, and 'female', for 'woman', γυνή).[55] Two lines of interpretation can be ruled out on the basis of these observations. One approach takes εἷς to mean 'one' in an abstract sense in which the differences are dissolved. This interpretative move neglects the connotation of the masculine gender of εἷς suggesting unity in one person. The second takes εἷς to mean 'the same person', and Paul's statement to mean that believers are now all the same, rather than distinct.[56] Here Christ is seen to replace earthly distinc-

---

52. So BAGD, s.v. εἷς, 1.b. Cf. for similar contrasts Rom. 12.5; 1 Cor. 10.17; 12.12, 20; 1 Cor. 3.8; 6.16; Mt. 19.5 (both citing Gen. 2.24); Eph. 2.14.

53. The variant reading ἕν at Gal. 3.28 in F G 33 is to be rejected in favor of εἷς, which is the *lectio difficilior*. The other readings, ἐστε Χριστοῦ (P46 A) and ἐστε ἐν Χριστοῦ (ℵ*), are probably harmonizations with 3.29.

54. Note, however, that both the masculine (εἷς) and the neuter (ἕν) are used to refer to the same 'one' in Eph. 2.14-15. Cf. Rom. 12.5; 1 Cor. 10.17; 12.12, 20 (ἕν σῶμα); 1 Cor. 6.16; Mt. 19.5 (εἰς μίαν σάρκα); 1 Cor. 3.8.

55. Cf. Mussner 1977: 264: 'εἷς wird ganz deutlich als Oppositum gesehen zu Ἰουδαῖος und Ἕλλην, δοῦλος und ἐλεύθερος, ἄρσεν und θῆλυ'. The adjectives ἄρσεν and θῆλυ are used as substantives with the article (and synonymous with ἀνήρ and γυνή) in Rom. 1.26-27, presumably because the emphasis here is on sex. Cf. BAGD, s.v. ἄρσεν, s.v. θῆλυ. For a discussion of the substitution of the biological terms for the social designations 'man' and 'woman', see de Merode 1978: 184-88.

56. Against Mussner 1977: 264-65, who takes εἷς to refer to 'the Christian' ('der eschatologische "Einheitsmensch" ["der Christ"]'); Schlier 1965: 175, who takes εἷς to denote 'Christ', such that each Christian is Christ to the other; also Tannehill 1967: 20; Meeks 1973–74: 181 n. 75; Lietzmann 1932: 24, who argues that 'you are all one' refers to the one 'seed' to whom the promise was given, namely Christ (3.16), so that we should expect to read 'you are Christs' in 3.29 instead of 'you are Christ's'; also Burton 1962: 208.

tions between Christians with one and the same 'personality'. But the context distinguishes between Christ and believers, as noted above ('you are Christ's').[57] Furthermore, this line of interpretation ignores the fact that εἶς connotes unity (as implied by the contrast with πάντες) rather than sameness. As Betz has astutely observed, 3.28d 'stresses the oneness', in contrast to 3.26 and 3.29, which stress the sameness (or equality) of believers: 'you are all sons of God' and 'you are seed of Abraham, heirs according to the promise' (Betz 1979: 200). If then 'you all are one' refers to the unity of believers in one person, does that unity include the differences between them or exclude those differences?

If we take 'one (person) in Christ Jesus' to presuppose the Pauline notion of σῶμα Χριστοῦ, as Betz has proposed (though the expression itself does not occur in Galatians),[58] then not erasure but retention of human differences is implied, for the body is made up of many (diverse) members (cf. Rom. 12.5; 1 Cor. 10.17; 12.12, 20), including ethnically and socially diverse members (cf. 1 Cor. 12.13, where the differences are *not* negated: 'and we were all baptized to one body, whether Jews or Greeks, whether slaves or free').

In addition, we should carefully examine Eph. 2.15b as the closest parallel in the New Testament to the idea of 'one (person) in Christ Jesus' (Gal. 3.28): '...that he might create the two into one new person (εἰς ἕνα καινὸν ἄνθρωπον) in him, making peace'.[59] 'One new person' (εἰς ἕνα καινὸν ἄνθρωπον) makes explicit what is implied in 'one' (εἶς, masc. sg., referring to a male person) in Gal. 3.28. 'One new person' is created out of 'the two' (τοὺς δυό), who are the Jews and the Gentiles, or 'the ones called circumcision in the flesh by human hands', and 'the ones called uncircumcision' (2.11-13). The implication is that circumcision is the issue that divides them, or the Law that ascribes ultimate significance to circumcision and uncircumcision (2.15).[60] How is the unity achieved? Not through the erasure of fleshly differences and the merging of the two into an undifferentiated one, as we can already guess from the image of

57. See also Eckstein 1996: 223-24 n. 230.
58. Betz 1979: 200; see also Bruce 1982: 190; Käsemann 1960: 115.
59. The relationship of the 'new person' to Christ is debated. According to Best, the 'new human' is distinct from Christ—'he' is created 'in Christ' (1955: 61). Lincoln, however, sees the notion of the 'new human' to be dependent on Paul's Adamic Christology with the associated ideas of Christ as an inclusive representative of a new order and of believers being incorporated into him (1990: 143).
60. With W.S. Campbell 1991: 113-14; contrast Lincoln 1990: 144.

the 'far off' who have been 'brought near' (2.13), rather, through the destruction of the 'barrier of the dividing wall, the hostility' (2.14), 'the law of commandments in ordinances' (2.15), which happens 'through his flesh' (2.14), referring to Christ's body on the cross. The result of Christ's death is 'peace' (2.15; cf. 2.14) or reconciliation: 'he reconciled both in one body to God' (2.16). 'One body'[61] implies the reconciliation of the two to each other, not only to God, and parallels the idea of 'one new person'.[62] We are thus to understand 'one new person' as a corporate person made up of the different members that have been reconciled to each other through Christ's death. 'One body' (implying different members) can be taken to suggest that the differences are retained in this one new person. The concluding statement that 'through him we both have access by one Spirit to the Father' (2.18) also presupposes the retention of differences, since without differences there is no need to stress equal access by the same Spirit.

Thus, though there are clear differences between Galatians and Ephesians, both epistles address the question of the place of Gentile Christians in the eschatological community and their relation to Jewish Christians, and answer that question similarly in terms of oneness in Christ.

In addition, we should also consider the suggestion of Gerd Theissen that 'you are all one in Christ Jesus' is to be thought of in analogy to sexual union (1974: 298-99). The idea is somewhat speculative; nevertheless, it may be warranted. Paul conceived elsewhere of the 'body of Christ' in analogy to man and woman becoming 'one flesh'. In 1 Cor. 6.15-17 he uses this metaphor to express the union of individual believers with Christ, and in 2 Cor. 11.2 to express the union of the whole community with Christ (Theissen 1974: 299; cf. also Park 1988). Therefore it is not implausible that he also thought of the unity between the diverse believers who comprise the body of Christ in analogy to the sexual union between a man and a woman (Theissen 1974: 299). 'You are all one in Christ Jesus' would then refer to a union like sexual union in which the differences are not erased but members 'cleave' to each other (by virtue of 'cleaving' to Christ), as in the hebraic paradisiacal ideal of man and woman cleaving to each other and becoming 'one flesh' (Gen. 2.24). It is conceivable that Paul had this ideal of sexual union in the back of his mind when he wrote

---

61. σῶμα here refers not to the crucified body of Christ, but to the body made up of the members of Christ, i.e., Christians (with Lincoln 1990: 144-45).

62. Lincoln (1990: 145) draws a parallel between the 'one body' and the 'new person'.

Gal. 3.28, since the immediately preceding phrase, 'there is "no male and female"', evokes Gen. 1.27-28, which alludes to the sexual union of male and female for procreation.

If, then, 'you are all one (person) in Christ Jesus' refers to the creation in Christ of a new humanity composed of *reconciled and united opposites*, not an undifferentiated oneness, Gal. 3.28d goes beyond the formally parallel statement in 3.26 stressing the equality of all in Christ—'you are all sons of God by faith, in Christ Jesus'—and instead stresses the *unity*. The 'one person' is the community of Jews and Greeks, slaves and free, men and women, that is, those who were formerly divided by their differences but are now united despite those differences through Christ.[63]

(4) *The Problem behind Galatians 3.28.* If my contextual arguments are cogent, the ideal Paul projects in Gal. 3.28 is not unity in Christ through the erasure of differences. And if the solution does not entail the erasure of differences, it is reasonable to assume that the problem does not lie in the differences as such—against the tacit assumption of Wire and Boyarin and the exegetical tradition they represent. The basic problem Paul is addressing in Galatians, to which 3.28 is a preliminary response, is not that there exist different peoples, Jews and Greeks. 'Jewishness' was not a 'problem' for Paul; he could even regard it as an advantage (Rom. 3.1; 9.4-5; 11.1, 24, 26, 28). Neither was 'Gentileness' something to be overcome (Gal. 5.6; 6.15; 1 Cor. 7.18-19). The problem is rather that salvation cannot be had either by 'race' (fleshly descent from Abraham [4.21-31]) or by 'law' (observing all that is written 'in the book of the law' [3.10]). Salvation cannot be by 'race', for that would contradict the promise given to Abraham (3.6-9; cf. Rom. 4.1-22) and go against the free electing grace of God on which Israel's existence was grounded throughout its history (Rom. 9.6-18; Hofius 1989: 178-81), as well as create inequality between Jews and Gentiles with respect to salvation—the salvation of the Jews would be by race and of the Gentiles by grace (Wright 1991: 166)—and fail to produce the single people of God corresponding to the one God of Abraham (Rom. 3.29; 10.12). Salvation cannot be by law-observance because neither the fleshly children of Abraham—those who are 'by birth' Jews (2.15)—nor the Gentiles are justified by the works of the law (3.11). And if no one is justified by the works of the law then *a fortiori* the promised blessing of

---

63. Cf. Eckstein 1996: 223. 'Ungeachtet aller menschlichen Unterschiede sind die Glaübigen in Christus Jesus jetzt εἷς, "einer"'.

Abraham cannot be mediated through the law to all the nations so that they all can belong to the single family of God.

At a deeper level, the problem that Paul is addressing in Galatians, and that stands behind his denial that salvation can be either by 'race' or by 'law', is *not the differences* in the flesh but *a certain kind of sameness*, the *sameness of Jew and Gentile as prisoners of sin* (cf. Wright 1991: 173). 'The scripture has imprisoned all things under the power of sin' (3.22). The statement 'you all are one in Christ Jesus' (v. 28d)—explicating 'there is neither Jew nor Greek, there is neither slave nor free, there is no male and female' (v. 28a-c)—gives a solution ultimately for *the common imprisonment to sin* of Jew and Gentile, slave and free, male and female. The differences in the body only seem to be the real problem, whereas in fact they are not. And yet they contribute to disunity and discord. How so? They insinuate themselves as having salvific significance and thereby hide the fact that all people are equally locked out of the promised blessing on account of sin. Underneath the *differentiated* body all are the *same* in this respect. And this sameness is precisely what divides them. Bound together by the invisible cord of sin, they are set apart by the visible walls that divide. Paul's response to the common imprisonment to sin of those who are divided by the differentiating body is his insistence on *the same way of salvation for all*, which results in the unity of those who remain different in the flesh within the single people of God, the recipients of the blessing of Abraham. 'All' are one in Christ is the solution to 'all' are imprisoned to sin. Expressed in the vocabulary of Romans: the negative background to the soteriological claim 'there is no distinction between Jew and Greek' (10.12) is not the culturological and creation-theological claim that there are 'Jews and Greeks', 'slaves and free', 'men and women' but the *hamartiological* claim that 'there is no distinction [between Gentile and Jew] since all have sinned' (3.22-23). If we trace the line of Paul's thought from the problem to the solution, it does not run from 'difference' to 'undifferentiated unity', but from 'sameness in sin despite outward differences' to 'unity with outward differences in Christ'.

Conclusion

My basic argument has been that Paul's claim in Gal. 3.28, 'there is no male and female', in no way implies that the differences between male and female have been abolished. Instead, these differences have been adiaphorized: (1) the problem is located not in the differences themselves, but *behind* them, so to speak, in the commonality of sin, and (2) the solution is found *outside* of the differences, in the common faith in Christ that creates unity and equality of all. In Paul we are witnessing a model of thought in which unity does not presuppose all-out sameness (dissolution of femininity or/and masculinity) but sameness *in some respects*—with respect to sin and with respect to the way of salvation.

'THE WOMAN OUGHT TO HAVE CONTROL OVER HER HEAD BECAUSE OF THE ANGELS' (1 CORINTHIANS 11.10)

Joan E. Taylor

[2]Now I praise you because you have remembered me (in) everything and you keep the traditions just as I have handed (them) to you. [3]So I want you to know that Christ is the head/source of every man, and (the) head/source of a woman (is) a man, and (the) head/source of Christ (is) God. [4]Every man who prays and prophesies (while) having (something) on the head shames his head. [5]But every woman who prays or prophesies with the head uncovered shames her head. For she is one and the same as a woman who is shaved. [6]For if a woman does not cover herself, also let her shear herself, but if (it is) dishonorable for a woman to shear or shave herself, let her cover herself. [7]For a man ought not to cover his head, since he is an image and glory/honour of God, but the woman is a man's glory/honour. [8]For a man is not from a woman, but a woman from a man. [9]For indeed a man is not brought forth on account of the woman, but a woman (is brought forth) on account of the man. [10]On account of this the woman ought to have control over her head because of the angels. [11]However, in the Lord, neither (is) a woman independent of a man, nor a man independent of a woman. [12]For just as the woman (is) from the man, so also the man (is) through the woman, and all the(se) things (are) from God. [13]Decide amongst yourselves! Is it proper for a woman to pray to God uncovered? [14]Doesn't Nature herself teach you that if a man (is) long-haired it is a dishonour to him? [15]But if a woman (is) long-haired it is an honour/glory to her, because the long hair is given for the sake of a covering. [16]But if any person appears to be obstinate, we have no such custom, nor (do) the communities of God.

In the final lines of 1 Corinthians Paul exhorts the congregation with the rousing words, 'be manly, be strong' (ἀνδρίζεσθε, κραταιοῦσθε: 16.13). Whatever egalitarianism one may discern in this letter is thereby thrown to the wind by a phrase of pure androcentrism. To be a real man is of course to be strong. To be a real Christian is presumably to be like a man and be strong. In a sense this exhortation may not have seemed entirely inappropriate to the women of the Corinthian congregation who were—according to Antoinette Clark Wire's reconstruction (1990)—in various ways being like men and being strong. One wonders if Paul has temporarily forgotten their presence as hearers and readers of his letter in the church of Corinth, given his words in ch. 11, in which women are apparently not meant to be like men at all. Or is Paul self-consciously speaking only to the men of Corinth?

The recent studies by Antoinette Clark Wire (1990) and Judith Gundry-Volf (1994b, 1996, 1997a) have built upon the feminist reconstructive historiography of Elisabeth Schüssler Fiorenza[1] in pointing to the significance of Gal. 3.28 for women (and men) at Corinth. After all, if Jews and Greeks, slaves and free, are all to worship and eat together without inequality or distinction, it would follow that men and women would do the same. Wire and Gundry-Volf both identify that a transformation of gendered social roles was taking place in the Christian church of Corinth. The neglect of women's gender-specific clothing or head-dress may have resulted from an understanding that in Christ there is no male and female (Gal. 3.28), which the women ascetics of Corinth interpreted as a mandate for a new social order 'in Christ (in the church)'.[2] Without sexual differentiation there is of course no sexual inequality, and women made social gains by means of this liberating message, especially when this was translated into the celibate lifestyle of *pneumatikoi*. Judith Gundry-Volf has explored how the celibate Corinthian *pneumatikoi* may be understood within a tradition of inspiration asceticism both in the wider Graeco-Roman world and in Judaism (Gundry-Volf 1994b: 110-12). She examines how Paul's complex argument responds to the situation by insisting that men and women are

---

1.   Schüssler Fiorenza 1993: 205-41. For issues of method in the reconstruction of the Corinthian women (which inform the present study), see her 1987 and 1994a.

2.   The roots of the celibate ideal may well go back to Jesus and his earliest disciples. If in Gal. 3.28 there is no 'male and female' (Gen. 1.27), there is no sex. In the Marcan tradition also, Gen. 1.27 is used to explain human sexuality: 'at the beginning of creation, "he made them male and female" so for this reason a man will leave his father and mother and be joined together with his wife and the two will become one body/flesh' (Mk 10.6-8a; cf. Mt. 19.4-5). However, in Q this is for 'the children of this world' who 'marry [i.e. males] and are given in marriage [i.e. females], but those who are judged worthy of a place in the other world and in the resurrection of the dead do not marry, because they can no longer die. For they are the same as the angels and, being children of the resurrection, they are sons of God' (Lk. 20.34-36; cf. Mt. 19.11-12 and 22.30). Here, those who look forward to the resurrection are already like angels. Angels, despite the unfortunate incident of Gen. 6.2-4, are generally considered to be celibate, even de-sexualized, heavenly beings (though apparently male in form). For a wider discussion and an argument for the origin of 'there is no male and female' in the earliest pre-Pauline Christian tradition, see MacDonald 1987.

inculturated, and identifies that Paul affirms equality with difference 'in the Lord'. She finds Paul emerging as neither 'culturally insensitive nor theologically unimaginative, neither totalizing nor arbitary' (Gundry-Volf 1997a: 171). Both Wire and Gundry-Volf point to the importance of the shame–honor system in antiquity for an understanding of the issues. While Wire and Gundry-Volf are not in perfect agreement about the situation of the Corinthian women, their work has greatly moved forward the feminist discussion of early Christian women's history by their careful attention to Paul's rhetoric and their nuanced reconstructive approaches.

In this chapter I wish to respond to these studies by building on their constructions, with some amendments, and by concentrating on one feature of 1 Cor. 11.2-16. I shall in this examination lay aside the various conundrums of Paul's ambivalent attitude to gender (see Schottroff 1993: 50; Gundry-Volf 1997b) and the focus will be exceedingly narrow. Here I want only to analyze one verse of Paul's first extant letter to Corinth: 11.10. The verse is grammatically peculiar, and semantically ambiguous, but it informs the understanding of the entire passage 1 Cor. 11.2-16, and Paul's attitude to gender overall, and therefore warrants careful treatment. 1 Corinthians 11.2-16, which treats the issue of the subordination of woman to man in creation, is a passage which is notoriously dense. One detects Paul's jumpiness on the issue in his sharp switches from one argument to another. Interpretations have been diverse, and the passage continues to exercise exegetes. The convenient solution of dubbing the passage an interpolation is generally rejected.[3]

As the title of this chapter indicates, I have translated the verse as, 'On account of this the woman ought to have control over her head because of the angels' (1 Cor. 11.10). There are two major issues of translation and exegesis here. First, what is the meaning of ὀφείλει ἡ γυνὴ ἐξουσίαν ἔχειν ἐπὶ τῆς κεφαλῆς?, and, secondly, does the phrase διὰ τοῦτο refer backwards or forwards: to the preceding argument, or to the concluding phrase διὰ τοὺς ἀγγέλους?

Control over the Head

Translations up until recently have generally reflected an understanding that a woman should be under a visible sign of authority, so that 1 Cor.

---

3. The authenticity of the section is generally now considered likely. The view that it is an interpolation (in three parts) has been presented by Walker 1975; cf. Trompf 1980, and Cope 1978. The authenticity of the passage has been well defended by Murphy-O'Connor 1976, 1980.

11.10 is translated along the lines of 'the woman ought to have [a sign of] authority on her head'.[4] A traditional translation 'a woman ought to have an authority on her head' has been argued for by Morna D. Hooker (1963–64), but Hooker does not think that the authority refers to male control of women. The authority is the covering which enables her to pray and prophesy when otherwise she would not have this authority, because of her lesser status in creation. Hooker's exegesis, however, implies that in Judaism women were not able to pray or prophesy in public (1963–64: 415-16), which is just not so. Women prophets were extolled in Judaism (cf. *b. Meg.* 14a), and contemporary 'inspired' Jewish women could model themselves on their example (cf. Philo, *Vit. Cont.* 85, 87).[5] The alternative translation is to consider the phrase ἐξουσίαν ἔχειν ἐπὶ τῆς κεφαλῆς as referring to the fact that a woman should 'have control over her head'. The word ἐξουσία generally defines the active power to control someone or something or the authority to do something, while ἐπί can be used to indicate power 'over' something.[6] This is in fact the simplest reading of the text. Hooker argues against this obvious translation by stating that it is 'quaint' to think that a woman somehow controls her rebellious head by covering it, but she misses the point that the woman is in an inspired state, in which the head may well be 'rebellious'.

It is important to note that 1 Cor. 11.2-16 does not tell us how many of the congregation were failing to follow Pauline instructions in regard to head-dress. Paul's language is entirely in the singular in regard to this practice apart from making his generalizations about what every man or woman should do. Especially noteworthy is the comment '*the woman* ought to have control over her [lit. the] head' (v. 10). This singular form can be put down to literary style, so that a singular woman is then made representative of many or all women (= Eve), but a literal reading would indicate there is only one woman who ought to have control over her head, even though she does not.[7] Let us then read this literally. This woman

---

4.   See for a summary of the diverse translations of this phrase Kistemaker 1993: 375-77.

5.   See below.

6.   See for these meanings LSJ 1968: 599, 621; and, also, importantly, the usage in Rev. 2.26; 11.6; 14.18; 20.6; cf. also Schüssler Fiorenza 1993: 228. For arguments proposing this translation see Gundry-Volf 1997a: 150-60. Fee (1987) notes that ἐξουσία is never used passively as a sign of man's authority anywhere else.

7.   In this case, there is a clear shift from the indefinite and definite forms of v. 9 to the definite form of v. 10: 'For indeed a man [Adam] is not brought forth on account of

would have been sufficiently confident of her practice that she felt quite able to defend it, to the horror of some other members of the congregation. Such an issue would have been one of those responsible for divisions (cf. 1 Cor. 1.10-11; 11.18-19), and hence we have a question put to Paul (by letter or word of mouth) or a situation described to him. The indication we have of a faction in favor of a woman not necessarily having her head covered is at the end of the passage, when Paul states rather flatly: 'If any person appears to be obstinate, we have no such custom, nor (do) the communities of God' (11.16). The reference to the obstinate person is masculine, the inclusive masculine of Greek: Εἰ δέ τις δοκεῖ φιλόνεικος εἶναι. It is pointedly not: 'if *any women* appear to be obstinate...' (contra Héring 1962: 110). The issue is one that has caused factions; it is the pro-'uncovered head for a woman' faction that is addressed in 11.16, not the woman or women alone.

So why would the woman not cover up? Paul writes that 'the woman ought to have control over her head *because of the angels* (διὰ τοὺς ἀγγέλους)'. The angels suddenly appear here, and have baffled exegetes ever since. Various different explanations have been given as to why angels are mentioned: they are the keepers of order on earth, especially in the Christian congregation (Hooker 1963–64: 414-16; Fitzmyer 1957–58: 48-58); they are liable to lust after human women if they see them exposed to view (Héring 1962: 107); they are in danger of worshipping Adam as God's glory in confusion (Wire 1990: 121-21, 127-28). But, as Elisabeth Schüssler Fiorenza has pointed out, it is the prophetic role of angels that is actually the point (1993: 228). The whole issue here is what should be done in the instance of prayer and prophecy. Elsewhere, Paul mentions that the law has been given through angels (Gal. 3.19). In the speech of Stephen in Acts 7 it is angels that have ordained the law (7.38, 53) for they are those who inspire the prophets. In roughly contemporaneous Jewish literature, the law is considered to be written by prophetic inspiration (Josephus, *Apion* 1.29, 37-40; *m. Ab.* 1.1). The angels do indeed look upon the world (1 Cor. 4.9; 1 Tim. 5.21) and keep God's order, but they also

the woman [Eve], but a woman [Eve] on account of the man [Adam]. On account of this the woman ought to have power/control over her head because of the angels'. The definite articles of v. 9 indicate that the references are back to Adam and Eve, but the definite article with γυνή, 'woman', in v. 10 does not seem to refer back to Eve. The meaning of the sentence indicates that the concern is with the woman in the congregation who does not have power/control over her head, rather than to Eve, who was created with long hair to cover herself before God (cf. v. 15).

enter into the human soul and inspire prophecy (see Gundry-Volf 1997a: 164).

Why do angels appear in this discussion? It seems likely that they appear here because they appeared in the reason given by the woman as to why she had her head uncovered. We may reconstruct the particular issue which Paul is addressing as being to do with the unnamed woman's argument in regard to prophetic inspiration. There was a woman who said: 'I do not have control over my head because of the angels'. The angels inspire, she becomes possessed, and in a possessed state control over the head is lost. Whatever head-covering she may have had is cast aside and, as she may have said, 'What does that really matter when in the Lord there is no real distinction between men and women? According to Paul's tradition which we carefully follow men should not wear a head-covering, while women should, and yet he says that in Christ there is no "male and female?" This practice endorses the distinction. Surely, either we all cover, or no one covers'.

Paul responds by asserting precisely why men and women are different in the sight of God, and claims that the very reason she gave for throwing off the covering is the reason she should keep it on: because of the angels. The angels do not throw off women's head-coverings, or condone such a practice. The angels keep God's order, and (as everyone knows) they have inspired the Scriptures. The angels would not want the woman's covering to fall off and could not have inspired her to do this, because they recognize the primordial distinctions between male and female and wish human beings to maintain these distinctions. Moreover, in the final analysis, the spirits of the prophets are subject to prophets (1 Cor. 14.27-32). Therefore, the woman ought to have control over her head because of the angels rather than have no control over her head because of them.

'On Account of This...'

This then helps to explain Paul's usage of διὰ τοῦτο at the beginning of the verse, for everything that has gone before explains the proper ordering of the universe in regard to gender that the angels would wish to maintain. Paul explains on the basis of creation that 'a man ought not to cover his head, since he is an image and glory/honor of God, but the woman is a man's glory/honor. For a man is not from a woman, but a woman from a man. For indeed a man is not brought forth on account of the woman, but a woman (is brought forth) on account of the man. On account of this the woman ought to have control over her head because of the angels'. As is well known, Paul here uses words with ambiguous or double-meanings in Greek, which cannot be rendered easily by single English words. In particular he plays with the word for 'head', κεφαλή, which carries the intimation of authority (see Fitzmyer 1989; Grudem 1985), but also means 'source', as in the source of a river, or the life of some being.[8] The foundation of this usage goes back to the creation of humanity: a man's source (via the prototype of a man, Adam) is Christ and a woman's source (via the prototype of a woman, Eve) is a man (Adam). But, in this patriarchal society, a woman's 'head' is also as a rule ultimately a man: a free woman's father, brother, husband, son or other male relative, or a slave woman's master, or an independent woman's 'guardian'. A woman is secondary in creation and has the source of her being in a man (Gen. 2.18-23) and a man will usually be her 'head' in society. Paul plays on the language of social norms, though ultimately the woman shames the source of her being: Adam, rather than her 'head' in terms of societal order, viz. an individual man. Nevertheless, just as she would not wish to shame her 'head' in society, so she should not wish to shame her (Eve's) 'head/source', Adam.

The word δόξα is usually rendered as 'glory', so that 'the woman is a man's glory' just as a man (as Adam) is 'an image and glory of God' (11.7). But δόξα has the basic meaning of 'opinion' (LSJ 1968: 444). It can mean 'glory' or 'splendor' certainly and Paul used it in this way to render Hebrew *kabod* (e.g. Exod. 16.10 [LXX)]), but more commonly δόξα means 'good opinion, credit, or honor', i.e. the opinion others have of one's reputation.[9] A woman with her head uncovered while praying and prophesying brings shame on Adam when she should bring him glory.[10] As Antoinette Clark Wire has noted, in society someone's 'glory' is intended to reflect credit on that person;[11] a wife was supposed to be a

8.   So Bedale 1954. Some early manuscripts make this understanding plain by using the word ἀρχή here. For κεφαλή see LSJ 1968: 945.

9.   LSJ 1968: 444. Dishonor, ἀτιμία, is contrasted with δόξα in 2 Cor. 6.6; 1 Cor. 15.43 and 4.10: see Gill 1990: 257.

10.   There is justification for us to translate ἀνήρ generically in v. 7, so that a woman will shame all men (= Adam) by not covering up on the basis of the indefinite forms of 'man' and 'woman' in 1 Cor. 11.3, 8.

11.   See Wire 1990: 120 and also p. 280 n. 8, which has rabbinic examples of wives who have shamed their husbands, when they should have been a glory to them. Wire considers the reference to a man here as being to the men of the Corinthian congregation with whom the women were connected (p. 280 n. 9), but the reference is to a (singular) man who is the woman's 'head'.

credit to her husband, and he was either honored or shamed by his wife's behavior. The same was true for a daughter in regard to her father, or any other woman in regard to her 'head'. As noted above, both Wire and Gundry-Volf emphasize the importance of the shame–honor system for understanding this passage (see particularly, Gundry-Volf 1997a: 153-60). However, here the issue is not to do with propriety and order in society, or shame of a man in society or in the church, for in the context of the church all Christians were brothers and sisters, and there were a large group of independent χῆραι ('widows') whose very name, 'bereft ones' indicated they were bereft of male 'headship'.[12] The only male 'head' of an independent and inspired celibate virgin or widow in the church of Corinth would be Adam himself, in as much as all women are Eve. For Paul also all men are Adam as much as they are physically in the image and glory of God, and therefore the woman without a cover while praying or prophesying shames all males everywhere in the entire world. As such, Paul does not ask women to be subordinate to individual men, but rather he asks them not to shame Adam. The issue is about the supposed sensibilities of God.

Inspiration and Control

For some comparative material which we may turn to in order to understand Paul's rhetoric, we may look to the Jewish milieu of Hellenistic Egypt and the evidence of Philo. Philo writes of possession-behavior in his description of a group of Jewish men and women living outside Alexandria (*Vit. Cont.* c. 41 CE). In describing the climactic singing and dancing at the 'feast' of the fiftieth eve, Philo identifies the participants as being intoxicated by heavenly inspiration:

> When each of the choirs [of men and women separately] has sated itself by itself, just as in the Bacchic rites [the revelers] are drinking the liquor of a god's love, they mix [the choirs] together and become a single choir from out of the two. [This is] a memory of the one established of old by the Red Sea, by reason of the wonderful works there... [At this time] both men and women were filled with inspiration and became a choir singing hymns of thanksgiving to God the Savior. The men [were] led by Moses the prophet and the women by Miriam the prophetess (*Vit. Cont.* 85, 87).

---

12. For explorations of the nature of these 'widows' and other celibate women and their roles in the nascent church, see S. Davies 1980; cf. Thurston 1989, and McNamara 1983.

Philo notes that they are 'drunk…with this beautiful drunkenness' (89). In this heavenly state they are truly 'citizens of heaven and also world' (90). According to Philo, this state of intoxication, though intense at this time of communal singing and dancing, is continual in the lives of the contemplatives in their regular day-to-day routines, both during sleep and waking. Philo writes that 'the [divinely] attending type of people who are taught always to see, may desire the vision of the Living One and fly past the perceived sun and never leave this [heavenly] company leading to perfect happiness' (11). They go about their divine attendance (*therapeia*) 'because they are seized by a heavenly passion [and]—just like the Bacchic revelers and Corybants—they are inspired until they see the object of desire' (12). So 'possessed' are they that 'they keep the memory of God' constantly and 'in dreams nothing else is dreamt of apart from the beauty of the divine attributes and powers. In fact, many [of them] call out the famous decrees of the sacred philosophy in [their] sleep while dreaming' (26). The 'decrees of the sacred philosophy' are, of course, words of Scripture. They ask in the sunrise prayers that 'their minds will be filled with a heavenly light' (27). The emphasis is on vision, of seeing the light of God that is higher up in heaven than the sun. They are inspired until they *see* the object of desire. In Philo's writings in general, there is a clear theme involving the quest to 'see' God, which is the height of human joy. The experience of seeing God is, as Ellen Birnbaum puts it, 'unmediated' by other human beings, and the God that is experienced is 'transcendent and immaterial'.[13] 'Israel' itself is frequently described by Philo as having an etymology meaning ὁρῶν θεόν, 'one who sees God' (e.g. *Leg. All.* 2.34).[14]

The people Philo describes concentrate also on the writings of Moses the prophet, and sing his song, the Song of the Sea (Exod. 15), and that of the prophetess Miriam in their feast. The emphasis on inspired (prophetic) Scripture and song links well with their wider mystical purposes, for prophets were of course thought to be those who had a special connection with Heaven. The identification of Miriam as prophetic prototype for the

---

13. Birnbaum 1996: 5. For other treatments of Philo's mysticism see Goodenough 1935 and Winston 1985. Völker (1938) considered Philo's mystical language purely metaphorical.

14. For a full list of these passages, and wider discussion, see Birnbaum 1996: 61-127. The false etymology may be arrived at by dividing up יִשְׂרָאֵל, with some additions, into אִישׁ, a person, a man; רָאָה, he sees/saw; אֵל, God. For other suggestions of possible Hebrew and discussion see pp. 70-77.

women of the group identifies the legitimacy of women's inspiration within this community. With prophecy, we find the ultimate justification for the inclusion of women in mystical enterprise, for women, just as men, had been prophets in Israel's past. There was not only Miriam but Huldah (2 Kgs 23.4-7), and inspired leaders like Deborah (Judg. 4–5). The Babli lists seven prophetesses in Scripture: Sarah, Miriam, Deborah, Hannah, Abigail, Huldah and Esther (*b. Meg.* 14a). If God could choose women as vehicles for the divine word, then it would follow naturally that women could live a life which was designed to increase one's chances of being permitted to share in the light of the divine splendor. Even Philo, whose rhetoric is usually hardly pro-feminine or pro-women, implicitly concedes this in his description.

However, Philo emphasizes that there is an order in this intoxication, and this order is reflected by intense concentration and quietness at appropriate times: the elder who gives the Sabbath discourse speaks 'with a composed appearance and quiet voice, and with reason and thoughtfulness' (31); music is governed by dignified rhythms (29); self-control is laid down as the foundation stone of the soul (34); their common meal on the fiftieth eve is governed by 'the utmost seriousness' (66) and there is silence during any time apart from when there is the appropriate moment for the singing and dancing (75-77). Above all, there is usually a segregation of the sexes in common assemblies designed to ensure that the modesty appropriate to women be maintained, though the separation is only by a wall high enough to prevent men seeing the women, but low enough to ensure sound carries easily (32-33, 69). Philo's rhetoric is designed to ensure that his readers do not mistake his inspired group for others who may be considered inspired in the Graeco-Roman world: they are indeed 'intoxicated' like the Corybants and Bacchic revelers, but they are restrained.

In contrast, and much to Paul's alarm, it seems clear from Paul's comments that he understood that in the Corinthian Christian meeting a number of people all speak at once in tongues, people interrupt, prophets speak simultaneously, and there is confusion as each person responds to the Spirit individually (1 Cor. 14.26-33). Along with this certain Christian men's wives appear to be present, perhaps taken along by their husbands, and they interrupt everything by asking questions, wanting to learn about what is taking place (1 Cor. 14.34-36).[15] It is all absolute chaos. Paul is

15. I see no reason to see this passage as an interpolation. If the issue is one of inquiring wives who are trying to learn about matters in the meeting, and are

disturbed by this: 'Let all things be done properly and in an orderly way' he advises (1 Cor. 14.40) for God is a God of peace, not confusion (1 Cor. 14.33). His ideal model of inspired but orderly behavior appears to be close to the model Philo presents in his description of the group of *De Vita Contemplativa*.

Spirit-possession was well known in Graeco-Roman antiquity. Spirit-possession may have given women some release from the constraints of the *oikos*, as Ross Kraemer (1989; 1993: 36-49) has argued in relation to the cult of Bacchus/Dionysus, the god of wine (see also Kroeger and Kroeger 1978). We cannot know precisely what took place in the ceremonies associated with the cult of Dionysus, but in general it was understood that people were possessed by the god and went into a frenzy. Such worshippers 'drunk the liquor of a god's love', as Philo noted (*Vit. Cont.* 85). Losing control was expected. In literature concerning Bacchic rites, women in particular were seized with frenzy, and in the foundational mythology of these rites women leave the household, neglecting the world of domesticity and childcare to run into the context of untamed nature, where they suckle wild animals rather than their own children. In the story of the maenads as described by Euripides, they are wild, immensely strong, and very dangerous. They lose control, and let their hair fall loose, down over their shoulders (Euripides, *The Bacchae* 695).[16] In the first century, the festivals of Dionysus were celebrated in many Greek cities every other year and appear to have been participated in mainly by women (Diodorus Siculus, *Bibliotheca Historica* 4.3.3, quoted in Kraemer 1989: 49). If Ruth Padel is correct, women were considered especially susceptible

interrupting in order to question people directly about what is going on, Paul's comment is essentially in keeping with his desire to keep (patriarchal) order in terms of marriage: the wives are supposed to be subjected to their husbands, as the law says (Gen. 3.16), so let them ask their husbands at home. In fact, the evidence for the outspokenness of the wives may well reflect the presence of women speaking, praying and prophesying in the meeting, for only in a context where women are doing these things would inquiring wives have felt the freedom to ask questions at all. In a context in which women were silent, the visiting wives would have remained silent also. As for the men bringing their wives, it is probably more likely, given the authority of the husband, that a man who had converted to Christianity would bring his wife than that a woman who had converted to Christianity would bring her husband. For the authenticity of the passage see Wire 1990: 149-52.

16. See *The Bacchae* (Vellacott 1973: 191-244). For other possession-cult instances of loosing of the hair, including in the mysteries of Isis, see Schüssler Fiorenza 1993: 227.

to possession in classical Greek literature.[17] The evidence for mystical seizure in Jewish sources is late, and harder to interpret, but an interesting mention of what happens to Asenath in the novel *Joseph and Asenath* may reflect a notion that angelic or heavenly inspiration involved lack of control over the head, as Judith Gundry-Volf has noted. The angel puts his right hand, shooting sparks, on Asenath's head and shakes it (*Joseph and Asenath* 16.12-13).[18] Quite clearly, she does not have control over her head because of the angel.

Covering the Head

Recent discussions of 1 Cor. 11.2-16 have raised the possibility that the real issue was not about covering the head with some kind of draped veil, but rather about hairstyles. This is proposed because in a Roman context such as Corinth the evidence suggests that there was no necessary social shame as such associated with a woman not covering her head.[19] The issue must therefore have been the shamefulness of either transgressing social codes of gendered head-dress or hairstyle, or else in transgressing what was considered proper in regard to hairstyle.[20] Such suggestions imply that Paul was mainly concerned with social propriety.

However, if the real point of Paul's rhetoric is not actually to do with social shame in itself, even though he uses the language of shame and honor, then one may still imagine he is talking about covering the head, which his language most obviously suggests. Despite the strangeness of what Paul is saying (given social convention), the passage reads more coherently if some kind of veiling or covering of the head with a cloth is

17. Padel 1993. In Greek, to be 'possessed' or 'inspired' is expressed by the word ἔνθεος which seems to reflect a pun on 'god inside' (see Padel 1993: 13) though the word is in fact derived from ἐντίθημι. Perhaps women may have seemed fitting receptacles of the divine spirit by virtue of their capacity to be receptacles of growing human life inside their bodies, a woman may be ἔντεκνος, 'having children', from the male seed which is ἔνθετος, 'implanted' within.

18. Gundry-Volf considers it then explicable why Paul might speak about a woman needing to control her head, 'for the experience of inspiration could be so dramatic as to make one lose control over one's body and speech' (1997b: 206).

19. For discussion of the use of head-coverings for men and women see Thompson 1988 and Galt 1931.

20. Schottroff 1993: 109-10, 127-29; Gundry-Volf 1997a: 151 and *passim*. Schüssler Fiorenza 1983: 227-30, argues that 'control over the head' implies keeping one's hairstyle in place, rather than shaking the hair out loose.

writing a work 'On Piety' as well as with several apophthegms indicating her exemplary modesty.[27] In one story, when a man comments that her forearm is beautiful she retorts: 'but it is not [for the] public' (ἀλλ' οὐ δημόσιος).[28] Such modesty is used by Plutarch to argue for even more modesty. He notes that her arm was glimpsed as she drew her *himation* around her, indicating that she was usually well hidden by her outer garment, and that 'not just the arm of the virtuous woman but also her speech too should be not public' since for a woman to speak in public is an exposure, ἀπογύμνωσις (or 'stripping bare') of herself, for 'in her speaking her feelings and character and disposition may be seen' (*Moralia* 142D). A virtuous woman should then, according to Plutarch, speak in public through her husband, 'and she should not feel vexed if—like a flute-player—she sounds more impressive by means of another tongue'. Such ideals are clearly relevant in the discussion of 1 Cor. 11.2-16.

Therefore, covering up was an ideal to which virtuous (generally élite, wealthy) women should aspire. Covering the head was distinctively *feminine* in terms of dress only insofar as it represented the ideal of modesty appropriate to a virtuous woman. Furthermore, it seems that if the issue was really gendered clothing as defined by society in general—like wearing a skirt in modern Western contexts—one needs to ask why any woman would have stopped at head-covering. It seems that the Corinthian woman did not dress as men, as the female disciple of Plato, Axiothea, may have done (Diogenes Laertius, *Lives* 3.46; 4.2), the Cynic Hipparchia (Diogenes Laertius, *Lives* 7.96-98) or later Thecla (*Acts of Paul and Thecla* 40), or else surely Paul would have addressed this much more significant situation.[29] She did not cut her hair either; Paul uses this hair cutting as an example of what would bring shame, trusting that any woman would

Plutarch, *Moralia* 142C, 145F; Theodoret, *Therapeutike* 12.73; Diogenes Laertius, *Lives* 7.42; 8.42-43; Iamblichus, *Vita Pythag.* 55, 132.

27. See Thesleff 1965: 125; Stobaeus, *Anthology* 1.10.13.

28. Clement, *Strom.* 4.121.2; cf. Diogenes Laertius, *Lives* 8.43.

29. Cross-dressing was widely known in the Graeco-Roman world in cultic practice, marriage ritual and initiation rites: see Bullough and Bullough 1993: 2-38, and Delcourt 1961: 1-18. Cross-dressing in religious or festive contexts tended to emphasize the usual gendered norms. In a Jewish context cross-dressing was usually considered wrong (cf. Deut. 22.5). The Dead Sea Scrolls contain a halakha banning men dressing as women or women dressing as men (4Q159, frgs. 4-6, ll. 6-7). See also later Christian writers such as Clement of Alexandria, *Paidagogos* 3.3.20.3, *Strom.* 2.18.81.3; and Tertullian, *De Pallio.*, on men looking like 'men', though some later women ascetics in Egypt adopted men's clothing. See Anson 1974.

find the notion repellent. Shaving may have been inflicted on women for adultery in certain places (see Héring 1962: 105 nn. 9, 10; Gill 1990: 256), but whatever the explicit meaning for the Corinthians, Paul takes it for granted that this is an 'unthinkable alternative', as Wire puts it (1990: 119). Throwing off a veil or other head-covering in a sense seems quite a minor statement, especially as this is only in a very specific situation: of prayer and prophecy in a private house, presumably, among people one is accustomed to thinking of as being one's spiritual family, one's brothers and sisters, ἀδελφοί.[30] Wire has therefore suggested that the Corinthian women (she sees them as a group) were in fact doing what other women would do in the presence of family: you only wear a veil outside in the public domain, not in the private space of a family home.[31]

The issue is made even more perplexing when consideration of what was appropriate for Jewish men is brought into the picture. In fact, it is unclear whether all Jewish men covered their heads while praying in the first century, but it seems quite possible at least that most (if not all) did. Alan Segal, in his book *Paul the Convert*, raises this issue in particular in regard to 2 Cor. 3.15-18 in which we have the same link between 'veiling' and 'glory' (1990: 152-54). Here, Paul seems to be making a play on the Jewish (versus Christian) male practice of covering the head and partially obscuring the face and upper part of the body, when he writes that Moses used to place a veil over his face so that the children of Israel could not see the remainder of the shining glory of God there (Exod. 34.19-35). Paul states that the old veil, over the face of Moses, remains, because whenever Moses (the Torah) is read: 'a veil lies over their heart', a veil which is taken away when someone turns to the Lord. His language is metaphorical, but may allude to known practice. With this turning to the Lord, the veil is lifted away, and 'we all with unveiled face behold as in a mirror the Lord's glory (δόξα) and we are being transformed into the same image from glory to glory, just as from the Lord's spirit' (2 Cor. 3.18). In view of 1 Cor. 11.2-16, the reference is apparently androcentric, in alluding to the practice of Christian men versus the practice of Jewish men; Christian men see with unveiled face the Lord's glory as in a mirror (which they look into). They see therefore their own reflection without any covering. In

---

30. Apart from the numerous Christian sources indicating this notion, cf. the second-century anti-Christian diatribe by Lucian, *The Passing of Peregrinus*: Christians' first lawgiver (Jesus) 'has convinced them that they are all brothers [and sisters] of one another' (13).

31. Wire 1990: 183.

1 Cor. 11.4 Paul asserts that every man who prays and prophesies while having something on the head shames his head (namely Christ). It seems likely that he says this to alert the reader to the Jewish male practice of having something on the head during prayer, to which Christian practice forms a contrast.

Segal points to the great weight of evidence in rabbinic sources of Jewish men praying with their heads covered, also when studying mysticism (*b. Ḥag.* 14b; *b. Taʻan.* 20a). All priests had headgear, according to Torah (Exod. 28.4, 37, 40). Covering the head indicated grief, modesty or embarrassment in biblical times (2 Sam. 15.30; 19.5, Jer. 14.3-4) and therefore it seems quite likely that we then get a development of this so that proper humility before God is expressed by a covered head; this is what we find emphasized in rabbinic literature (*b. Šab.* 10a; *Midr. Ps.* 2.99), and in the first century, says Segal, a man would have covered his head with his *tallith*, or prayer shawl (1990: 152-54). Nowhere in Jewish literature do we have the slightest suggestion that it was proper for men to have uncovered heads before God. The evidence is that Jewish men would wear a head-covering in a ritual context. In pagan practice, some men appear to have covered their heads when actively sacrificing.

There is no reason to assume that Paul is then promoting Jewish convention in Corinth, whether for men or for women. Jewish women are never singled out in any sources as being especially distinctive in terms of their attire, and therefore we may assume that they probably conformed to wider social norms: Jewish women who wished to demonstrate special modesty (and virtue) would do so (*3 Macc.* 4.6; *b. Giṭ.* 90a), while others would not. There is also nothing to indicate that it was a norm for Jewish women to wear a *tallith* or *himation* during prayer. The wearing of a *tallith*—covering the head—was distinctively masculine attire in terms of prayer. If anything, then, Paul is completely inverting Jewish norms, rather than maintaining them, because Christian men do not wear *talliths*. This argues against the kind of argument used by Susanne Heine, who extrapolates a paradigm of what Christian women should do at prayer from a supposition that all Jewish women were veiled in public (Heine 1987: 96-97; cf. Conzelmann 1975: 185 n. 39). Paul insists upon the Corinthians following wider Jewish-Christian contexts where an attempt was made to modify the usual Jewish tradition for polemical purposes.[32] In 1 Cor. 11.2-16 he gives his reason for it. It is nothing to do with propriety before the

32. The attempt to be distinctive over against Jewish norms is found also in the *Didache* regarding the right days for fasting: *Didache* 8.

public, or general custom, or Jewish norms, or even equality, but involves propriety or proper modesty *before God* in front of whom Christian women, but not men, should cover up.[33] It rests on his reading of Genesis.

In conclusion then, it is Paul who 'genders' head-covering in the specific context of prayer and prophecy for the Corinthians, insisting that it is a tradition that he himself is passing on, appropriate to the 'communities of God' (1 Cor. 11.16). The evidence from Graeco-Roman culture indicates that both men and women could cover their heads for modesty in certain contexts, though women of high status would do so more commonly in public than men in certain areas to show their exceptional virtue by means of such modesty. If a woman was throwing off her head-covering during prophecy and prayer and arguing that a veil was a distinctive form of *feminine* attire that was irrelevant in view of Gal. 3.28, it was because Paul himself had asserted that it was a distinctive form of feminine attire in one context only: that of prayer and prophecy. It was then this tradition that was the problem in Corinth. It seems that the Corinthians took pains to stress to Paul that they followed his traditions (11.2), and it is in regard to these traditions that the issue of head-covering for women then arises. It is as if they have said, 'we want you to know we follow your traditions in everything, *but*...why have you recommended different clothing practice for men and women when praying and prophesying? Why should women be more modest than men in this particular context?'

The issue for Paul seems to be about how it all looks to God when prayer and prophecy is taking place. In the specific instance of praying and prophesying—that is, when God/Christ is present—a woman, but not a man, should be covered up. A covering of the head with the *stola* or *pallium* (or for Greek-style clothing, *himation*) meant much more than a hat or a little veil for the hair. The cloth of the outer garment fell forward and provided covering for the upper part of the body also, like long hair, as we can see in sculptural images of veiled women such as of Eumachia

---

33. One may 'psychologize' that Paul was used to covered women from his home context in Tarsus, and sought to inflict his own sense of propriety on the Corinthian church by means of creation theology, but that may be too speculative, and possibly may isolate Paul from Jewish-Christian churches. His final dismissive assertion that 'we have no such custom, nor (do) the communities (or churches) of God' (v. 16) would seem to be a direct appeal to link his notions of gendered attire while praying or prophesying with the practice of churches governed by his 'we' (Ephesus, Antioch?) as well as others in Judaea, Rome and elsewhere.

from Pompeii.[34] In the Christian community this is a dress code that applies to all women, not only to high-born wealthy women in public pious situations, the kind of élite women who were particularly concerned to show virtue and modesty, but also to slaves and artisans who might otherwise not cover up. All women, regardless of class, must show due modesty before God, and hide themselves with a head-covering, for all women in the context of Christian prayer and prophecy are equalized as virtuous women before God, who should be concerned not to shame their heads; after all, God is looking down from above![35] This circumstance would apply in public or private worship: the focus is God, not other people.

Paul does not advocate that women cover up in front of all men. In fact, the logic of Paul's argument suggests a commonly recognized situation in which a woman would not cover herself in front of a man, but *only* before God. If a man must not cover up before Christ/God because he is the glory of God, then a woman should not cover up before her 'head' (Adam), because she is the glory of a man. Paul's words here are context-specific, not a rule on gendered clothing to be adopted by all men and women in all circumstances. The context is only prayer and prophecy, in which both men and women are equally active and powerful, virtuous and honorable, brothers and sisters in Christ.

The rest of Paul's rhetoric makes sense when this is borne in mind. Paul writes in a rather pseudo-Stoic fashion that a woman is given long hair by Nature (= God) as a covering to her, and that long hair is her δόξα, 'glory' or 'honor'. In fact it also maintains her honor, as a draped head-covering does. The long hair is given to her as a covering before *God*, not before men, for when she was first created God draped her in order to preserve her modesty before him, dignifying her as a virtuous woman was dignified by modesty. A covering was a representation of God's acknowledgment of her virtue. God has created a woman with long hair to function in a natural state as a cloth cover functioned among the élite in civilized life in cities, where women tied their hair up in braids and curls. One could argue that since God intended women to have very long hair as a covering then perhaps this would suffice and all women should grow their hair very long

34. This statue is now in the Mansell Collection: see Haward 1990: 86.

35. Nowhere does Paul indicate that the issue is between husband and wife. The issue is between women and God. This has been well argued by Morna Hooker (1963–64), who thinks that woman should cover her head to veil modestly the glory of man (her head).

and wear it loose to completely cover themselves up, but Paul did not assume that any of his hearers would take this inference;[36] rather, they would prefer to cover up when Christ/God was particularly present. God has not made men with particularly long hair because he did not require it that men should cover themselves up before him.[37] As a man could see another man naked without it signifying loss of virtue, so the male God could see a naked man, but not a naked woman.

Conclusion

One may, after all this, now return to the woman we have distinguished who first may have let her head-covering fall during prophecy and prayer, and who defended herself against criticism by reference to the wild power of angels. Paul retaliated by claiming that the angels guard the order of creation, and therefore would not condone such behavior. The woman is shaming Adam in a situation in which God is clearly present, and she is not recognizing that she needs to show due modesty befitting a virtuous and honorable woman before the divine. God gave Eve long hair to cover herself before him, but since women of Paul's time wore their hair braided and curled up on their heads, this covering was no longer employed. They should therefore wear veils to cover the upper parts of their bodies and their heads in front of God.

How might the woman responsible for the faction respond to Paul? Paul claimed to know more about the angels than she herself, who was inspired by them. He put her in her place in creation, even while yet perhaps conceding a kind of gender mutuality 'in the Lord' (1 Cor. 11.11-12). The head-covering would soon take on a new meaning for women as a symbol of subjection. Paul's letters would soon be collected and defined as authoritative, and his words addressed to a particular situation of inspired prayer and prophecy would take on a resounding significance for all.

---

36. In Elisabeth Schüssler Fiorenza's reconstruction it seems that Paul's argument from Nature could have been turned around against him. The women could say: 'We do have veils: our long hair!' The point may be rather that they do have their hair up, and are therefore like a shaved woman, with necks and breasts exposed to view, which brings shame on their 'heads' (1983: 227-28).

37. I do not see this as a fashion issue. Even when European and/or Mediterranean men do not cut their hair it seldom reaches below the waist and usually comes down to a point not far past the shoulders. It is therefore not the same kind of covering afforded by women's hair when it is uncut.

Clement of Alexandria would interpret the passage as indicating that while the souls of men and women could equally attain virtue, their bodies were different, which led to women's roles in child-bearing and housekeeping; women should practice the Christian philosophy just as men, but the men 'are better at everything' (*Strom.* 4.8.62.4). Prophecy would dry up in the 'orthodox' church, reviving only for a time in Montanism. Women in the church were left with the head-covering as an indication of proper dress, not only at times of worship but elsewhere also, and were soon bereft of the joyful, vibrant prophecy that had once made the cover slip. Women's voices were no longer to be heard in worship contexts, apart from in responses to liturgical initiatives of male priests, formulated song or whispered prayer. No matter how well-meaning we may assume Paul's motives to have been in promoting honor, modesty and order in recognition of the presence of God and the angels, one can only wonder at how astonished the woman of Corinth may have felt at his words, given the strength of the prophetic power with which she was animated. The woman's silence may itself speak volumes.

THE LOGIC OF ESCHATOLOGY: THE IMPLICATIONS OF PAUL'S GOSPEL FOR GENDER AS SUGGESTED BY GALATIANS 3.28A IN CONTEXT

Douglas A. Campbell

Introduction

Galatians 3.28 must be one of the most widely cited texts from the Pauline corpus if not from the entire Bible. But in my view it is not so widely understood. There are various reasons for this which I do not have time to document in full here; partly a long history of interpretative resistance, especially on matters of gender, abetted in more recent times by a number of unfortunate methodological decisions.[1] The result is a text whose formulations are very well known but whose substance has for most of its interpretative history been almost systematically avoided. This is doubly unfortunate because, correctly understood, it is an excellent summary of the Pauline gospel, stating clearly if compactly that the reconciliation effected by God's action in Christ contains a set of staggering negations as the necessary reflex of its still more staggering event of transcendence.

---

1.   The interpretative tradition has long been nervous of suggestions of Marcionitism or Gnosticism; has often endorsed nature-grace progressions; and also tends to layer different passages together uncritically from Paul, not to speak from the rest of the New Testament, in order to overlay and to qualify the present section's radical thrust. In the modern critical period these tendencies have been exacerbated, even as the recovery of the text's argument has been stimulated, by feminist concerns. Layering continues, especially premature introduction of material from 1 Corinthians; form-critical readings decontextualize the argumentation, perhaps within highly speculative reconstructions of early church development and history; the slippery question of androgyny has been central to analysis since the 1970s (when it was fashionable); the section's binary oppositions tend not to be contextualized very effectively—and their discussion is also not usually connected with the same oppositions, writ large, discussed in the Household Codes; while ostensibly presuppositionless exegesis continues to table distinctly Western ontological assumptions about the person, the body, time, and so on, in relation to a text that challenges many of these assumptions, and certainly does not share them as a matter of course (on this last set of issues cf. Zizioulas 1985).

Furthermore, both these claims (which reflect divine actions) must be embraced—even as they embrace us—if we are to understand God's reconciling action in Christ correctly. As such I table Gal. 3.28a here—in deliberate disagreement with most of its current expositors—as a useful scriptural yardstick, a κανών, for our broader theological reflections on reconciliation (which I have taken broadly to mean 'salvation' and therefore to denote soteriological concerns).

But before analysing this text in detail, we need first to emphasize a commonplace concerning the circumstances surrounding the composition of the broader text within which it is embedded, namely, Paul's letter to the Galatian Christians. The primary[2] focus of much of that letter is a problem Paul refers to once, perhaps a little loosely, as 'judaizing' (2.14). He means by this the wholesale adoption of traditional Jewish practices by his Gentile converts in Galatia.[3] In effect, they are to become Jews, although they will probably retain many of their Christian commitments.

Suffice it to say that Paul seems unambiguously opposed to this step, and deploys various arguments designed to dissuade his audience from taking it.[4] Indeed, he sees high stakes as present in this move and argues accordingly with one of his crudest remarks (see 5.2, 4, and also v. 12). However, at this point—mercifully—we can set aside the further difficult historical questions in relation to Galatians.[5] It is the basic and incontro-

---

2. It is not the sole focus.

3. The precise details of this are debated, but it seems clear at least that any males will undergo circumcision (see 4.21, 5.2-3—cf. vv. 1, 11 and 12!—and 6.12, 13; cf. also v. 15), and the observation of basic Jewish temporal and dietary practices will probably follow on this (cf. 2.12 and 4.10). Consequently, the dictates of 'Moses' will also be quite central (cf. 3.10, 12, 17, 19b, and 24).

4. That is, however we understand the previous and present loyalties of the Galatian Christians, and even the motives and arguments of Paul himself, he seems primarily occupied with an attempt to prevent them from taking up the yoke of the Torah.

5. That is, of the opponents' precise identity, chronological issues—which are bound up to a degree with the timing of the arrival of these opponents—and also interpretation of the letter's opening biographical argumentation (1.13–2.14—many of the difficult questions surrounding the interpretation of 2.15–3.14 and 3.15-18 can also be bypassed here). Longenecker gives an excellent account of the more conservative, Acts-based account of the letter's provenance (1990: lxi-c); Luedemann (esp. 1984) of the more radical epistolary approach, informed ultimately by John Knox 1987. Corroborative argumentation is also found in Luedemann 1989. We can also set aside the brief recent text-critical assertions concerning the readings of p[46], and the assumption that Paul is quoting an early church confession here. Longenecker 1990 canvasses the relevance of p[46] accurately at each point of relevance. And as we account

vertible anti-judaizing thrust of Paul's discussion that will be surprisingly useful for adjudicating interpretations of Gal. 3.28a in its broader setting (3.19-29). This is because in the light of this we will prefer those readings that attack Jewish law-observance in some way; or, given an alternative, that attack it most strongly.[6] With this basic matter of provenance in the back of our minds, we can turn to the details of our famous text.

Key Localized Decisions

The interpretation of 3.28a in its immediate setting—scholars have traditionally been especially interested in, and quoted, the first half of this verse—must begin by carefully considering seven lexical and phraseological questions,[7] although I will merely summarize here conclusions argued for in detail elsewhere (D.A. Campbell 1997).

for the text in its setting and reveal its thoroughly Pauline character the form-critical hypothesis, although very popular, will prove unnecessary on all counts, and therefore also unfounded. (I offer detailed criticisms of the form-critical thesis in relation to this text in 1997, §1.3. These follow on from my observations concerning the same methodological application in relation to Rom. 3.21-26 [1992: 37-57].)

Finally, the question of the opponents' teaching can also largely be set aside. Martyn (1997a) has offered a fascinating and skilful, but also at points highly speculative, reconstruction of this. In so doing he runs foul of some of Barclay's methodological strictures (1987). The simpler concerns here focus on the uncontroverted and most basic thrust of the text—which also arguably addresses encoded rather than empirical opponents; a distinction Barclay himself could profit from making (cf. Stowers 1994: 21-33, 44, 74).

6.   It may also be noted that the letter is probably very incomplete in terms of its articulation of the situation, suffering both from widespread assumption concerning Paul's own position, and from considerable distortion of that of his opponents. We should consequently expect a sharp answer from Paul in Galatians concerning Gentile observance of the Torah, but we should not necessarily expect a self-sufficient or especially accurate one.

7.   I would suggest that two further questions apparent here are not so immediately germane, namely, the meaning of 'sonship' and 'the son', and the contribution of v. 29; decisions justified in more detail in my 1997 study. The latter concern picks up an important extended case for continuity in some sense with Abraham (although not as widely distributed as the argument for discontinuity with law-observance [etc.], this theme is also quite prominent in the letter-body: see 3.6, 7-9, 14, 15-18, 19, [21-22], 29, 4.[4-6], 7b, and 4.21-31); a concern not argued for in 3.26-28, however, which focuses on the letter's complementary argumentative concern for discontinuity. Similarly, the meaning of 'the son' for Paul in Galatians is grounded primarily in 4.4-7 and perhaps also in 4.21-31; texts beyond our present concern.

(1) *The Meaning of* οὐκ ἔνι *in Verse 28a*

οὐκ ἔνι is often translated as the mere negation of 'to be' giving the statement 'there is no Jew or Greek'. This is then usually supplemented by the adverbial phrase 'no longer' (cf. NRSV). But this last phrase is unsupported in the Greek text and such a reading also shifts the focus of the argument away from the Galatians themselves—who are the focus of sustained attention everywhere else—to the categories being negated. So I would suggest that a better rendering takes οὐκ ἔνι as a shortened form of οὐκ ἔνεστι yielding the emphatic negation 'it is not possible to be...' ('to be' must be supplied here but this is quite normal for Paul). This construal can then take an implicit subject for that verb, and in context this links up in turn with the baptized of v. 27, thereby retaining the context's broader emphasis on the Galatian Christians. Hence I would translate these famous negations as 'it is not possible for you to be a Jew or a Greek; it is not possible for you to be a slave or a freedman...' (and so on); a rather stronger and more personal set of negations.

What, however, is the origin of the three antitheses that Paul negates here so firmly?

(2) *The Meaning of the Binary Couplets in Verse 28a*

New Testament scholars often appeal to early church tradition at this point, observing that Paul is not discussing class or gender in context, and hypothesizing primarily on that basis that he is therefore reproducing a fixed liturgical fragment that somewhat exceeds its current usefulness (a fragment also attested in 1 Cor. 12.13 and Col. 3.11). But this common assertion overlooks the ubiquity of this analysis of society in both Paul and his background (here, intriguingly, attested in both Greek and Jewish sources). These three binary oppositions summarize a Hellenistic ideology concerning human society attested at length in, for example, Aristotle's *Politics*, but found vestigially in many other places as well,[8] including

---

8.   Martyn lists Stoic and neo-Platonic traditions as well as proto-Gnostic or Apocalyptic possibilities as possible backgrounds to the formula (observations still valid even if the theory of quotation is abandoned; see 1997a: 379-80). One of his famous earlier studies also deploys neo-Pythagorean parallels (1985). Moreover, a closely parallel text to v. 28a is attributed to Plato in Plutarch's *Marius* (46.1) and to Thales and Socrates in Diogenes Laertius's *Lives* (1.33) and Lactantius's *Divine Institutes* (3.19.17). Betz also notes possible influence from the Sophists (1979: 192 n. 87 and 193 n. 95—he also notes a fascinating *Persian* parallel on p. 185 n. 26). For possible Cynic parallels see Downing 1997. Important broader background material

Jewish prayers.[9] So Paul is no more citing a liturgy or confession here than when current reporters of international politics speak of 'East versus West' or 'North and South'. It would seem that multitudes, including popular folk, thought of human society in terms of a horizontal ethnic opposition between 'us' and 'everyone else', and two further, more internal, vertical oppositions of class and gender—the élite versus the great unwashed, and the fair versus the uncouth sex; horrible analytical oversimplifications it is true, but better than nothing.

The third couplet in Paul's citation also contains a tell-tale divergence, however, when it negates not 'male *or* female' (or even 'man or woman') but 'masculine *and* feminine'. This is probably an allusion to Gen. 1.27 (LXX) where God made humanity in his image, 'masculine and feminine'. So Paul seems to have Adamic or created humanity in mind here; a broad canvas indeed.[10] But on what is this striking negation, essentially of the present cosmos, grounded? And at this point we are forced to appeal to the statements that immediately precede v. 28a in v. 27: ὅσοι [γὰρ] εἰς Χριστὸν ἐβαπτίσθητε, Χριστὸν ἐνεδύσασθε.

(3) *The Suggestions of Verse 27*

Verse 27 begins to supply a positive warrant for the negation of the foregoing categories using the two 'whole body' metaphors of immersion and re-clothing drawn from the ritual of baptism.[11] These also employ the metaphor of spatial movement to suggest something: the baptisands have moved, as into water, into Christ, and have also been clothed in Christ (and note the object of the movement, namely, Christ himself; *not* 'the people of God', or, even worse, 'the primal androgynous one'). This

---

may be found in Cartledge 1993. I analyse the closely related Col. 3.11, specifically in relation to the puzzling appearance of 'Scythian', in 1996.

9.   The now infamous text is attributed to R. Judah ben Elai (c. 150 CE) in *t. Ber.* 7.18 and *j. Ber.* 13b, but to R. Meier (his contemporary) in *b. Men.* 43b.

10.   The case is not decisive but see my 1997, § 2.2.3. Gundry-Volf makes the case with characteristic precision in her 1997c. Paul's overarching concern with transcending law-observance in the present crisis lends considerable weight to this 'more radical' construal. *Not* to stress the transcendence of created dimensions would give argumentative hostages to Judaizing fortune; something virtually inconceivable in the letter's original setting.

11.   The discussion of baptism in Paul is complex and cannot be rehearsed in detail here. Betz gives an interesting account informed by cautious *Religionsgeschichtliche* concerns: 1979: 187; see also his 1995. However, even his cautious use of this approach to the ritual in Paul is beginning to look threadbare!

movement also seems to denote a total or comprehensive change because it grounds the negation of the cosmic categories that follows immediately.[12] But in order to grasp this negation fully, the analysis must be broadened a little further.

(4) and (5) *Parallelism and the Notion of 'One-ness'*

At this stage it is helpful to note an important structural feature in the subsection that generates vital interpretative leverage, namely, a striking parallelism between vv. 26 and 28b that neatly brackets our particular text and its initial warrant in v. 27 (and this is a common device in Paul).[13] The first of these brackets in v. 26 states that 'in Christ' the Galatians are 'sons of God'; something clearly derived from Christ's sonship that Paul will give more details about shortly in 4.1-10. The parallel statement in v. 28b complements this claim with the important motif of 'one-ness' (εἷς). Most commentators now move rapidly to 1 Corinthians 12, where 'one-ness' is a prominent theme and some of our couplets are also cited, but this appeal is, I would suggest, misguided. Many of the key premises for that chapter's discussion of wholistic unity—namely, those creating a spirit-body analogy—are missing from Galatians 3. It is in fact more likely that the use of 'one' here by Paul, paralleling as it does the phrase 'sons of God', means nothing more than 'one and the same' (a meaning also attested elsewhere in Paul[14]), so it is not undergirding a part-whole analogy at all. And at this point we can dispense with a whole raft of interpretations that sail off into the nefarious realms of androgyny.[15] These judgments, in my

---

12. An important argumentative point often overlooked. These transformations symbolized by baptism seem to ground a complete ontological shift and change, so we can appreciate some of the force of the ritually grounded metaphors for Paul retrospectively.

13. The recognition of this inclusio also identifies the famous statements of v. 28a as an integral part of a larger subsection comprising three verses, hence they cannot now be considered in isolation from that carefully crafted setting.

14. Meaning 2a in BAGD. See perhaps Rom. 3.30, more clearly 9.10, 15.6; perhaps 1 Cor. 6.16-17 and 10.17, certainly 11.5, 12.9, 11, and possibly v. 13; and Phil. 1.27 and 2.2; cf. also perhaps Lk. 12.52, Jn 11.52, Acts 4.32, and Rev. 18.8.

15. The seminal—and very brilliant, but also distinctly dated—analysis was Meeks 1973–74. More recently Boyarin 1994—another brilliantly creative study—has greatly emphasized Gal. 3.28 and its supposed attestation to a Hellenistic ideal in Paul of undifferentiated metaphysical unity, that then generates awkward conceptual and psychological tensions with Paul's other commitments to Jewish historical particularity and individual bodiliness. Such constructs are undercut quickly and completely,

view, are based on a demonstrable misreading of the text, which I would suggest affirms clearly that the state inhabited by the Galatian Christians is a uniform but personal and pluralized condition.

(6) *The Import of the Spatial Categories*
By this point in my initial analysis a general sense for the subsection is beginning to emerge. Paul seems to be deploying spatial categories consistently in order to speak of categories of existence or being and their transformation in relation to the events of Easter. (The Galatians are said, in the space of three verses, twice to be 'in Christ', to be clothed 'in' Christ, and to be immersed 'into' Christ.) Interpreted this means that the Galatian Christians, irrespective of their previous positioning within the potentially diverse subcategories of present society, have been shifted into a mutually exclusive category of uniform sonship in Christ that displaces their previous existence, whatever it was—a dramatic set of claims!—in a shift best symbolized in certain respects by the ritual of baptism. When Paul states that someone is 'in Christ', he is making a statement about their new Christian ontology derived from their involvement (through the Spirit as it turns out[16]) in the events of Easter; events that centre of course on Christ himself.[17] Which brings us to my last detailed decision, namely, the interpretation of πίστις in v. 26.

(7) *The Meaning of* πίστις
In the light of the foregoing it seems that a christological reading of ἡ πίστις in v. 26, '[by means of] the faithful one', is the most apposite as

however, by the foregoing observation that the oneness Paul is speaking of, in its immediate setting, is a oneness of sonship (in the sense that all are now 'sons' in Christ)—this is not their only problem in relation to the text, but it is perhaps their most significant one. Paul's rationale is explicitly christological, and no analysis that ignores this dimension in his argument can lay claim to much plausibility.

    16. See 3.2, 5, 14; 4.6, 28; 5.16-18, 22-25; [6.1?], and 6.8.
    17. The literature is copious and again cannot be discussed here, but see perhaps especially the parent of the position, Deissmann 1912 (a better starting point than Albert Schweitzer), popularized accessibly in Stewart 1935: 147-203. Longenecker is also sensitive to the importance of the phrase and gives a nuanced analysis (1990: 152-54), although it differs somewhat from the above suggestions, loading—in the manner of Deissmann—too much into the grammar of the dative. Paul, in my view, is simply talking of 'Christ-being', that is, of being governed by Christ (hence the frequent trivial use of the phrase). Just what that entails in turn must be left open for further analysis of his texts and arguments.

against a more traditional rendering in terms of belief or trust, since the former reading speaks in martyrological terms of the event of the cross, which lies at the heart of the rather extraordinary process of termination and reconstitution that Paul is describing.[18] The Galatians are, in Christ, sons of God, *and by means of Christ's great act of faithfulness*, namely, his execution—a claim that Paul also makes exactly and overtly in 6.14-15. This is the point where God has acted to terminate the divisive categories of the present cosmos. Over against this suggestion, the traditional reading in terms of 'faith'—an essentially anthropocentric view—really inserts an alien set of soteriological assumptions into Paul's present argument *and with no other textual warrant for that in context.* Only the incontrovertible establishment of Arminianism elsewhere in Paul would permit such a reading; something I would dearly love to debate here but space forbids it.[19] (Suffice to say that the Arminian reading of Paul, so beloved of much of the New Testament interpretative community, is in my view possibly assisted by the projection of several unrecognized but distinctly modern European assumptions.[20])

With these seven localized decisions made, I would suggest the following translation (within which Paul's argument hopefully appears a little more clearly; see also Figure 1 below):

> For all of you are (by means of the faithful one)
> sons of God in Christ Jesus.

18. This phrase also reaches back to Paul's previous stretch of argumentation where πίστις is a recurrent motif: it appears only in the summary section 5.5-6 after this point in the letter! So its detailed interpretation is really bound up with our understanding of 3.15-25.

19. For a representative sample of the debate see Dunn 1997 versus Hays 1997. Hays's original published doctorate remains especially important in the present setting (1983); while Dunn expresses the traditionalist anthropocentric reading frequently in his 1993a and b, and 1998. (I engage with the issues within the latter study raised by this decision in Campbell 1998). Like most scholars, I am also reading the prepositional phrases independently of one another, the first adverbially and the second adjectivally (in the predicate), so Gal. 3.26 is *not* a pristine example of a πίστις Χριστοῦ genitive in Paul (and the reading of p[46] ought to be rejected as a later scribal harmonization: see Longenecker 1990: 150).

20. Karl Barth remains extremely useful here, esp. 1959; also Colin Gunton, esp. 1985. I hope to detail these specific charges in a forthcoming monograph tentatively entitled *The Individualist Reading of Paul: A Preliminary Account of the Neo-Lutheran Paradigm's Nature, Problems, and Solution.*

For you have been immersed into Christ;
you have been clothed in Christ.

It is not possible (for you) to be a Jew or a Greek;
it is not possible to be a slave or a free person;
it is not possible to be 'male and female';

for all of you are one and the same
in Christ Jesus.

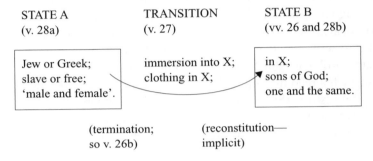

STATE A	TRANSITION	STATE B
(v. 28a)	(v. 27)	(vv. 26 and 28b)
Jew or Greek; slave or free; 'male and female'.	immersion into X; clothing in X;	in X; sons of God; one and the same.
	(termination; so v. 26b)	(reconstitution— implicit)

Figure 1. *The Argument of Gal. 3.26-28a*

Substantive Issues

With these localized exegetical decisions in place we can now move on to
a consideration of certain more substantive issues. Three interest me in
particular (and discussion of these is followed by two briefer sets of historical observations): first, what we might call Paul's uncompromising
eschatological logic; secondly, the theological limitations imposed by the
contingent setting of Paul's argument; and thirdly, the detachability of the
Hellenistic social ideology that he uses here.

*The Heart of the Matter: The Uncompromising Eschatological Logic of
Paul's Reconciling Gospel*
The clear contingent force of Paul's statements in Gal. 3.26-28 concerns
Judaism. His point seems to be that the distinction between Jewish and
non-Jewish lifestyles and peoples has been subsumed in the broader
supersession of all created human existence, hence the apparently redundant claims concerning the abolition of class and gender actually
participate significantly in his argument by indicating the cosmic sweep of
this assertion. Law-observance, claims Paul, participates in the general
state that has been left behind: from within that state its observance or

non-observance would be meaningful, but given the universal transfer effected by and within Christ such concerns are now redundant. The point is especially clear if Paul alludes to Gen. 1.27 in v. 28a. This textual echo would suggest that Paul's framework is creational (which is to say that the symmetrical counter-point to Christ's work for Paul is Adam; another plausible suggestion surely). So the view backwards is a dramatic and far-reaching one.

The reason for Paul's complete and universal negation seems to lie in the event he presupposes, namely, the execution of Christ. Death is a total negation. Moreover, Christ in all his humanity died, therefore humanity as created has been executed in him. In addition, resurrection reverses a condition that according to Jewish tradition began in Eden (hence also perhaps Paul's allusion to Gen. 1.27). So the mutually reinforcing elements within Paul's probable reasoning here seem apparent. In essence:

> To be in Christ is *not* to be in humanity as it was created.
> (It is to have died.)
> Judaism is part of humanity as it was created
> (a distinction arriving in fact some time after creation with Abraham).
> Therefore,
> to be in Christ is to be beyond Judaism and non-Judaism:
> it is to have died to this particular distinction in created reality.

Complementing these suggestions is the subsection's inference that the new state in which the Galatian Christians now live is *eschatological*. That state is denoted in 3.26-28 by existence 'in Christ' as 'sons of God', but its discontinuity with preceding creation, its universality and comprehensiveness over against that former creation, and its implicit consequence on Christ's resurrection, all point ineluctably in this direction. Hence Paul's abolition of created dimensions is complemented by eschatological expectations of another creation. The complete termination of humanity in Christ's death—the death of a martyr—is followed by the dramatic affirmation by God of this in a new creation beyond this event—the eschatological reflex in martyrology of resurrection. (Moreover, as a result of this the presupposition of that new reality—its *eikon*—is Christ's resurrected state denoted here by Paul in terms of sonship.) So the dualism of states that Gal. 3.26-28 speaks of is almost certainly a sharp eschatological dualism comprising creation and a new creation, with Christ's execution and resurrection both separating and connecting them.[21]

---

21. We have also seen that Paul's chosen vehicle for denoting Christian participation in this process is baptism.

As a direct result of this stark eschatological framework I would suggest that Paul's contingent point concerning the transcendence of Jewish law-observance *is necessarily transferable to all the other differentials he discusses as well*. Consequently, class and gender distinctions *must* also be deemed transcended for those in Christ.[22] This necessary extension of the logic of abolition also of course includes ethnicity *per se*. Paul understandably targets here the distinction between Jews and Gentiles—in fact the distinction that the New Testament is primarily preoccupied with. But any ethnic differential is also implicit in this abolition, and not merely that between Jews and non-Jews. So this argument contains potent significance for other ethnic conflicts within the early church; an application that is especially clear in Col. 3.11 (which I suspect Paul composed) where divisions within barbarity are targeted, specifically between Phrygian and Scythian.

Furthermore, if Paul's understanding of the consequences of the Christ event—as this subsection presupposes—is valid, then this extended set of negations is also a *necessary* inference of his thinking about Christ. So if they prove unpalatable, *a different interpretation of the impact of the Christ event needs to be found*, and that in defiance of Paul's creational-eschatological view as outlined here. In short, I would urge the realization that *universal abolitionist consequences, based themselves on a retrospective perception of eschatological supersession, are utterly intrinsic to Paul's gospel of eschatological reconciliation*.

I am especially confident of this realized eschatological aspect to Paul's argument in view of the particular contingency of the situation that was noted at the outset of my discussion. Only such a realized view can impact negatively on Jewish law-observance, Paul's principal goal in composing Galatians. Any mitigating of the force of the supersession experienced by Christians—and any corresponding muting of the presence of the new creation in the lives of those 'in Christ'—must open the door for a certain validity to be attached to ethnic behaviour in the old age, in this case observance of the dictates of Moses as Judaism suggests. If the old age is still even partly in force, with the Christian living in it, then there is still something to be said for transferring from a pagan to a Jewish category within that dimension. But I cannot see Paul granting such concessions here. His intention and argument are both clearly directed towards a com-

---

22. Biological procreative functions, productive work, and eating and drinking, are hence presumably also transcended in the new creation (cf. Rom. 14.17; also Mk 12.25).

plete and irrevocable transcendence of such concerns.[23]

The *a posteriori* structure of this argument is also especially note-worthy. Paul argues *in view of* existence in Christ, *in the light of which event* conclusions are dictated about previous existence. Clearly, only Christians can make or understand such contentions—the text reasons from within the circle of their experience (and this is also not surprising in the context of the Galatian crisis—it is not a conversion document). Moreover, this is perhaps the only *a posteriori* eschatological argument on offer. Comparable Jewish discussions of course tend to be resolutely futurist and hence necessarily speculative in a way that Paul's is not.[24]

In short, we can say that Gal. 3.28a in context is an irreducibly radical, abolitionist, and therefore also political and liberational text. It is this because more fundamentally it speaks of a gospel that is ontologically concrete, universal, markedly dualist (correctly understood), and eschato-logically transcending (in qualification of the preceding). Two realities are in play here, and Christians have been transferred in and through Christ from the one, characterized by various complex bisections, to the other, characterized more uniformly by sonship. And as Paul looks back he can see no reason to affirm the primacy of the categories that he has left behind. This is, in my view, the essence of the martyrological, participatory, and eschatological logic of Paul's reconciling gospel as it is revealed by Gal. 3.26-28.

The Rhetorical Shape of the Argument
But these stringent proclamations of abolition and transcendence may seem to some a little dangerous, not to mention counter-intuitive. At this

23. Paul's view of the law is much discussed these days. Less seldom discussed is an explicit justification for its abrogation (or at least a coherent one). But Gal. 3.26-28 supplies that (which is not to say that it is Paul's only argument against the law): his eschatological view of the effects of Christ's death and resurrection impacts directly on the question of law-observance and the function of the Mosaic Torah. These are now for him quite small—although perhaps especially nostalgic—components of a redundant reality. When viewed in these terms, any return to law-observance by his Gentile converts amounts to *a betrayal of the way Easter has effected reality at its most fundamental levels*; reason perhaps for some of Paul's passion. As W.S. Campbell puts it: '[t]o retract this [although I differ a little from W. Campbell on what "this" is] would be tantamount to acting as if Christ had not come, as if the new age of the Gospel had not arrived' (1991: 100).

24. Although degrees of inauguration should at times be admitted: witness esp. Qumran.

point then it may be helpful to note the impact of the contingent situation in Galatia on the rhetorical shape of Paul's argument, and also the exact nature of his negations.

As we have already noted, Paul's argument in Gal. 3.26-28 contains a distinctive *a posteriori* structure, viewing present reality from the vantage point of existence in Christ and hence emphatically beyond the categories of creation. This in turn generates typically *a posteriori* arguments— 'where you are is good, so why go back to where you were—which is also, incidentally, bad'. We can surmise now that, in the light of this basic structure, Paul's specific contentions will have certain important limitations:

(1)   It is unlikely that Paul will nuance the pre-Christian state at all positively. That state must be depicted in tortured terms as much as this is possible, and a glance at the rest of the letter confirms this where a great deal of imagery is drawn from minority and slavery (minority being an essentially negative category in ancient society). It is a state that Paul wants the Galatian Christians to feel glad that they have left behind, and to contemplate a return to with shame, disgust and horror. It therefore seems monolithically negative.

(2)   The finality of the transition will be emphasized as well. Paul wants his converts to think of themselves as having made the decisive shift—they must think of themselves as having left issues such as law-observance behind. So we would also not expect qualifications of the partiality of this transfer. This would also blur Paul's point.

(3)   And (corresponding to [2]) the nature of the new reality in Christ should also be depicted in realistic terms, that is, it too can hardly be presented in a diluted form. The Galatian Christians must be confident that they really are living in a new creation, otherwise the argument from transfer loses much of its force. It will also of course be presented in a very positive light, here in terms of 'divine sonship'.

Three important but unanswered sets of issues are now more comprehensible.

(1)   Corresponding to (1) above, there is little theology of creation in Gal. 3.28a in context. As we have just seen, articulation of any positive dimensions in that state will not serve Paul's present rhetorical purposes. This is of course not to say that Paul does

not have positive perspectives on creation: of course he does, but he will not be talking about them here.

(2)   Corresponding to (2) and (3) above, there is also little eschatological nuancing. We do not receive here an account of the degree to which Christians participate in the new creation because any admission of partiality will also mute Paul's contentions. So we should not expect detail concerning eschatological inauguration or remaining futurity from Gal. 3.28a in context; merely statements of its actual realization—which we are nevertheless irrevocably committed to in some sense.

(3)   There is also little articulation of *how* we are transferred into Christ and into the new creation, and of how his death is related to Christian baptism. We are given a few motifs to follow through further, namely, divine sonship, the phrase 'in Christ', and more generalized references to Christ's martyrological faithfulness and to Christians' immersion and clothing in him, but that is all. Paul can largely assume here the past facticity of that event and go on to build on it. Key soteriological premises are therefore also missing, notably the role of the Spirit, which becomes apparent in the letter shortly.

In sum, the rhetorical exigencies of Gal. 3.26-28 contain implicit warnings against extrapolating Paul's positive views on creation, on the detailed mechanics of soteriology, and on the degree of eschatological realization, from this subsection. The text's particular focus dictates that these concerns will probably be muted and, correspondingly, any silence on such matters should not be overinterpreted.

But is this model dangerously negative about creation in any case?—is this an irreducible structural propensity in what Paul seems to be saying here?, and not merely a matter of rhetorical (dis)emphasis (perhaps thereby creating permanent vulnerabilities to Gnosticism). Paul's *a posteriori* approach is, I would suggest, seriously misunderstood if these conclusions are drawn.

That is, although it has long been traditional to counter the dangers of Gnosticism through an appeal to creation and its goodness (principles we should note that an *a posteriori* approach will not necessarily deny), Christ's entry into our condition in order to redeem humanity can also speak powerfully concerning the status of that prior state (something Paul tables in Gal. 3.19-25; 4.4-5). The incarnation inherently affirms the goodness of creation—although it does not follow from this that creation cannot be eschatologically superseded in any way, that is, within some-thing better. Hence I would suggest that in theological terms it simply does not follow that Paul's resolute christological presuppositions, as they are expressed here, entail an impoverished theology of creation.[25]

In addition to the resources in relation to creation implicit in his Christology—which I think Paul recognized at times—careful attention must also be paid to the nature of the negations that Paul is deploying. Whereas Gnosticism and much Hellenistic thought in general made *a priori* negative claims about 'what is', that is, creation in and of itself, as we have seen, *Paul's* negations are comparative judgments made on the basis of a new superior state; they are therefore relative and external nega-tions.[26] It is a metaphysic of transcendence, admittedly with a negative

---

25. Actually, I suspect that Paul himself recognized these incarnational resources at times, although not especially consistently. His use of Wisdom Christology (which is admittedly disputed), if present, implies a pre-existent and/or prior role for Christ vis-à-vis creation (pre-existence perhaps supplying a strictly speaking meaningless temporal metaphor for the very meaningful notion of *ontological* priority). Wisdom Christology is present in isolated patches in 1 Corinthians and arguably also in Romans 8 (see 1 Cor. 1.30; 2.7, 16; 8.6; Rom. 8.3, 29), although its clearest Pauline repre-sentation is in the disputed captivity letters (see Eph. 1.3-14; 3.3-11 [and v. 19?]; Col. 1.12-20; 2.2-3). This material is much discussed. W.D. Davies, as ever, is insightful (1980: 147-76); more controversial is J.D.G. Dunn (1980: 163-212); E. Schüssler Fiorenza briefly presents the case for 'Sophia Theology' at Corinth (1983: 219-20). Creation was through Christ for Paul, therefore, it must be 'good', but his primary christological interest—and certainly in Galatians—is the establishment of the new creation, effected at Easter.

26. I sometimes use for pedagogical purposes at this point the somewhat banal example of transport. Horses were considered for millennia to be a superior, faster and more comfortable mode of transport than one's own legs; indeed, they were quite a status symbol—a good Turkish stallion was the mediaeval equivalent of a Porsche. However, with the invention and production of the motor car, we moved beyond the horse-drawn era. Now, on the one hand, this shift should not be taken to imply that horses were not superior to auto-perambulation: they were. They were a good mode of transport, and better than the other options. But they were also emphatically superseded by the motorcar to which they stand in a decidedly negative relationship. Hence, my children never ride to school, although my parents usually did. So we are entitled to view horses negatively in modern comparative terms (except perhaps for recreational purposes), although favourably in absolute terms. Paul's argument vis-à-vis creation is structured in exactly the same fashion. To remain attached to creation on his view is the equivalent of remaining committed to horse-drawn transport in the modern era; an eccentric commitment, one might say.

element, as against a metaphysic of sheer negation, and there is a world of difference between these two types of negation.[27]

In short, I would suggest that implicit in the gospel of reconciliation as Paul deploys it presuppositionally in Gal. 3.26-28 is a strong affirmation of the goodness of creation—although, importantly, not the latter's *unconditional* affirmation. Creation, which Paul tends to speak of in terms of 'the cosmos', is good enough for the divine son to enter, to assume, to reconcile, and to redeem, while in so doing a set of relative negations also inevitably takes place. The Pauline gospel's advocates need not be ashamed then of its *a posteriori* structure on these counts. To accuse Paul of Gnosticism is to misunderstand what he is trying to say. Indeed, perhaps to assert this charge repeatedly against an eschatological reading of Paul's gospel may betray not so much an anti-Gnostic vigilance as a fundamental commitment to a type of Western theology premised on an underlying nature-grace progression. Paul's statements in Gal. 3.26-28, construed in the foregoing manner, are rightly perceived to be hostile to this entire approach, but the problem is not their Gnostic propensity so much as their resolutely *retrospective* theological epistemology—an approach that offends our desire to contribute something significant or fundamental to the articulation of our theology?[28]

The Argumentative Status of Hellenistic Social Ideology (v. 28a)
I want now to explore briefly an intriguing question stemming from the *a posteriori* nature of Paul's claims: What is the precise relationship between the specific content of the negated couplets in v. 28a—that is, the fundamental binary dimensions of creation that according to Paul are being transcended—and his argument for their abolition? Perhaps some-

27. Indeed, despite its negations, arguably only such an *a posteriori* claim, rooted in redemption, *can* effectively ground a positive view of creation because one might entertain doubts about the viability of an *a priori* project that attempts to do the same independently and prior to redemption: see here especially Buckley's powerful analysis (1987).

28. It is also worth noting that, when we examine the Corinthian correspondence closely, we find that Paul was no friend of Gnosticism or of any more generalized Hellenistic gnosis. He fights a bitter battle in the context of that community against a powerful and essentially gnostic preacher, crafting a series of devastating rejoinders against its various aspects (*although he does not really appeal to creation in this connection*).

MacDonald's (1987) imaginative and thorough study is intriguing in this connection, although I do not find his thesis ultimately probative.

what surprisingly, closer analysis suggests that the content of the state being negated, here supplied by Paul in terms of stereotypical Hellenistic antitheses, does not affect the validity of his argument *and hence is largely detachable from his christological claims*. Put differently, v. 28a, although perhaps the most interpretatively famous component of this subsection, is the least important theological element in vv. 26-28b (and perhaps mercifully so, since arguably its perspectives are not 'theological' at all). If this is true, then we must now read the celebrated negations of v. 28a in a new way.

In a little more detail, the validity of Paul's argument, as we have seen, depends on the positive state into which Christians have moved. If this state of existence—being 'in Christ'—is valid *and* exclusive of all other categories then it simply follows that anyone transferred into it has left their previous categories behind (or at least has begun to decisively). Hence it does not matter what those categories were—they are a point of origin only. So the definitions here can be changed substantially without altering the validity of the argument one jot. We might say that in Christ's death the relevance of any internal categorical analysis of existence prior to Christ in relation to soteriology has also been terminated. The *a posteriori* structure of Paul's argument leads inevitably to this conclusion, as the following analogous argument suggests:

> To be transferred into Pink (P) is to be pink (p).
> To be p, in P, is to be entirely p;
> that is, to be p is to be in no way nor in any element not p
> (i.e. p is an exclusive and exhaustive category).
> X has transferred into P and therefore is p.
> Therefore, it is impossible for X to be (now) in any way not-p.
> Therefore, X is now not red, or rough, or oval, or biological, etcetera
> (*supply any category*).

This feature of Paul's argument introduces an important dislocation into his statements (which I doubt he himself was especially aware of: that is, he seems to deploy the couplets reasonably seriously). His specification in v. 28a of the created state being negated 'in Christ' bears no valid relationship to the central premises on which his broader argument depends. Furthermore, those central premises are his properly basic theological axioms, so they can hardly be abandoned. From this it follows that (1) Paul must coordinate any statements about creation with his basic axioms if they are to share in those axioms' validity; and (2) his present statements, not being so coordinated, are invalid (or, at least, they possess a different order of validity).

All this is not to say, however, that Paul's claims that social status and gender difference as well as Jewish or non-Jewish ethnicity have been abolished 'in Christ' are invalid. His *abolitionist* claims (as we have already noted) are entirely correct, *but not because the frame of reference within which they have been asserted is also valid.* They are valid as part of the broader argumentative validity that we have already reprised, namely, the exhaustive supersession of created humanity—whatever it is—effected in Christ and retrospectively perceived and articulated. Hence Paul's couplets in v. 28a really denote salient features of this Christian negation only. *They articulate specific points where the universal abolition of the gospel must be contingently emphasized*; in the context of Galatia, at the point of Judaism; at Corinth, mere difference *per se* (although for contingent reasons perhaps deliberately avoiding emphasizing any abolition of gender differences); and arguably also at Colossae, at the point of intra-barbarian ethnic differentials. Hence we do not have to accept that humanity ought to be divided into the two categories 'Jew' and 'non-Jew' (or, still worse, 'Jew or Greek'), nor do we even have to accept the fundamental validity of a single ethnic category for the description of Judaism or of non-Jewish ethnic groups, to accept the Christian claim on the basis of the premises stated here that any reification of such distinctions ought now to be abandoned in Christ.

We might summarize this distinction as follows: as general categories of human existence the couplets in Gal. 3.28a bear little relation to Paul's gospel and its basal validity and can be treated as such. As specific points in a given context where the negation of the universal gospel needs to be grasped, however, they remain valid. We can learn then from v. 28a and its context about contingent negations (including the negation of inappropriate gender differences), but we should eschew the construction of any theology of society on the basis of Paul's analysis of human creation here (i.e. some 'theology of nature'). And this conclusion links up with my previous suspicions that Paul is informed at this point primarily by Hellenistic social ideology. We would not necessarily expect a tight correlation between those categories and Christology, and neither do we find it. Ironically, it seems that Paul's binary analysis of society can itself be abolished, along with any contingently prominent reification of racial, class, or gender differences.[29]

Two further more historical points can now be noted.

29. This reduction in the significance of Paul's binary social categories in Gal. 3.28a is not especially dramatic in its interpretative consequences for that letter—as the

Pointers Elsewhere in the Corpus

Galatians 3.26-28 summarizes in my view the central argumentative dynamic in Galatians as a whole, although I do not have time to demonstrate that thesis here; however, Galatians remains incomplete and hence famously obscure on certain points. So it is worth asking if Paul explicates the critical complex tabled rather summarily in Gal. 3.26-28 more fully elsewhere in his corpus. And at least we can cross-reference a series of motifs in order to find any such discussion: Christ as God's son; Christians as sons and hence as probably receiving υἰοθεσία; a dualistic framework comprising the new age's eschatological displacement of creation (where discussion of Genesis 1–3 and/or Adam might also be expected); and Christian transition between these two states being described in terms of baptism and consequent existence 'in Christ'.

In fact an obvious answer to our queries lies to hand, namely, *chs. 5–8*

form-critics have long pointed out, slavery and gender issues are hardly salient there. So the question of their theological integration with Paul's gospel does not really need to be faced during the exegesis of Galatians. It is in 1 Corinthians and, granting authenticity, Colossians and Ephesians, where any rub lies. In those locations, however, the awkward implications of Gal. 3.28a in context need not necessarily be faced by exegetes—although, intriguingly, recent proposals have placed that text more centrally to some of these discussions; a suggestion which is to be welcomed although not necessarily accepted on the delicate form-critical and historico-biographical grounds supplied (see, *inter alia*, Schüssler Fiorenza 1983: 218-19; Wire 1990; and Gundry-Volf 1997c).

The crucial point to be grasped here is that, as we have seen, in Gal. 3.28a Paul baldly negates three standard bifurcations of society that include gender on the grounds of the eschatological existence of Christians in Christ; negations that he intends radically and seriously *and that his gospel is intrinsically committed to*. That is, *we now have a theological criterion from Paul's own hand of the (correct) ethical implications of his gospel* (and not merely of a putative early church confession), here specifically for questions concerning ethnicity, slavery and/or gender. The question that now begs to be asked is whether Paul's advice elsewhere measures up to this criterion; an interesting task for another study—although there are many in existence already, if not from this particular perspective. If it does not, that may be due to theological incompetence or to dissimulation, but it cannot now be (οὐκ ἔνι...) because the Pauline gospel *itself* is either confused or inherently subordinationist! And hence there is also no need to urge the presence of the principles of Gal. 3.28 and context in 1 Corinthians and/or Ephesians and Colossians on form-critical and/or historico-biographical grounds: insofar as Paul's gospel is present, he can be evaluated simply in these terms.

For identical 'liberative' goals but a rather different—and in my judgment seriously flawed—textual strategy see Elliott 1994.

of Romans.[30] These chapters are framed by an eschatological discussion focused on sonship (5.1-11; 8.1-39); contain numerous creational allusions (5.12-21; 7.7-25; 8.29); interpose a transition in terms of baptism (6.1-11); and speak repeatedly in spatial terms of Christian existence, that is, of being 'in Christ' (see especially 5.21; 6.11, 23; 7.1-4, 25; 8.1, 39). Christ is spoken of as 'his', that is, God's son, and in a context heavily informed by the Spirit, so that Christians receive sonship or υἱοθεσίαν and so cry 'Abba Father'. And there are further, less immediately apparent, similarities. The momentum against law-observance is also maintained. And the analysis of ch. 7 is now increasingly referred to the story of Adam and Genesis 3 in continuity with the suggestions of 5.12-21. Indeed, with the exception of the ethnic and class categories (although slavery is deployed extensively as a metaphor for salvation in 6.12-23) *every motif in Gal. 3.26-28 and its ensuing argument is specifically reprised in Romans 5–8 in an expanded form* (assuming Christ's πίστις to be largely the same as his ὑπακοή[31]). Hence, chs. 5–8 in Romans can legitimately be viewed as an extended discussion of the theological programme that Paul pithily summarizes in Gal. 3.26-28. We might say that *chs. 5–8 of Romans are Gal. 3.26-28 writ large*.[32]

---

30. As noted especially by Longenecker 1990, although not especially programmatically, and also by Martyn 1997a.

31. See esp. 1.5 and 16.26; also 8.25 (ὑπομονή).

32. Given that many of the key motifs in Gal. 3.26-28 recur in the parallel form-critical texts as well (baptism, the Spirit, allusions to creation, 'oneness', the 'in Christ' motif, and so on), it is plausible to suggest that they too, like Gal. 3.26-28, are summaries of one of Paul's key theological packages that is explicated more fully in chs. 5–8 of Romans. That is, these texts too are symmetrical to that longer discussion; they would therefore indicate that at these points as well Paul is bringing fundamental theological axioms to bear on the issues at hand, namely, disunity at Corinth and perhaps also the matter of ethnic cleavage at Colossae (so they are almost certainly indicators of centrally contingent matters at the time of writing).

Moreover, now we can explain the puzzling similarities and differences between all these texts. As summaries, rather than quotations or confessions, they recapitulate broader theological positions *using key motifs but not fixed syntax*. The order of those motifs would also be expected to vary, as well as the in part contingently controlled selection of those motifs, and this seems to be the case. They are not therefore pre-Pauline, so that they can be decontextualized from Paul's texts and communities. Theories of specific quotation between letters are also too precise and, in addition, limit the content of the subsections too severely.

Fascinating opportunities arise now for the reconstruction of Paul's original preaching and most basal teachings (which are probably quite similar, although

Possible Historical Location

A final set of observations seem intriguing in response to the following question: Where can we locate this basal theological package of Paul's historically?

An important clue is given here by the uncompromising law-free dimension in the argument that we have already noted repeatedly. Many scholars speak of Paul formulating this aspect of his theology 'under fire' so to speak, that is, in the context of the Galatian crisis itself. But while this may arguably be the first *extant* evidence of such theology, this original provenance for the theology itself seems unlikely—that would presuppose an odd cleavage between the advent of the law-free mission and Paul's theological reflection on that event.[33] Are we to believe that this reflection was only apparently undertaken under the pressure of circumstances at Galatia and so perhaps considerably later than the law-free mission itself? (Paul's unbending relations with the Jerusalem leadership recounted in Gal. 2.1-14 are also not very comprehensible on this view.) This all seems highly unlikely.

The obvious point at which to place this powerful and radical piece of theological reflection is (roughly) the actual advent of the law-free mission

---

development must be allowed for). These sections create the possibility of identifying a family of such theological summaries that may function intermediately between the very abbreviated 'in Christ' formulations and the extended discussion of chs. 5–8 in Romans. We would not expect every motif to be repeated in each instance—their deployment will still be contingent—but with an initial sample of between two and four instances (including perhaps also 1 Cor. 11.11) a useful stylistic profile of these summaries is now possible (that is, a family resemblance could be attempted), which could then possibly be broadened (e.g. for 3.26-28, cf. 5.5-6 and 6.14-15; also 1.4 and 2.19-21), and also pursued in relation to the contingent argumentation of each individual letter. Thus the intriguing similarities between Gal. 3.26-28 and 1 Cor. 12.13, and perhaps also Col. 3.11, may be far more significant than mere mutual attestation to an early church liturgy, interesting though any such insight might prove. Rather, they may well comprise windows into an intermediate level within Paul's gospel that allow scholars in turn to unpack that gospel, on the one hand, within its most coherent extant statement and, on the other, in relation to each contingent letter—something that would also, however, highlight more clearly any inconsistency in the recommendations of his letters.

33. Unless the writing of Galatians follows the onset of that crisis very closely; a traditional, Acts-based position followed, *inter alia*, by Longenecker. Although not to be underestimated, I am not (now) convinced that Galatians is Paul's first extant letter, but the rehearsal of arguments for and against this question is notoriously complex. Luedemann is a useful advocate of the later placement of Galatians (1984, 1989).

itself. Paul, a textually trained Jew and originally a fierce advocate of Torah,[34] would almost certainly not have participated in this movement, and then later vociferously defended it, without some articulated rationale for this in terms of the will of God as effected in Christ and attested to by Scripture—and the Jerusalem leadership would also doubtless have failed to be impressed by anything lacking this. Yet here we have just such a rationale that can exactly explain Paul's subsequent behaviour.[35] So our questions devolve into a related set of queries: When and where was the first advent of the law-free mission?[36]

These are controversial questions that again we cannot pursue in detail here.[37] Suffice it to note that this event probably ought *not* to precede Paul's first visit to Jerusalem (as a 'Christian') as recounted in Gal. 1.18-24, for then the deliberations of 2.1-10 would almost certainly have taken place 14 years earlier. Are we really to suppose that Paul and his law-free gospel slipped through Jerusalem, not to mention a meeting with Kephas and James, for a fortnight unnoticed?! However, in the light of this we ought to abandon Damascus and/or the early Arabian mission in Nabataea as a likely point of origin for the position; an often-overlooked corollary. But any point after this first visit to the holy city and preceding the later

34. Commitments that, we should note, were not completely abandoned in his Christian apostleship: see e.g. Rom. 1.2, 3.21.

35. For more explicit scriptural function see Romans 5–8, notably the use of Genesis 3 and the story of Adam and Eve (see esp. 5.12-21 and 7.7-25), and also the references to a son and to sons in ch. 8 (references variously interpreted, but usually in some relation to Scripture). There is also a vestigial citation of Scripture with Gen. 22.12, 16 being used in Rom. 8.32 and Ps. 44.23 (LXX) in 8.36. Paul's use of baptism is also, in one sense, an appeal to an authoritative tradition, although not to a Jewish scriptural one.

36. Are we to suppose, alternatively, that Paul radically changed the rationale for this event rather later? There is no need to suppose this, and no evidence to suggest it either.

37. For a seminal methodological statement again see Knox 1987; and for more detail (the early) Luedemann 1984 and 1989. Watson 1986 is also an especially insightful study in historical terms, although the thesis's theological reductionism should be disavowed (as it is, rather courageously, by the author).

The Aretas datum is generally badly handled by Pauline chronologers, perhaps principally because it is so awkward for Acts-based schemes: see, e.g., Riesner 1998: 42-43 and 75-89. However, this judgment must also include radical chronologers ostensibly following Knox and initially detached from Acts, like Luedemann: so 1984: 31 n. 10. As was the case for my claims concerning Western projection assisting an Arminian reading of Paul, I hope to document these chronological claims and the resulting structure in a monograph in the not-too-distant future.

ructions in Galatia seems formally possible. Can we supply hard chronological markers for these visits and problems? Fortunately, Paul's letters
supply useful information at just this point.

Paul's first innocuous Jerusalem visit ought to be coordinated with the
Aretas datum (see 2 Cor. 11.32-33; also Acts 9.23-25), that is, his escape
from Damascus and the control of its ethnarch who was currently responsible to Aretas IV. This yields a *terminus a quo* of c. 37 CE since Aretas
only acquired control of Damascus—and quite tenuously—during the
campaigning season in 36. Paul arrived in Antioch after this escape and a
subsequent fortnight in Jerusalem, therefore probably some time in early
37 (or late 36). He had already been a Christian for three years. And at
roughly this point Acts 11.26 makes the highly plausible observation that
'the disciples were first called Christians in Antioch',[38] that is, the Christians there no longer looked like Jews because they were no longer law-
observant and so a new name had to be coined for them. Now assuming a
little time had elapsed for Paul to make his presence felt at Antioch, and
also for these extraordinary law-free conversions to take place, a date as
early as 38 CE (give or take a year) could then be urged for the origin of
the theology that Gal. 3.26-28 summarizes, along with a likely location of
Antioch.[39]

Incredibly then, the germ of the dramatic theological programme sum-
marized by Gal. 3.26-28 may well have been in Antioch c. 38 CE.[40] Most
importantly, its Christology, revolving around 'sonship'—and presupposing a related filial pneumatology—of which the radical position on law-
observance is merely a reflex, could date from this period as well.[41]

---

38. This remark is in my opinion a historical triumph for Acts—which is not to say
that Acts' suggestions are *always* so accurate. A critical control and sifting is simply
indispensable. So cf. here Gal. 1.21, and also Phil. 4.15b, where the primary evidence
of the letters confirms the suggestions of the secondary Acts.

39. This will also as it turns out arguably coordinate with Paul's 'revelation'
recounted in 2 Cor. 12.1-4. So the law-free Gentile mission may have received
apocalyptic visionary confirmation—something it might well have needed: cf. Acts
10.1–11.18; also Gal. 1.12, 16; 2.2.

40. This mission and its theological justification's collision with more orthopractic
Jerusalem theology can in turn be placed much later (viz. the early or mid 50s). Gal.
3.26-28 itself is probably penned in the context of that later conflict, whenever it was,
as the preoccupation of the first phase of the letter with Jerusalem suggests, but the
historical origin of its theological position and rationale is earlier, and possibly considerably so.

41. So Longenecker's historical concerns, which he pursues using a form-critical
method I regard as dubious, are still answerable.

Conclusions

In the final analysis we must interpret Gal. 3.28a in context in terms of what it is attempting to say and not in terms of what it, quite understandably, does not attempt to address. Hence one of our primary conclusions is that the subsection, although it says certain things quite clearly, fundamentally lacks self-sufficiency, pointing beyond itself to the crucial discussion that follows immediately in 4.1-9 and, beyond that, to the much fuller analysis of chs. 5–8 of Romans (while it also points to exciting, and possibly quite early, events in the early church). I suspect that a full understanding of Paul's gospel requires then, ultimately, a full understanding of that discussion and its construal of sonship, to which Gal. 3.28a in context stands as an important way-station. Nevertheless to grasp this is to grasp one of its most important secrets.

Meanwhile, its famous abolitionist thrust in my judgment remains incontrovertible, although the Hellenistic framework within which those negations are asserted is, perhaps more surprisingly, expendable. Far more important is the grounding of those negations in an *a posteriori* fashion upon an uncompromisingly radical set of claims rooted in a corporate experience of eschatological salvation in and through Christ's crucifixion; a process symbolized in baptism. Here, a theology of the cross succinctly proclaims that the Galatians should leave their present anxieties—contingently, about traditional Jewish practices—behind. While that such redundant preoccupations necessarily include any reification of gender differentials, as v. 28a states, is also a valid recognition which, somewhat sadly, still requires uncompromising proclamation in our own day.

Part II

Theological Perspectives

GOD, GENDER AND IDENTITY

Linda Woodhead

Introduction

A great deal of contemporary academic discourse and debate, particularly in the social sciences, circles around the notions of 'self' and 'identity'. This reflects a much broader cultural trend which some have spoken of as 'the turn to the self' or 'the subjective turn' (see, for example, Taylor 1989). Though it has much older antecedents, not least in the Christian tradition, the turn is characteristically modern. Used substantively, the 'self' is a word that dates from the late seventeenth century.[1] It signals a shift from a view of the human person from a third person perspective—caught by the gaze of God or of another human person—to a view of the person which privileges the first person perspective and does not objectify the subject to the same degree. The self, we might say, becomes subjectivized.

In the attempt to explain this shift towards a concern with self-identity, sociological and cultural commentators tend to focus on two opposite yet reinforcing processes. On the one hand, the conditions of modernity make the self stronger. Money-based economies, for example, give most selves —in the developed West at least—new scope to express themselves through both work and consumption. Similarly, the spread of political democracy invests the self with the right, the duty and the 'weight' necessary to make its own choices in the spheres that most affect it. So the self becomes sovereign. On the other hand, the conditions of modernity destabilize the self. Sociologists tend to speak in terms of the 'fragmentation' and 'fragility' or 'destabilization' and 'decentering' of the modern self. Social differentiation and the division of labour, the speeding up of time, cultural pluralism, de-traditionalization—all these characteristics of the modern or postmodern condition—are said to lead to the increasing fragility and frag-

---

1.   According to the *Oxford English Dictionary* (2nd edn; XIV: 906-907) it is first used thus by Thomas Traherne in 1674.

mentation of the self.[2] The modern self is a cipher whose identity hangs in the air. As given social roles disappear, it encounters itself as the cross-roads of a host of conflicting and unstable multiple identities.[3]

My main purpose in this chapter is to relate this contemporary concern with identity to an older but still influential style of feminist theology. In so doing I hope to open up a fresh and potentially revealing perspective on such theology which can perhaps help to take forward some debates within and about the discipline. My argument is that some enduring aspects of feminist theology can be viewed as a manifestation of our anxiety about identity, and that its characteristic stress upon the essential difference of women and of women's experience can be viewed in part as a strategy to resolve contemporary anxieties about identity. In the final part of the chapter I shall argue that this is in many ways a misguided strategy, and propose what I believe to be better feminist—and Christian—alternatives.[4]

Feminist Theology and the Quest for Identity

Gender as Primary Identity

All feminist theology is, of course, not the same.[5] But a feature of some feminist theology is an insistence that *gender identity is primary identity*.

2. For a useful summary account of this position see Hall *et al.* 1992: 274-316.

3. For more on this theme see Woodhead 1999, and, again, Taylor 1989.

4. This paper was originally written in 1996, and its age is evident in the archive to which it refers. My critique was focused on a particular tendency within what might be called the 'first generation' of feminist theological writing which was still highly influential when I wrote. Though this tendency persists, it has since been critiqued by other writers besides myself. Secular feminist theory has long abandoned a crude understanding of women's identity and experience, and is currently at the cutting edge of thought about identity and gendered identity/difference. There are encouraging indications that contemporary feminist theology is learning from these debates and experimenting with new methods that interrogate and explore women's experience rather than imposing an essentialist understanding of it. In this respect, I believe that feminist theology may be able to forge new and constructive links with the social sciences in a way that 'mainstream' theology has failed to do. I have in mind, for example, an excellent thesis by Ellen Clark-King (2003) which employs empirical research methods to explore the spirituality of working-class women in Byker, Newcastle, and which begins to build a feminist theology informed by their voices.

5. By even speaking of 'feminist theology' one lays oneself open to the charge that there is no such uniform or homogeneous body of discourse. I know this to be true, and in what follows I do not for a moment wish to suggest that my critique applies to all feminist theology.

Many feminist theologians agree on this whether they are Christian or post-Christian, liberal or radical, and whether they believe that gender is naturally given or socially constructed. In order to see just how central the assertion of gender primacy is in much feminist theology there is no better place to start than with the claims which the discipline makes for itself. For in many cases, feminist theology does not present itself as one school among others within the wider discipline of theology—as parallel, say, to Thomistic theology or liberal theology. Rather, it understands itself as more radical than that, as an entirely new departure, an entirely new way of doing theology which calls into question the methods and self-understanding of *all* traditional (male) theology. Rosemary Radford Ruether, for example, presents feminist theology as a whole new way of doing theology because it is based upon *women's experience*. As she says,

> The uniqueness of feminist theology lies not in its use of the criterion of experience but rather in its use of *women's* experience, which has been almost entirely shut out of theological reflection in the past (Radford Ruether 1983: 13).

The claim made in passages like this is that one's gender determines one's experience and so one's knowledge, including one's knowledge of God. So gender identity has a primacy, a primacy which determines even one's knowing. In its weaker forms the claim is that our experience of God is always determined by the subject who experiences, the most salient characteristic of that subject being his or her gender. In its stronger forms, the claim is that the divine is actually *constructed* according to gender. Many feminist theologians agree with this strong claim where the traditional Christian God is concerned, viewing him as a male construct serving patriarchal interests. Not all feminist theologians are willing to take a step further and suggest that women construct their own God, but some get fairly close to this position by maintaining that God must conform to women's interests. As Rosemary Radford Ruether famously puts it in *Sexism and God-Talk*,

> Theologically speaking, whatever diminishes or denies the full humanity of women must be presumed not to reflect the divine or an authentic relation to the divine, or to reflect the authentic nature of things, or to be the message or work of an authentic redeemer or a community of redemption (Radford Ruether 1983: 19).

This position can easily slide into the more radical one which acknowledges that women are free to construct the divine in the way they find most helpful. Post-Christian feminist theologians who have embraced goddess worship have been the most ready to admit this. As Carol Christ says,

> Women, who have been deprived of a female religious symbol system for centuries, are in an excellent position to recognize the power and primacy of symbols. I believe women must develop a theory of symbol and thealogy congruent with their experience at the same time as they 'remember and invent' new symbol systems (Christ 1992: 279).

Thus in *some* feminist theology, God himself/herself comes to be subordinated to gender identity. The assumption is that women's experience is competent to judge and construe both revelation and God. Women's experience becomes the primary knowledge which trumps even what has been previously understood as God's communication of himself/ herself. In this way, I want to suggest, women come to swap places with the Godhead. Whereas in traditional Christian thought God was believed to create humankind, now it is humankind who creates God. No longer are we made in God's image, but he or she is made in ours. In this way, the self comes to occupy centre stage in some feminist theology as in so much modern thought. Here the modern preoccupation with self-identity works itself out in terms of gender-identity. It is woman who makes God. She becomes the measure of all things.

Problems with the Elevation of Gender-Identity

The claim made by some feminist theology that gender-identity constitutes primary identity and determines the whole religious and theological enterprise has clearly won many supporters. And in the forms in which it is so forcefully stated by some feminist theologians, it does at first sight seem to have some plausibility and an immediate attractiveness. (I will say more about this attractiveness below.) On closer examination, however, I believe that feminist theology's assertion of the primacy of gender-identity is in fact beset by a number of serious problems.

One cluster of problems concerns the very notion of women's identity and women's experience. In the sorts of feminist theology I have cited above these notions are absolutely central, and the claim that feminist theology is unique is built upon belief that there is such a thing as a clear and distinct female identity and experience. But in practice these notions prove elusive. Carol Christ and Judith Plaskow divide women's experience into two categories: 'women's *traditional* experience' which includes 'marriage and motherhood', 'intuition, expression of feeling', 'women's body experiences such as menstruation, pregnancy'; and 'women's *feminist* experience', which includes 'the experience of liberation itself—recognizing oppression, confronting sexist culture and institutions, and moving into freedom' (Christ and Plaskow 1992: 8; authors' italics). This way of specifying what constitutes women's experience and women's identity in terms of the experience of liberation and oppression on the one hand and bodily experiences on the other seems a fair summary of the approach adopted by a majority of feminist theologians, and a number of more recent works identify women's experience in nearly identical terms.[6]

More recently there has been yet another development in feminist theological thought about women's experience, namely an increased stress upon women's experience of nurturing, connectedness, relationality and sisterhood. Mary Daly was one of the first to speak about women's orientation towards sisterhood.[7] Her comments seemed to win empirical backing from Carol Gilligan's *In a Different Voice* (1982), a work much cited in subsequent feminist theology. Since then, Rosemary Radford Ruether's work has also displayed an increasing stress upon this aspect of women's experience, and one finds similar ideas in the work of Isabel Carter Heyward, Rebecca Chopp, Mary Grey, Anne Johnson, and in many of those feminist theologians influenced by eco-feminism. Indeed it is a measure of the increased popularity of the construal of women's experience in terms of relationality and connectedness that in her book *Jesus: Miriam's Child, Sophia's Prophet* (1994b), Elisabeth Schüssler Fiorenza feels the need to attack it for its lack of political awareness, and to reassert the primacy of women's experience of oppression and liberation over against that of relationality (1994b: esp. 50-57).

A final construal of women's experience—and so of women's iden-

---

6.   For example, Lisa Isherwood and Dorothea McEwan write of women's experience that, 'when it is authentic for the individual, [it] is normative... It may have very many different expressions; it might be the acceptance of the traditional understanding of women's bodily experiences, menstruation, pregnancy, lactation, menopause and illnesses connected with the female physiology or it might be the understanding of liberation in the spirit beyond those biological givens, and any combination on the spectrum that extends from the one to the other' (1993: 81-82). Compare Linda Hogan's more nuanced study *From Women's Experience to Feminist Theology* (1995), which, while it makes a plea for a more pluralistic understanding of women's experience, continues to insist that the most fundamental aspect of this experience is the experience of oppression.

7.   See, for example, the chapter entitled, 'The Bonds of Freedom: Sisterhood as Antichurch' in Daly 1986.

tity—which has long been influential in feminist theology is one which speaks of women's experience as linking women directly with the divine. Very often the suggestion is made in feminist theology that authentic women's experience is transparent to the divine or participatory in the divine. This goes hand in hand with the suggestion that women are naturally spiritual and naturally connected with the divine. As the South African feminist theologian Felicity Edwards expresses it,

> spiritual experience…is moving evolutionarily beyond masculinist consciousness, which is mental, conceptual consciousness *par excellence*, to the level of spirit. Spirit is beyond or above or deeper than the ego developed in the separatizing masculinist mode… [N]eo-feminist consciousness, epitomized in this luminous, radiant aliveness, the perception that 'I am I insofar as I am in you' has all the incisive clarity of masculine consciousness, along with the holistic consciousness of the feminine. This identifies it as a definite advance in the evolution of consciousness, and to live this way is to love (Edwards 1995: 189-90).

As Edwards' comments show, this understanding of women's experience is one which ties in neatly with an emphasis upon women's naturally relational, nurturing and 'holistic' qualities, and which often goes hand-in-hand with the latter.[8]

Here then are four of feminist theology's most characteristic attempts to specify what women's experience is: experience of motherhood, menstruation and other things related to women's bodies; experience of oppression; experience of connectedness; and experience of Spirit. As I have explained at greater length in an article in *Modern Theology*, I am seriously suspicious of *all* these attempts to give content to women's experience—and indeed to the very *notion* of women's experience (Woodhead 1997). To me, each one of these attempts to specify what women's experience actually amounts to seems beset by difficulties. Take the claim that women's experience is constituted by the experiences of oppression and of resistance to oppression. For a start, not all women would agree that oppression has been such a defining feature of their lives. And even if they did, there seems to be something highly problematic about the strategy of building women's sense of selfhood upon victimization. To do so is to suggest that women have a vested interest in maintaining oppression and that without it their identity—not to mention their ability to do theology—will collapse. What if the opposite pole is stressed: not victimhood but struggle against

---

8. Again, Daly seems to have been a pioneer in establishing this complex of ideas, a complex which is already present in *Beyond God the Father* (1986).

oppression and liberation from oppression? To see self-identity in these terms is certainly one option open to women, but the model of woman as liberator, far from saying anything distinctive about woman's identity, seems merely to buy into a long-established male paradigm: man as freedom-fighter, deliverer of oppressed peoples, the political or martial hero, the fighter for rights.

In some ways I believe that the claim that the distinctiveness of women's identity is based on experience of connectedness and relationality is therefore more promising than its alternatives. At least it has no vested interest in victimhood. In addition, there is some (limited) experimental evidence for the claim—Gilligan's study, for example—and it receives additional support from some everyday observations.[9] Moreover, there seems to be an obvious plausibility about the claim that women's role as mothers and child-rearers should affect the way in which they relate more generally, and might influence them differently from men. But not all women are mothers, and, increasingly, not all mothers are child-rearers. Equally, many women resist the self-image of themselves as nurturing and relational and see it as an attempt to restrict their identity. And as women increasingly enter into public life it is clear that some can be just as ruthless, independent and self-determining as men.

An additional problem with the claim that women's experience is essentially one of relation and that women are naturally in tune with one another and with the divine, is that it can easily begin to sound like something an evangelical cleric might have said in the last century in order to maintain women in their role as 'angel(s) of the house'. Here is William Wilberforce on the subject: 'That sex...by the very constituency of its nature, is more favourably disposed to the feelings and offices of religion'.[10] His friend Hannah More adds, 'Their hearts are naturally soft and flexible, open to the impressions of love and gratitude, their feelings are tender and lively; all these are favourable to the cultivation of a devotional spirit' (More 1990: 238). In other contexts, feminist theologians are rightly keen to protest against such 'stereotyping' and 'essentialism'; it is strange therefore to endorse such views in the course of trying to specify the nature of women's experience and identity.

---

9.   Gilligan's conclusions about the differences between male and female moral development have not gone unchallenged. For an account of the debate see Wilson 1993: 179-82.

10.   Wilberforce 1797: 376. My attention was drawn to this and the following quotation by Plant 1996.

Feminist theologians' attempts to give content to the notion of women's experience and women's identity are therefore fraught with difficulty. The attempt is, I think, admirable in its recognition that there are real differences between men and women, and that these differences can and should affect the way we organize our thought, our lives, our society. And yet the way in which these differences are explained by feminist theology, and the way in which they are thought to account for women's identity in its entirety, seems to me problematic.

On these issues I believe that an engagement with the thought of the Belgian-born feminist Luce Irigaray can be illuminating.[11] Following Irigaray, I would want to affirm the importance of women's sexed differences, but recognize that these are not such that universal declarations can be made about them. They are differences which are bound up with our shifting cultures and discourse, which are affected by women's different locations, and which are not simply the product of a given and fixed women's 'nature'. Like Irigaray I would want to affirm that our sexed differences should not be simply suppressed by the invocation of universal 'human' nature, for the latter can indeed turn out to be a cover for predominantly male (or other dominant) interests. But that does not mean that women need claim an identity entirely different from that of men, nor that this identity can be clearly and universally specified.

In its attempt to give clear and universal content to women's identity and experience then, I believe that the direction taken by much feminist theology should be resisted, and that there are good *feminist* grounds for this resistance. In denying the complex, shifting and multi-faceted nature of women's identities I believe that some feminist theology lays itself open to the charge of being reductionist. It seeks to reduce my identity as a woman to less than it really is. It tries to foreclose prematurely on my richness, variety, contradictions and possibilities. One can often see the same process at work in secular feminism. Reading a feminist collection on *Heterosexuality*, for example, I was interested to see that most of the

---

11. Indeed Luce Irigaray seems to me one of the most interesting and fruitful dialogue partners for Christians in relation to the whole debate about gender. Not only is she aware of the Christian tradition and in some ways sympathetic to it, she is critical of just those elements of feminism and feminist theology that seem to me the most antithetical to Christianity. A bibliography of Irigaray's works can be found in Whitford 1991. See also Chanter 1995. Irigaray engages directly with feminist theology in her critique of Elisabeth Schüssler Fiorenza's *In Memory of Her* in 'Equal to Whom?' (1989).

contributors acknowledged that this was a topic which feminist theory had hitherto excluded from its agenda. Heterosexuality and heterosexual relatedness had therefore become invisible aspects of women's lives. Consequently, the contributors to this volume struggled to speak about the topic. They felt guilty in acknowledging the importance of their relationships with men and the centrality of this important aspect of their identity. As one commented, 'having a good husband seems to be many feminists' well-guarded secret' (Wilkinson and Kitzinger 1993: 22).

Feminist theology can also be guilty of such reductionism. Those aspects of my identity which are affirmed as 'authentic' women's experience are acceptable, enabling me to acknowledge wholeheartedly my sisterly endeavours, my ecological ones, my nurturing ones, my spiritual ones. But those aspects of my identity which have been labelled inauthentic—or simply not written or spoken of—become problematic. In *Changing the Subject* (1994), Mary McClintock Fulkerson points out how the discourses of American Pentecostal and Presbyterian women have thus been excluded by academic feminist theology's tendency to a hegemonic and reductionist understanding of 'authentic women's experience'. 'Women's experience' has become a tool of exclusion and a political device. Women who are not like women are supposed to be, who believe things that women are not supposed to believe, or who willingly belong to institutions deemed oppressive by feminist theology find themselves either having to repress the 'inauthentic' parts of their identity, or feeling that they are not proper women at all.

The Attraction of Innocent Gender-Identity
Why, given that it faces such problems, has a reductionist strategy of identifying a narrowly defined gender-identity as primary identity seemed attractive to some feminist theologians and their readers? One reason is surely that it provides such a neat solution to the contemporary anxieties about identity to which I alluded at the start of this article. Currently these anxieties are perhaps more acute for women than for men as women enter into roles, offices and institutions only recently opened to us, and in so doing leave behind the clearer and more stable roles, duties and identities that our mothers and grandmothers were likely to know. How appealing then to be told not only that one has a clear identity—one's identity as a woman. This identity is made secure and attractive in a number of ways:

First, it is presented as a natural, given identity. It demands no training, effort or exertion to attain, but must simply be 'owned' and 'celebrated'. It may require 'consciousness raising' or the banishment of 'false consciousness', but it is there to be discovered rather than achieved.

Second, it is an identity which is wholly my own, inalienable and autonomous. It is not bestowed by another nor given in relationship, but is entirely within my control and can never be taken from me.

Third, it is an innocent and a good identity, a state of natural and original blessedness. Women who get in touch with their true selves find there all the moral and spiritual resources they need. The self, it is suggested, is not merely good, but is in deep connection with the divine and ultimately one with the divine.[12]

Finally, woman's identity is often made yet stronger and more stable by defining it over against the 'other' of male identity. Any fragile identity may be made stronger by this oppositional strategy. Thus Christian fundamentalism reinforces its identity through opposition to a wider 'modern' and 'liberal' culture regarded as totally corrupt and enslaved to evil (see Ammerman 1987: 72-102). The blacker the enemy is painted, the sharper the definition in which the whiter-than-white group appears. Unfortunately, the same process can sometimes be seen at work in feminist theology. Thus a male viewpoint ('androcentric' or 'phallocentric') can be presented as a bad thing in and of itself, whereas a female standpoint is seen as having a natural legitimacy. As with forms of religious fundamentalism, my innocent identity here depends upon the ascription of a guilty identity to those who are not me. Some feminists thus persist in calling men 'the enemy', and it is still possible to read remarks like the following: men belong to a social group 'whose main relation to women is through rape' (Wilkinson and Kitzinger 1993: 76). Similar ideas play themselves out in feminist theology in the idea that all theology done by men is deficient and misleading, whereas all theology which articulates women's experience is helpful, authentic and good.

Christianity and Women's Identity

So far I have tried to show that feminist theology relies on a belief in gender as primary identity which is problematic on feminist terms. I have been trying to suggest that there are good grounds for women *qua* women to reject it. In the remaining part of this article I will suggest that there

---

12. Angela West offers a powerful critique of this cluster of ideas (1995).

are also good theological reasons for suspicion. I do so by reflecting on a few passages from Scripture and tradition which seem pertinent to the discussion of identity and which seem to me to have the power to move our thinking about identity forwards and to force it beyond some of the dead-ends in which it can sometimes become trapped in contemporary discourse.

'What do you have that you have not received?' (1 Corinthians 4.7)
In his dispute with the 'puffed up' Corinthians, Paul chastises them by asking: 'What have you that you did not receive? If then you received it, why do you boast as if it were not a gift?' As the context of his question makes clear, Paul is thinking here both of what is given to us by God and by other human beings. For Paul, as for much Jewish thought, human identity is not the creation of each individual, but is bestowed by God and by fellow-humans. Our existence is gift. It is the gift of God and it is the gift of those who have shaped and formed us, both directly and through the texts and institutions they put in place.

In this insistence that all we have is gift, biblical anthropology stands at odds with much modern thought about the self and self-identity—including some feminist theological thought. As we have seen, the very language of 'self' suggests a self-contained, autonomous subject rather than a subject formed by relationship with God and others. Feminist theology often reinforces this picture. It suggests that my identity as a woman is given and that it is my natural or essential substance. It maintains that all knowledge must be tested at the bar of an experience which constitutes my personal, individual criterion of right and wrong, true and false. And it proposes that women's goal is liberation, the flinging off of dependence and all the ties that bind us. Here the feminist theological hope is often articulated in terms of autonomy, freedom, independence, self-naming, and self-creation.

More recently, however, there have been voices within feminist theology which have begun to question this non-relational understanding of self. I have spoken already of those feminist theologians who wish to speak of women's predisposition towards relationality. Equally, Mary McClintock Fulkerson's *Changing the Subject* develops this theme under the influence of post-structuralism by stressing human intersubjectivity: the way in which every aspect of human existence is socially, culturally and textually constructed. She criticizes feminist theology for relying upon a notion of women's experience which is naive about these matters and which imagines such experience to be a sort of pre-cultural deliverance unique to each woman.

So there are some signs that, following the lead of secular feminism, feminist theology may be beginning to move away from belief in what Seyla Benhabib has called the 'unencumbered' self, the self viewed as asocial, acultural, wholly independent, self-determined, self-determining, self-possessed and autonomous (see Benhabib 1992). In doing so, feminist theology moves closer to a Christian understanding of the self, an understanding which asks, 'what do you have that you have not received?' Yet still there remains a crucial difference between the two understandings: when Paul asks this question he draws attention not just to what is received from other human beings, but what is received from God. Of course the two are often inseparable: God works through human beings and human culture, and particularly through Jesus Christ. But God is not reducible to the human, though the Holy Spirit may be directly present in creation.

So in biblical thought, as in traditional Christian and Jewish thought, to be human is not merely to be in relation with other human beings, but to be in relation with God. To be human is not to be a 'self' but *a creature*. It is to stand in relation to God as one's maker, and to the rest of the created order as a fellow-creature who has been granted dominion. Psalm 8 answers the question 'what is a human creature?' by saying that it is a being made by God and placed between God and other creatures: a little less than God, with dominion over what God has made. To be human is to be set within a network of relationships both with God and with fellow creatures, human and non-human. It is this which makes the person rather than any individual or autonomous substance. The human being is given by and with God and the rest of the created order. Yet it is too easy to speak of 'relationality' as if that closed the debate on identity. That is merely another essentialism.

'Your life is hid with Christ in God' (Colossians 3.3)

Talk of relationality needs therefore to be qualified by another theme in Christian thought on identity: that the self is *hidden*. As Paul puts it in his letter to the Colossians, 'your life is hid with Christ in God'.

In the face of anxiety about who we are, our natural response is to seek an identity which is not hidden but clear, revealed, easy to grasp. It is this, I have suggested, which can underlie an eagerness to seek identity in gender, an identity which is immediate and apparent, easily recognized, written in our very flesh. Yet there is much in the Christian tradition which should make us wary of seizing hold of a graspable identity in this way. Verses like that from Paul just cited remind us of a powerful tradition within Christianity which stresses that we are always more than we can know. Our identity in this life remains forever beyond our grasp. Our life is something which is hid with God, and which we can never fully know in this life.

Reflection upon the self in relation to God the Holy Trinity may help flesh out this idea. First, God creates. The biblical assurance is that persons are not made by God in a moment of absent-mindedness, or in the fashion of identical objects on a factory conveyor-belt. As Psalm 139 says,

> thou didst form my inward parts,
> thou didst knit me together in my mother's womb
> I praise thee, for thou art fearful and wonderful.
> Wonderful are thy works!
> Thou knowest me right well;
> my frame was not hidden from thee,
> when I was being made in secret,
> intricately in the depths of the earth.
> Thy eyes beheld my unformed substance;
> in thy book were written, every one of them,
> the days that were formed for me,
> when as yet there were none of them... (Ps. 139.13-16).

Compare this with the Lord's words to the prophet Jeremiah,

> Before I formed you in the womb I knew you,
> and before you were born I consecrated you;
> I appointed you a prophet to the nations (Jer. 1.5).

The creator God shapes us, has a task for us, and gives us the talents with which to fulfil that task. But the task and the talents lie hidden unless discovered and actualized by each person for him or herself. Their hiddenness safeguards human freedom. We are not programmed like robots to fulfil our task and grown into the image of God; we may or may not accept our calling and grow with God's help into what God has made us.

Second, as God the Son, God is the God through whom all things were and are made. He is 'logos', the principle by which the whole creation is ordered, the 'order and coherence in which it is composed'.[13] In Jesus this order is embodied and made clearly visible to other human beings. As the

---

13. This phrase occurs in a slightly different context in O'Donovan 1986: 31.

Letter to the Hebrews puts it, 'in these last days [God] has spoken to us by a Son, whom he appointed the heir of all things, through whom also He created the world' (Heb. 1.1). All things exist for Christ. He is their *telos*, that for which all was created and towards which all tends. The creation is, as Karl Barth puts it, 'the external basis of the covenant'.[14] The world was created in order that human beings might exist in covenant relationship with God, and they exist in such relationship through Christ, the *telos* of creation towards which all things move.

Human beings then are made *by* Christ and made *for* Christ. The Gospel of John says of Jesus Christ that he comes 'unto his own' (Jn 1.11). He comes to a humankind created through him, whose life and conditions of life he has chosen to share. The Christian belief is that in coming to Christ, human beings come to their true selves. He is the pattern of true human existence and abundant human life, and thus he is also depicted in Christian tradition as the judge who will reveal who we truly are. But as he reveals the criteria of judgment in his own being—the being in which we are offered incorporation—Christ comes as saviour as well as judge. He comes to earth to bring humans to their true selves. He shows in his words and his deeds what full humanity means and what a truly human life looks like. And the 'good news' is that he is more than just teacher and exemplar; he does not remain external to us, an exemplary figure from the past, but by his death and resurrection gives us the gift of Spirit, and by this gift comes to exist *in* us, incorporating the believer into his body, the church.

So third, as Spirit, God is immediately present to creation. This is not an aloof and distant God, but the God who stands at the door of each person's heart and knocks. In the biblical understanding God is closer to each person than they are to themselves. God is the basis of our life, our inspiration, and all that is authentic about us. The Spirit is not an 'optional extra' in human life, but the only possible ground of a truly human life. Such a life, in other words, comes from God and not from 'we ourselves'. The purely human is what Paul calls 'flesh', and its nature is sin. Without God humans are sin. They are less than they should be, and less than God intended. But those who open their hearts to God and to neighbour are promised the gift of the Spirit and new life through the Spirit. They become a 'new creation', a creation which begins in this life, but which is completed only after this life, in resurrection. In this life, therefore, the new creation remains partially hidden and the full revelation when God will be 'all in

14. See, for example, Barth 1958: 95-97.

all' is still awaited. In the meanwhile we struggle, partly redeemed, and partly still in thrall to what is not of God.

By thinking through our relation to the trinitarian God it is thus possible to see something of what is meant by the statement that our lives are hid with Christ in God. The source of our life comes from outside us and lies in the God who made us, redeemed us and sanctifies us. If we think that our identity is our own possession, something within our control and within our comprehension, we deny the true source of our life and become less than we should be. We are more than we can know or lay hold of: as Paul says, 'you are not your own' (1 Cor. 6.19). Only God knows what we really are, and this will only be fully revealed to us on the day of judgment.

Yet the insistence that our life is hid with Christ reminds us that it is not entirely hidden, not absolutely mysterious: we are not left completely without clues, for God is a God who is revealed, most notably in Jesus Christ. We have had 'glimpses' of our true identity in Christ. Our lives must therefore be lived in conformity to Christ's, a conformity made possible by the gift of Spirit. The Spirit unites Christians with one another and with Christ. They become more than they would otherwise be, and more than they can know. This does not mean that they cease to be the particular individual God created, a unique and irreplaceable man or woman. Nor does it mean that they become clones of Jesus of Nazareth. Rather, it means that their individuality, their unique identity, can only be perfected in relation to Christ and to one another. 'Your life is hid with Christ in God'. It is hid with Christ, not absorbed without remainder into Christ. It is your life, not someone else's.

It is at this point that some feminist theology becomes most suspicious of Christianity, for it views the Christian God not as the one who perfects humanity—particularly women—but as the one who threatens to destroy them. Thus Mary Daly and Daphne Hampson, for example, reject belief in a transcendent personal God and in Christ as the Son of God, because they believe that to submit to them is to submit to heteronomy. Both Father and Son threaten the autonomy of the individual just as much as they threaten women's gendered identity. I do not for a moment question the force of this critique. Both feminist theology and women's history leave us in little doubt that women's identities have often been cruelly constrained within the churches, and that tradition and Scripture has been used to prevent women from becoming what God intended them to be (in body as well as spirit). I have tried to show, however, that Christianity does not necessarily speak of a wholly transcendent (male) God set over against us. In its teachings and symbolic reservoir it also offers us a picture of God and God's people not in a relation of domination but of love and co-creation.

'Put on the new nature…' (Ephesians 4.24)
I have spoken above of how Christianity holds before us the hope of a new life lived in the Spirit, and speaks of our life hid in Christ as a 'new creation'. The corollary of this is that what may be called our 'natural' lives are neither good nor innocent, but less than they should be, less than human, less than what God intends. Our 'natural' life is a life in which we try to draw only on our own resources, or on diabolic sources of energy which transcend the individual. Such natural life stands in direct opposition to the life which God holds before us, a life energized by the Spirit. So Paul instructs the Ephesians: 'Put off your old nature which belongs to your former manner of life and is corrupt through deceitful lusts, and be renewed in the spirit of your minds, and put on the new nature, created after the likeness of God in true righteousness and holiness'.

Feminist theology has always been critical of Christianity's emphasis on human fallibility and sinfulness. Valerie Saiving's early critique of Niebuhr's identification of human sinfulness with pride as an analysis appropriate to men but not to women was powerful and telling, and many feminists since Saiving have argued that if women are tainted by 'original sin' it is more likely to be the sin of faltering self-worth than of pride (Saiving 1992). There is no doubt that the doctrine of original sin continues to be used by people made confident by their positions of power to keep others in their place. Indeed the same illicit use may be made of this doctrine as may be made of gender identity: it can be used to limit and restrict a person's identity, to tell them that they are less than they actually are. To tell someone that they are completely corrupt and to say no more is a distortion of the gospel which results in human distortion. It is, moreover, a distortion with which we are all too ready to cooperate, for there is that in all of us which already whispers insidiously that we are not good enough, not the sort of person who can perform heroic tasks, not worthy to associate with other people or accept their affection, that we are bound to fail in what we attempt, and that we are likely to corrupt what we touch.[15]

But to believe such things is to refuse to believe the good news that human beings are offered new life by and in God. It is to refuse to believe that our lives are hid with Christ in God, and it is to succumb to the desire

---

15. I owe this insight to Harvey 1985 and 1991.

to believe that our identities are entirely within our possession and knowledge and known to us in their entirety. It is to cling to the old nature and to *refuse* to put on the new nature.

The attempt to grasp at an innocent gender-identity is thus no antidote to the distorting effects of a misuse of the doctrine of original sin, for it is but a mirror image of the same reductionist strategy. Both attempt to bind and fix human identity in an idolatrous way. Both exalt a part of human identity at the expense of the wider whole, and so reduce human beings to less than they really are. Human identity should not be identified with a person's present identity, or with any identity which may be grasped hold of in its entirety. Any such 'fixed' identity must always come under judgment. Both those who believe they are all good and those who believe they are all bad are guilty of wanting a control and certainty about themselves which the gospel will not allow. The gospel tells us that our identity is not our own in this way, that it is always more than we think, always transcendent, because caught up with God in Christ through the Spirit.

At its best, the Christian doctrine of sin is one which, like Paul speaking to the Ephesians, speaks in the same breath of the old life which we must put away and of the new life which we must put on. It is a distortion to mention only the old life just as it is a distortion to mention only the new. Christianity has sometimes been guilty of the former distortion, but feminist theology can be equally guilty of the latter. The belief that our natural identity is innocent and good is dangerous because it stands at such variance with the evidence, particularly the evidence of the modern age; it is a denial of the terrifying realities of human sin and evil. The *hiddenness* of human identity provides a good reason for being highly suspicious of any such blanket evaluations of human worth. 'Judge not', Jesus commands, for no one knows what lies hidden in the human heart. Human identity and human motivation are not open and accessible in this life, and judgment is always provisional.

'A woman's sex is not a defect; it is natural... Thus He who established the two sexes will restore them both' (Augustine)[16]
My suggestion is that Christianity resists reducing identity to gender identity. It insists that identity is more than we can grasp, and that any grasping at identity cuts us off from our larger identity, that identity which is a new creation, hid with God in Christ. Yet it is not part of my argument to deny the reality and the importance of gendered identities, so long as

16. *City of God*, bk 22, ch. 17.

they are understood within the wider context of our God-given identity. Indeed I wish to argue that there is much in the Christian tradition that safeguards sexed identity and insists upon its importance, not least by viewing gender as part of the order of redemption.

The most quoted piece of Scripture in the gender debate must surely be that from Paul's letter to the Galatians: 'There is neither Jew nor Greek, there is neither slave nor free, there is no male and female; for you are all one in Christ Jesus' (Gal. 3.28). In the days when feminist theology was very much under the influence of liberal feminism, this passage was taken to endorse the typically liberal insistence that there is one basic human nature shared by all God's creatures which ensures a perfect equality between them, compared to which all differences including cultural, economic and sexual differences are relatively trivial. The passage was therefore interpreted as saying that women should be treated as the equals of men by the church. Now that liberal feminism is no longer so popular, however, the passage is sometimes viewed a little less favourably. The suspicion may be that it is advocating a sexless, spiritualized existence which renders women's reality invisible.

In fact, I think that the passage is doing something rather different from what both the liberal and postliberal readings suggest. It is not speaking about some universal human nature which underlies all other differences and which is more real than those differences; it is speaking about the new life which is consequent upon incorporation into the body of Christ. It insists that this life is open to all comers. No one is excluded on any ground whatsoever and no one is any more or less a member than any other. As the preceding sentence says, 'For as many of you as were baptised into Christ have put on Christ' (Gal. 3.27). What this passage speaks of, in other words, is the new identity offered in Christ, an identity which is offered to all and which in that sense relativizes our 'old' identities. It establishes our identity on a new foundation, it places its centre of gravity in Christ and fellow members of his body, the church, and it establishes our primary identity as children of God and heirs of the promise.

As we have seen above, putting on this new identity does indeed mean letting go of some aspects of our old identity. That in us which is corrupt will be exposed in the light of God, and should be renounced. But we are not all corruption, and we are not to be transformed out of recognition. There is also that in the 'old nature' which is 'natural' in the sense Augustine intends in the quotation above: part of what God has created, which must not be discarded but transformed and perfected. And our sex, according to the overwhelming (though not entire) weight of Christian tradition, falls into this category.[17] This is why (even) Augustine says, 'a woman's sex is not a defect; it is natural... Thus he who established the two sexes will restore them both'. This insistence is bound up with another: that the new creation, brought to completion only in the next age, is a creation in which bodies are not excluded. For Christianity insists that human beings are an inseparable unity of body and soul. Christianity goes further than feminist theology in this insistence, for it suggests that this unity is a God-given unity and will persist beyond death: the resurrection life is a life of renewed body as well as mind and soul. The entirety of the human person is gathered into the order of redemption: we continue as sexed and embodied persons rather than as the ethereal, sexless, sub-personal manifestations of spirit which some older feminist theology envisages.[18]

This does not mean, however, that our sex will remain unchanged in the order of redemption any more than our bodies will. Augustine speculates that though women will retain their sex they will not indulge in sexual intercourse nor give birth, for he does not believe that such things belong to the order of redemption. Both he and Paul speculate on what our transformed bodies will be like: 'spiritual bodies' Paul calls them, and Augustine insists reassuringly that they will neither be too fat nor too thin, too short nor too tall, too old nor too young, and that physical defects will be removed.[19] As there is so little evidence on which to base such remarks, this detailed speculation about the order of redemption may be interesting, and even theologically profound, but is probably not to be relied upon too heavily! Its importance lies rather in the reminder that we do not really know what our redeemed gender-identities will be like, and that they certainly cannot therefore be simply equated with their current manifestations.

So important strands in the Christian tradition tell us that our gender identities are a real part of us, and that they will persist in the order of redemption. They insist that gendered identity has an eternal significance

17. See Ramsey 1988, where he shows the importance of Augustine's insistence that both sex and the body must be viewed within the context of the history of redemption.

18. As Radford Ruether says of the afterlife, '[i]n effect our existence ceases as individuated ego/organism and dissolves back into the cosmic matrix of matter/energy... It is this matrix, rather than our individuated centers of being, that is "everlasting"' (1983: 257).

19. See, for example, *City of God*, bk 22, chs. 15–20.

and must be transformed along with every part of us in order to conform to the image of God in which we are all made. But there is also a refusal to let our gendered identity become so important that it prevents us from taking on this new nature, or completely determines what this new nature is to be. Our gendered identity is to be understood as part of our God-given nature, a nature that is bodily and spiritual, natural and cultural. Christianity has little interest in the distinction between sex as natural and gender as constructed which has been so influential in feminist theory. For Christianity everything is constructed, and the key question is whether it is constructed by Godly or ungodly forces. The distinction which matters is not that between nature and culture or body and spirit, but that between old creation and new, between that which belongs to the old order of corruption and that which belongs to the new order of redemption.

Conclusion

I have been arguing against what I see as an unhelpful tendency in some feminist theology to seek refuge from anxieties about identity in the security of a defined, delimited and innocent women's identity. I have suggested that such a strategy is idolatrous: it reduces my God-given reality to less than it really is; it leads me to suppress some aspects of my identity and to cling uncritically to others; it restricts my freedom and ties me to an identity which reduces me; it limits and pre-ordains the nature of my relationships both with the divine and with other human beings; and it forecloses on my relationships with others of both sexes. In doing all this it acts to keep all my relationships within bounds and under control and prevents that openness to the Spirit and to others in which alone I can grow and flourish.

It has been no part of my intention to suggest that Christianity has been wholly on the side of the angels where these issues of identity are concerned. I have tried to point out that the church has also been guilty of wishing to foreclose on human—and gendered—identity (much more often at the expense of women than men). Likewise, much Christian theology and most Christian institutions continue to be spectacularly bad at accommodating women's differently sexed identities. Despite Paul's remarks about the distinct and individual nature of the different members of the one body, the church has often tried to force men—and more often women—into very narrow, restrictive and reduced identities. It often fails to accept that all are equally members of Christ's body in their difference and not in spite of it. Part of the extraordinary value of feminism and feminist theology lies in its having opened our eyes to these sins, failings, and distortions.

My intention in this article has not been to deny any of these criticisms of the Christian tradition, but to show that there are also powerful and constitutive elements of that tradition which stand in judgment on such manipulations of identity, and which remind us that by God's grace we are always more than any attempt we or others may make to seize hold of our identity. To cling to my identity as a woman, a homosexual, a Barthian, a person of colour—or whatever—is not just to reject God, but to reject our true selves. I have tried to show that Christianity may have something more to say, that it can still speak to the contemporary situation, and that it may have the power to set us free from an anxious quest for an identity which is clear, fixed, contained and under control.

WHO IS THE CHRIST? ISSUES IN CHRISTOLOGY AND FEMINIST THEOLOGY

Elaine Storkey

Introduction

Feminist liberation theologians have presented us with a curious dilemma. They, more than many, have recovered what is fundamental to the Christian faith, that it is good news for the poor. They have exposed the false piety that has erected systems of power and manipulation and reinforced injustice, questioning whether a gospel which does not address the pain of the dispossessed can be a gospel at all. Liberation feminism offers an incarnational theology which rejoices that the empowering God is in our midst, the God who stands alongside the marginalized and downtrodden, and understands the reality of suffering. Yet there are niggling questions at the very centre of this particular incarnational perspective. *How* is God in our midst? In what way is God to be identified or recognized? Until these queries are resolved, the celebration of Christian liberation may yet be premature. For, with guests already arriving there is a rumour of absence. It would seem that no invitation has been issued to someone central to an orthodox understanding of incarnation. Jesus Christ, in whose name Christians have always gathered, is apparently unwelcome, unless he comes relinquished of his 'encapsulation in the structures of patriarchy' (Radford Ruether 1981: 47).

The concept of God incarnate has always been a demanding one. Some forms of Hinduism address it by positing frequent and multiple incarnations in a variety of forms. Fertility religions see God as recurrently incarnate in the birthing and rebirthing processes. The Romans and Greeks barely needed any doctrine of incarnation, since they represented their gods as half-human anyway, and often entering into human pettiness and indulging in competitive power-broking. The Semitic religions have thus rightly been cautious about any claims to divine incarnation, seeing God as ultimately other and jealously guarding the first Commandment. When, for Jewish worshippers, the holiness of God cannot be articulated in noun form, let alone be seen in a human body, Christians have needed good reason to identify the being of God with the human being of a man. The good reason has been seen in the promise of the Hebrew Scriptures; the covenants made and renewed by God, the kingship of the Davidic line, the Messianic hope of Ezekiel, the Suffering Servant of Isaiah, the Prophecies of Micah, the spiritual outpouring promised in Joel. It is this promise which has been given shape within the Christian Scriptures; its fulfilment is seen in the central concept of the Word made Flesh, located by John in the very life and death of Jesus, in whom 'dwells all the fullness of the Godhead bodily'. The *credo* of Simon Peter, 'You are the Christ, the Son of the Living God', is echoed in the response of so many whom the gospel writers record. The disciples who followed him, the women who touched him, the friends who loved him, the enemies who hated him, and the soldier who executed him, seemed united in the belief, or fear, that 'truly, this man was the Son of God'. Centuries of Christian worshippers have made that their own affirmation.

Feminist theology is, however, somewhat coy about viewing the incarnation quite so specifically. To start with, there is the age-old offence of the particularity of Christ. Surely it is inconceivable that one specific male, born within a distinct race in a particular century, could be *the* incarnation of the divine. For many feminist theologians this is not only inconceivable, but also outrageous. Radford Ruether's claim that 'Christology has been the doctrine of the Christian tradition that has been most frequently used against women' (1981: 45), is one echoed by eco-feminists and post-Christian feminists, for each has her own reasons for rejecting a traditional Christology. These different feminists seem united in the concern that the christological interpretation of the person of Jesus held by the church through the centuries, has reinforced patriarchy and subjugated women. At best the offence of Christ's particularity is too great. At worst he becomes the symbol of a necrophilic religion centring round a dead man on a cross. As womanist theologian Delores Williams said in the 1993 Re-Imagining conference in Minnesota, USA: 'We don't need folks hanging on a cross, with blood dripping and weird stuff'.

The Gendered Particularity of Christ

Various aspects of Christ's particularity therefore become pertinent to feminist theologians. His maleness is obviously one focus. For if Christ is God, then God is male, and the male is God (Daly 1973: 19). This syllogism may be logically deficient, but it has emotional resonances that carry weight. It echoes the strong sense that Christ's maleness, 'construed in official androcentric theology and ecclesial practice' (Johnson 1993: 52), has led to a diminution of the ontological status of women.

The central concern has hinged on the question of what it is to be male and how this is different from being female. If, as Plato points out, the difference is simply one of whether a person bears or begets it should be no crucial demarcation. It is merely a difference of biological function that should have no bearing on how men and women are included in the affairs of the state, or the process of leadership and education. The difference between bearing and begetting is similar in kind to the difference between having hair and being bald. A bald man is no less likely to make a good cobbler than a hairy man. However, despite Plato's charming inclusiveness towards men who were thin on top, his arguments did not win the day in Christian theology or the church. For Aristotle, more than Plato, held the vital sway. And for him biology was rather more crucial than baldness. Developing his own table of dualisms, already inherited from Pythagoras, he set the female together with matter, passivity and imperfection, and the male with form, activity and perfection, claiming that 'the woman is, as it were, an impotent male'. This impotence lies in the fact that she has little to contribute to generation and procreation; in fact she offers only the material substance of her menstrual blood, against the vital male contribution of form or soul. 'The female is, as it were, a mutilated male, and the catamenia [female secretions] are semen, only not pure; for there is one thing they have not in them, the principle of soul' (Radford Ruether 1983: 128). What distinguishes the male is thus the very 'principle of soul' which becomes the cause of new life, passed on in their semen.

With our more reliable understanding of biology we could have cheerfully relegated such nonsense to the bin, were it not for the fact that this ingenious piece of bigotry found its way into theology and into Christology. Aquinas, ever the devotee of Aristotle, suggested that God has to be incarnate as a male because of woman's ontological inferiority.[1] Christ's maleness was not in any sense optional. Nor, it would seem to many of his later followers, was it the result of God's choice of self-disclosure. It was rather logically and ontologically necessary. The normative human person is male; Christ must represent and reinforce that normativity. And for Radford Ruether, even when mystics have tried to 'androgynize' the

---

1. *Summa Theologica*, Pt 1, Qn 92, arts. 1, 2.

Christ to include female and male elements, '[f]emaleness is still cor-related with the lower side of human nature' (1983: 126).

Feminist theologians have explored the implications of this position for some decades. They have argued that it lies behind the many exclusions and prohibitions of women, not least behind the barring of women from the Catholic and Orthodox priesthoods. For, within such an androcentric symbol system, males can represent both the divine and the creaturely, whereas women can represent only the latter. Surreptitiously, the boun-daries of biology become co-terminous with those of necessity. Conceptual demarcations become blurred. When the 1976 Vatican declaration sug-gested 'there must be a physical resemblance between the priest and Christ', the confusion between 'representative' and 'representation' was made official. The concept of being a representative of Christ elided into the concept of being a physical representation of Christ, for the priest must bear some resemblance to the Saviour. But what kind of resemblance is required? Clearly not one of height, skin colour, Jewish facial charac-teristics or hair length (bald men are equally as acceptable as hairy men). It would seem that the requirement lies only in a resemblance of genitals. Radford Ruether can therefore be justified in concluding that from this perspective, 'the possession of male genitalia becomes the essential pre-requisite for representing Christ who is the disclosure of the male God' (1981: 45-56; 1983: 116-38). And she insists that notions of the maleness of God, through the logos-image of Christ, inevitably undermine the basic Christian faith that Christ indeed possesses a humanity that includes the humanity of women.

The great danger with Christ's particularity is that, when shaped by such philosophical assumptions, it is not particular at all. In fact maleness has now become a 'universal', an essentially required component of Christ's humanness. The concerns of liberation feminism here are perfectly legiti-mate ones. The weight put on Christ's maleness has forged much theology and ecclesiology to the detriment of women. Yet now another question emerges. If maleness is seen as essential to Christ in his humanity, how is it non-essential to Christ in his divinity? Radford Ruether is clear about her own answer, having argued it repeatedly since her chapter 'Can a male Saviour save women?' in 1981 (Radford Ruether 1983). 'Incarnation solely into the male sex does not include women and so women are not reckoned. That is to say, if women cannot represent Christ, then Christ does not represent women' (Radford Ruether 1983). Christ as God incarnate is God as male incarnate. And exclusion from redemption has to leave women with fundamental problems with regard to the Christian faith.

Radford Ruether is not the only feminist theologian who argues this way. Korean theologian Rita Nakishima Brock insists that the doctrine that only a perfect male form can incarnate God fully and be the salvific focus, makes our individual lives in female bodies a prison against God. For her, an exclusive divine presence in a 'perfect' man called Jesus, who came to be called the Christ, must be disallowed if Christology is to be reclaimed in feminist visions (Brock 1988: 68). We need to be able to accept our actual, sensual, changing selves as the lover of the divine. For Brock therefore, Radford Ruether's question 'Can Christ redeem women?' cannot be asked without simultaneously asking 'Can women redeem Christ?'

The odd turn in the argument here illustrates the impatience within liberation feminism towards traditional ways of doing theology. Having mounted a strong critique of the way in which Christ's maleness has become absolutized within some areas of the church, the way is now open for these writers to demonstrate that, from within a biblical framework, divinity cannot be held to incorporate sexuality. They would be on safe ground if they were to argue that the position being put forward is not valid from a New Testament perspective. But they do not. The work of feminist exegetes, such as Phyllis Trible, Letty Russell, or Catherine Kroeger, is largely ignored, as is the obvious point that since, in his representative function, Christ is *anthropos*, rather than merely *aner*, women must, quite legitimately, be included in his work of reconciliation. Although the liberation feminists rightly identify the problems caused by Greek influences on early theology, they do not respond to the problem with biblical and textual scholarship. For the text is perceived as too contaminated by androcentric assumptions to be of any help. Instead, they seem content to write Christ off as the 'Word Made Male' and to abandon traditional Christology without further investigation.

However, the swiftness here is unwarranted, especially when the conclusion is reached with such scant attention to the central sources of the Christian faith. The re-interpreting of the key question is also premature. For it becomes one of whether, within a new incarnational theology, the idea of the Christ can in any way be redeemed. Their proposals for that will be looked at later.

Race, Ethnicity and Particularity

Although the weight of complaints lean heavily on Christ's maleness, this has not been the only feminist concern surrounding his particularity. There is also the question of race and ethnicity. Christ's positioning as the rejected Jewish Messiah inevitably brings for many writers issues of anti-Semitism. Some see a strong parallel between the church's attitude towards Jews and women. Just as women were often blamed for the death of Christ ('You are the devil's gateway; it was because of you that Christ had to die'[2]), so were Jews. 'Jesus was used first against the Jew: saying that the Jews persecuted and so the Jews should be condemned' (Lan 1993). Even the stereotypes are similar: Jews, like women, were apparently viewed as 'impious, faithless, contumacious and lusty' (Radford Ruether 1975: 166). Much of Radford Ruether's own work in Christology has argued its relationship to anti-Judaism, seeing the roots of anti-Semitism in the Christian idea of the reprobate status of the Jew. For Radford Ruether, if the general struggle between Christians and Jews was, and is, a theological one, the core of this struggle is christological. 'Theologically, anti-Judaism developed as the left hand of Christology. Anti-Judaism was the negative side of Christian affirmation that Jesus was the Christ' (Radford Ruether 1975). Radford Ruether alleges that there are within Christology three assumptions that reinforce this development. The first is the belief that God's judgment is upon the Jew while Christians, through the person and work of Jesus, can claim God's promise for themselves. Second is the Christians' relegation of Judaism to an ethnic, or particularistic tribal religion, while they claim universality for their own faith. Third is the Christian identification of Jews with the Old Adam and themselves with the New: Jews possess the Old covenant of law and letters, whereas Christians hold the New of grace and spirit. For Christians to centre their worship on Jesus, as the crucified incarnation of God, puts the Jew beyond the boundary of inclusion in redemption.

Although racial particularity seems to have something in common with gender particularity, the argument here is very different. For what Radford Ruether does not consider in this context is the place of Christ's own Jewishness. If she had, she would have stayed with the logic of her first question and, applying it to ethnicity, would have asked, 'Can a Jewish Christ save Gentiles?' Instead her fundamental question now reverses and becomes, 'Can a Christian Saviour affirm Jews?' Her attack is on Christian, not Jewish, particularity. This means she largely ignores the other interesting argument, that if Saviours need to exhibit sameness in either race or gender, we are going to need rather a lot of them for the needs of the world to be satisfied.[3]

2. Tertullian, *On the Apparel of Women*, bk 1, ch. 1.
3. A point made well by Angela West (1995: 179).

Radford Ruether's focus is dictated more by the narratives of history than either theology or logic. For history is littered with pogroms, persecution and ethnic cleansing of the Jews. Christianity itself has had to contend with Jewish resistance to the idea that Jesus is the Messiah. And the chronicles of that contention have not been attractive. Because the church has not included unconverted Jews in a redemptive ecclesia, it has sometimes gone on also to exclude them from neighbour-love. It has been slow to protest against the violations of their human rights. Too often, ideologies other than Judaeo-Christian ones have found their way into some parts of the church; ideologies, for example, of Aryan superiority, ethnic purity, social demarcations, and strict gender hierarchies. The Shoah itself was carried out by those whose thinking blurred Christianity with profound anti-Semitism. When millions of their fellow humans were persecuted and killed simply because they were Jews, too many Christians were silent. When liberation feminism maintains that there is an intrinsic connection between Christology and anti-Judaism their evidence looks compelling.

Yet here again, we cannot argue from history to necessity. For historical processes are never straightforward applications of particular principles. The persecution of the Jews has never followed from the theology of the Incarnation, but from the ubiquity of human sin. Nor does the crucifixion of Jesus, the Jew, in any way justify the murdering of any other Jew. However much the argument focuses upon the defectiveness of the Christian story it cannot escape the fact that the biblical records offer us a different perspective; that Christ came to abolish the human barriers which create hatred and discrimination, and to reconcile both Jew and Gentile to God and to each other. When the very attitudes which Jesus preached against have been predominant in human wrongs, it is the fault of those who espoused them, not the Christology of the New Testament.

Nevertheless, the allegations continue, and others are added, for example, that Christology lies behind the development of colonialization, white racism and the endorsement of slavery. From the first days of its political establishment it has created oppression for those people whom Radford Ruether calls 'the underside of Christian imperialism': women, slaves, barbarians, Jews, pagans and heretics. For her, Christology became 'the apex of a system of control over all those who in some way or another are "other" than this new Christian order' (Radford Ruether 1983: 125). Womanist theologians have struggled against the early identification of Christianity with their own legacy as coerced people. The Jesus of the white man was the opponent of liberation: 'A ship named Jesus carted black people from Africa into slavery in America. White preachers presented Jesus as a supporter of slavery. Jesus was so clearly presented as an image on the side of oppression' (Williams 1993; see also Grant 1989). The same allegation is made from Asian feminists, and in the feminism of indigenous peoples. In fact, liberation feminism finds strong evidence to suggest that Christology can be identified with almost any manifestation of human injustice.

When the case for this identification has not been positively established (which, if we are looking for some biblical justification, is really most of the time) there is a suggestion that it can certainly be negatively established. The appeal is to the argument from silence. If traditional Christology is not responsible for racism and anti-Semitism, why have Christians been so lamentably slow to develop, from the doctrine of the incarnation, a theology which offers liberation of the poor, resistance to structures of inhumanity, and deliverance from servitude? The question is an important one. The church, especially within the affluent world, has a case to answer. When Christians in the less affluent world have built theologies of liberation on Christ's identification and compassion, we have been slow to show solidarity with this. We have not been ready to learn from black Christians in white majority cultures how they experience the meaning of the incarnation. As one writer suggests, there is a sense in which black Christians have always been in the business of re-imaging Jesus, but along lines which are entirely faithful to the New Testament accounts (Williams 1993). Yet we have shown little interest when they see in the gospel narrative something close to their own story of struggle, violation, injustice and resilience against defeat.

Nevertheless, for liberation feminists to take the reproof further and to suggest that the church through the ages has had the wrong Christology is an odd conclusion. A better conclusion is that we have not heeded the Christology we have had. For Christ applied to himself the Messianic vision of Isaiah; that he had come to bring good news to the poor, to set the captives free, to bind up the brokenhearted, and to release those who are oppressed. He came to bring life in abundance, not to the rich but to those who are poor in spirit, to those who mourn, and to the peacemakers who will be called the children of God. To fail to make this promise an actuality in our own time points not to a weakness in theology, but to human complacency and hardness of heart.

Particularity and Ecology

Liberation feminists with strong ecological sympathies see in Christ's particularity another sinister consequence; the encouragement not only of gender, race and class hierarchies but also human/non-human hierarchies. Some feminist theologians draw a close parallel between the subjugation of women and the subjugation of the earth. Summarizing Radford Ruether, Jacquelyn Grant explains:

> As men have dominated nature they have dominated women, as they have exploited nature they have raped women. They have been able to do this because of their believed superiority of men over nature and men over women (Grant 1989: 140).

Radford Ruether makes the point that not only does the so-called divinely created order of things (spirit over nature, mind over body, male over female) sanction social hierarchy and appear to be natural. It draws its strength from a traditional Christology (Radford Ruether 1981: 61). Christ, in his uniqueness and particularity, is seen as the most perfect of creation. He symbolizes the supremacy of the human male above all other forms of life. In fact, nowhere in the world has there been a more detailed and total statement of man's dominance over the natural order. Christ is worshipped as having complete authority and power over the natural world. He subdues the storm, turns water into wine, uses fish to pay his taxes, and walks on the water. But the fundamental model of relationship represented here is one of domination. Women must see that there can be no liberation for them and no solution to the ecological crisis within any society which accepts this model (Radford Ruether 1975: 204; see also Grant 1989: 137). As feminist theologian, Kwok Pui Lan, insists, 'if we cannot imagine Jesus as a tree, as a river, as wind, and as rain, we are doomed together; if we are ever anthropocentric in our search we are doomed' (Lan 1993).

Radford Ruether therefore rejects a Christology which speaks of a transcendent God with 'power over' the creation. She calls for a new way of communal egalitarianism, where old relationships of power and domination are destroyed to be replaced by a new humanity, a new heaven and a new earth. Toward this end, and along with a growing number of eco-feminists, she invites us to work with a notion of God as the ground of all being, the all-embracing source of life. This general life-form, cosmic-womb, world-soul contrasts sharply with the specificity of the incarnate Christ in Jesus.

> We can speak of the root human image of the divine as the Primal Matrix, the great womb within which all things, Gods and humans, sky and earth, human and nonhuman being, are generated. Here the divine is not abstracted into some other world beyond this earth but is the encompassing source of new life that surrounds the present world and assures its continuance. This is expressed in the ancient myth of the World Egg out of which all things arise (Radford Ruether 1983: 45).

For Radford Ruether, it is only when all strains of particularity, maleness, domination and ethnicity are gone that we can embrace God without fear of exclusion or alienation. It is only when we leave behind the 'once-and-for-all' idea of Jesus the Christ, that we are able to see the incarnation in its fullest possibilities. But what is left of Christology when this has taken place? And to what extent can what remains still be embraced as part of a *Christian* heritage?

Sin, Salvation and the Cross

My focus has been on the offence of Christ's particularity to liberation feminists. However, it is well known that the even greater offence is that of Christ's salvific mission. The arguments have been discussed very fully elsewhere (see Moltmann-Wendel 1991, and Storkey 1994, 2000), but it is important to rehearse a few of them here. A Christ-Saviour is dismissed by many feminists theologians, including Hampson, Heyward and Jantzen, as being a hero figure who prevents human beings (especially male humans) from accepting responsibility for their own actions. A Christ-Saviour also raises the important issue of what it is that we need to be saved from. Within much feminist theology sin itself is regarded as gender specific. The sins assumed by traditional Christian soteriology are identified by feminists as 'male' sins: pride, will-to-power, and egocentricity. For Hampson the very concept of sin in Christian theology has been shaped by male psychology, characterized as separateness, oppositions, fear of relationship, and 'angst' ('anxiety without an object'). So when we use themes of Christ's 'emptying' and 'self-abnegation' as a symbolic act in renouncing our sins, she finds it 'far from helpful as a paradigm' (Hampson 1990). By contrast, female sin, as first suggested over 40 years ago by Valerie Saiving, might be more properly regarded as triviality, self-negation, or under-development of the self (Saiving 1960: 100-12), for which, most feminists believe, there is no 'saviour' outside our own will-to-change. For Anne Wilson Schaef sin is being out of tune with our internal process and thereby distorting ourselves. Sexism offers a powerful distortion of reality, which is why women need to live within 'the female system'. There, we will find that 'living in tune with god means being in tune with what one already is' (Schaef 1985: 168). Grace Jantzen also challenges 'the patriarchal dimensions of the concept of salvation' and offers instead 'the luxuriant self-sufficiency implied in the idea of flourishing' which allows us to recognize that 'the natural condition of humanity is good: we need only to be allowed to develop normally' (Jantzen 1996: 66). In a series of short steps then we have moved from a redefining of sin so that it is 'relevant' to women, to its effective abolition as a meaningful concept within feminine experience. Sin has been 'eliminated' from *authentic* women's lives as 'a kind of false consciousness' (West 1995: 111). Women may still need to repent, but it is for our lack of mutuality and flourishing, not for our pride. And to overcome this, we certainly do not need a saviour to plead our case to God.

But as well as the 'why', there is also the 'how' of atonement. The Cross is seen neither as the place where God's power overcomes evil, sin and death, nor the place of reconciliation between God and humanity, but a symbol used to glorify death and to romanticize suffering. It involves ideas of sin, sacrifice, guilt, suffering and scapegoating, which many feminists see to be deeply offensive to women. The Cross not only justifies violence, but makes the passive acceptance of victim status a virtue. As Radford Ruether insists:

> Christ's cross is used to inculcate a sense of masochistic guilt, unworthiness and passivity in Christians. To accept and endure evil is regarded as redemptive. Liberation Christians say that God does not desire anyone's sufferings, least of all Jesus', any more than God desires or blesses poverty... (Radford Ruether 1981: 29).

Similar points are made by many others. Elga Sorge suggests that traditional Christology 'encourages an attitude of faith which is orientated more on suffering, torture and violence than on love, pleasure and joy' (quoted in Moltmann-Wendel 1991: 81). Mary Grey believes that this brings particular problems for women who have so absorbed the ethic of self-sacrifice and punishment, that they have assumed that their rightful place was just there, on the cross with Jesus (Grey 1989: 13). Delores Williams is sceptical of any religion which puts a high premium on suffering, for 'if those people are in power, they are going to find somebody to suffer' (Williams 1993). Regula Strobel asks, 'How can we think of the act of violence, the judicial murder of Jesus in connection with the theological concept of redemption... Can such a repressive, bloody act ever bring redemption salvation and blessing?'[4] The traditional focus on Christ's death is therefore seen as unhelpful for women. Even for those feminists who do not wish to abandon the special place in the theology of liberation there has to be some repositioning. The emphasis must now shift to what Jesus lived for rather than what he died for.

One move in this direction is to reinterpret the Cross, to empty it of the more barbaric aspects of Christ's suffering and abandonment by God. The cross does not have to be about a male 'saviour' dying in agony, but about the power of life-sustaining love in the community of women. Rita Naka-shima Brock echoes this when she explains: 'Jesus did not die totally abandoned, though he is described as feeling godforsaken. The divine erotic power illuminated through Christa/Community in Galilee and the woman at Bethany is sustained through Jesus' death by those who watch him die' (Brock 1988: 98). For Elisabeth Moltmann-Wendel, however, this is simply untrue to the story. She points to the distinction in the New Testament between being forsaken by human beings and 'godforsakeness' which 'cannot be done away with by any erotic power or power of relationship' (Moltmann-Wendel 1991: 83-84). For her, something in the very riddle of Christ on the Cross, forsaken by God, remains at the heart of Christianity. It gives us a glimpse into the abyss, into the dark night of the soul, and cannot be removed morally. When women domesticate it, simply to fit their own ideas, they have in fact 'de-crucified Jesus' (Moltmann-Wendel 1991: 82).

The Christology of the New Testament has, of course, one crucial answer to those who are apprehensive about the Cross. And that is the Resurrection. The central message is not one of violence, suffering, passivity and defeat. It is that God's love has overcome the deepest hatred that the human heart can find. The truest meaning of the Cross is one of vindication and victory over death summed up by both the angels' question to the women, 'Why do you seek the living among the dead?', and St Paul's cry, 'Where, Death, is your sting?' (Lk 24.5; 1 Cor. 15.55). But this is little comfort to many liberationist feminists who confess, at best, an agnosticism on this issue. Radford Ruether in particular has problems not only with the resurrection of Christ, but with any idea of personal eschatology, for she believes it goes against all we experience in life.

4.　'Wollte Gott Uns durch Blut erlosen?': lecture given in Stuttgart, 12 March, 1990, quoted in Moltmann-Wendel 1991: 84.

What we know is that death is the cessation of the life process that holds our organism together. Consciousness ceases and the organism itself gradually disintegrates. This consciousness is the interiority of that life process that holds the organism together. There is no reason to think of the two as separable, in the sense that one can exist without the other (Radford Ruether 1983: 257).

Even here, by offering us a model of personal survival, traditional Christology apparently distracts us from the real purpose of death, which is to absorb organisms back into the earth matter. We cease to be an 'individuated ego/organism' and become part of the 'cosmic matrix of matter/energy'; what Radford Ruether calls elsewhere 'Mother-Spirit'. And it is in this process that we find everlasting life, not that of following in the footsteps of a 'risen' and individuated Christ.

The liberation feminist dissatisfaction with orthodox Christology thus seems overwhelming. This comes as no surprise to post-Christian feminists, who, like Jewish feminist Naomi Goldenberg, find it impossible that such a masculine image as Jesus Christ should symbolize the liberation of women (Goldenberg 1979: 4). For Mary Daly, Christ, as the central symbol of Christianity, is inherently defective (Daly 1986: 72). For Daphne Hampson, Jesus is beyond redemption. The Christ of the Church and the patriarchy of the Church are so inextricably interwoven that there is no prospect of any extrication (Hampson 1990). Any attempt at corrective measures are a waste of time.

Yet many feminist theologians, including liberation feminists, do not want to abandon Christology completely, for its links with an incarnational theology are too strong. At the very least it is time to do some deconstruction and reassembling of the faith. Some believe that there is always the possibility of redeeming the Christ, of retelling the christological story, in a way that might after all be liberating to women. In this penultimate section I want to review some of their proposals.

Retrieving Christology

One of the earliest suggestions was to substitute an androgynous Christ for a male one. Just as equalitarian feminism emphasized the intrinsic sameness of women and men, its theological counterpart saw Christ as both male and female. This alternative symbol denotes inclusiveness and equality. This is evident in the thinking of womanist Delores Williams when she argues that because the incarnation came through the body of a woman, the feminine is incorporated into the very being of Jesus. Yet, elsewhere, androgyny has fallen out of favour, expecially since the attack from Luce Irigaray and other postmodern feminists. For, they argue, androgyny has never eradicated patriarchy, but has simply facilitated the incorporation of women into it. Any assertion of the equality of women begs the question, equal to whom? Because the answer is, inevitably, equal to men, this position never fundamentally destroys the notion of the male as norm.

One of Radford Ruether's own suggestions has been to bypass the equality-difference debate and opt for transformation. Her benchmark of true biblical faith, her 'canon within the canon', is the prophetic-messianic principle incorporating the cry of the prophets against injustice and idolatry, the bias to the poor and marginalized, and the servant-leadership of Jesus of Nazareth. The new hermeneutical principle is clear: 'Whatever denies, diminishes, and distorts the full humanity of woman must be regarded as nonredemptive' (Radford Ruether 1985: 27). Thus a new Christology must be one of social transformation. She expresses her own eschatological vision in one of the paradigmatic passages in liberation theology.

> Alienated power is overthrown. Those who presently have and represent power are called to lay this power down in service. The subjugated are lifted up. They will inherit the earth in the new liberated Kingdom of redemption. The despised of the present society lead the way into the Kingdom. Men leaders, even God, repent of domination; servants, women, the poor are liberated from servitude. This is a Christology of the process of conversion, the process of creating a new humanity of wholeness in mutuality (Radford Ruether 1976).

The question is, however, what happens to Jesus in this process? In fact a divorce occurs. The historical Christ and the redeeming Christ are split apart. The historical Christ was a specific, limited man. The redeeming Christ is an ongoing, liberating, messianic principle, revealed in a new community. 'Christ as redemptive person and Word of God, is not to be encapsulated "once for all" in the historical Jesus' but in the community of liberation today.[5]

> This kind of spirit Christology does not separate out a past perfect historical Jesus from the ongoing Spirit. Rather it sees Christ as a power that continues to be revealed in persons, both male and female, in the present. Christ is located in a new humanity that discloses the future potential of redeemed life. The reality of Christ is not completed in the past but continues to be disclosed in the present (Radford Ruether 1983: 131).

5.   Radford Ruether has argued this consistently since 1974 (see 1983: 138).

So Christology can be redeemed, Christ can be 'converted to liberation, to the defence of the life of the poor', but only with qualifications. (S)he has to become inclusive, indigenous and open. We have to be able to experience Christ 'in the form of our sister' (Radford Ruether 1983: 138). For the poor in Latin America, Christ can be incarnate among them, 'converted to care for the people in and through their land, only when the mestizo Christ acknowledges that he is the son of a dark Indian woman' (Radford Ruether 1996: 12).

This process of deconstructing Christ is therefore a demanding one. It requires us to go back over the history of Christianity, to recognize that the central place of Jesus has been the result of a misconception of him as divine. Carter Heyward advocates that we now must see Jesus not as the Christ, the Son of God, the miracle worker, the Saviour, or as the unique Incarnation of God, but simply as a human being who knew and loved God. We must 'de-idolatrise him', as the one who allows mutuality to flourish; re-image him as the one who 'reinforces the participatory nature of existence'. Then we are able to understand that what we had interpreted, for example, as divinely activated miracles are really 'statements of mutual participation in existence'. Heyward cites as evidence the woman with the menstrual problems in John's Gospel, ch. 7. Here, despite what the church has held, no divine miracle occurred. The woman healed herself; Jesus himself said so. For women have the divine within. The task of the new Christology is to allow women to find this divine within.

In most theologies ecclesiology and Christology have been seen as separate. Here they now merge. In abandoning a Christology that focuses on the person of Jesus as the unique incarnation of God, Radford Ruether and Heyward both deliberately blur the distinction between Christ and the Church. Rather than in the particularized Jesus, the Christ resides in the people of justice, of transformation, the women of faith.

Christ without the Cross, without violence, gender, race, creed, ethnicity or specificity, is the ultimate liberationist utopia. It is what Elisabeth Moltmann-Wendel calls 'the attempt to develop a gentle theology of non-violence and a utopia of feasible, achievable happiness' where ethics replaces dogmatics and God is to be grasped 'in immanence, in the process of life and an ethic of reciprocity' (Moltmann-Wendel 1991). It is there in Mary Grey's vision of a new kind of redemption, where the very lives of women become 'part of the divine dynamic for the transformation of the world' (Grey 1989: 58). In acknowledging the need for redemption, she does not 'pretend that living is pain-free' (1989: 4). So, redemption lies in the healing of relationships and the creation of non-dominative, non-discriminatory patterns of behaviour; and since at the basis of these ills has been sexism, overcoming sexism by women's power of mutual love will produce the new world order. So we, as women, can indeed become the Christ. We can discover our inner power to lose ourselves in one another.

The problem is, if we are the Christ in our mutuality, service, relationality and our freedom, how do we become so? What process takes us from brokenness and selfishness into mutuality and love? Mary Grey envisages that it is through the collective empathy of women. For her the dream will be redeemed when women's own experience of pain and exclusion reaches into 'the tragic situations of brutalised women at a world wide level to the pain of women throughout history. From there it reaches out to the suffering of all marginalised groups, women and men, the interweaving of all oppressions, and from there to the root of all suffering in the evil which grips the world and cries for redemption' (Grey 1989: 175). The result will be 'both the celebration of mutual loving actually experienced and a celebration in hope of authentic conversions to mutuality'.

Yet this seems greatly to overstate the power of empathy. For mere empathy seems unlikely, of itself, to be able to safeguard us from any participation in the 'sin of negating relationships', or from becoming part of the 'brutalization of the world'. Whenever the reality of sin is acknowledged, even if that sin is seen as gendered in expression, an insurmountable problem presents itself. How do we avoid its sway over us, and its consequences? In replacing Christ with the open community of women, we sinners have claimed salvific power for ourselves. We are now both redeemer and redeemed; co-creators of a transformed future and co-wrestlers against forces of darkness. But how long will it take before we find that this new 'Christology of interconnection' cannot bring the transformation that our struggling selves need? In fact this utopian vision can be possible only if we deny the niggling evidence of wrong in our lives, and (like Mary Daly in *Beyond God the Father*) see women as the wholly innocent. Rather than 'utopic' it is, rather, as Celia McDonald suggests, 'profoundly pessimistic, for without a clear sense of God's supreme re-creating power, the world as it is remains a battleground for forces of good and evil, with only human good intentions as hope for a positive outcome' (McDonald 1998).

In *Gaia and God* Radford Ruether expands the fusion of Christ and the Church, into that of the world and God. In her 'theocosmology' the world (*gaia*) and God are no longer seen as two overlapping realms, but metaphysically 'one', and God finally becomes the unity of creation (see Ansell 1994: 264). There is now no need for any Christ at all. We need only a mystical sense of the oneness of all life, the 'cosmic matrix', 'the total self that contains us all'. Our liberation becomes complete, not when we are freed from bondage by a redemptive God, but when individual persona-hood is infused by 'the encompassing matrix of all things' in which 'Gods and humans' have their beings. And although, unlike post-Christian feminists, Radford Ruether still writes from within the Church, we would be hard pressed to justify calling her a theist (Hampson 1990: 29). She shows reluctance not only to accept the uniqueness of Christ as the incarnate revelation of God, but to think of God as transcendent, personal, or even existent. Instead, 'God's Shalom is the nexus of authentic creational life that has to be reincarnated again and again in new ways and new contexts in each generation' (Radford Ruether 1981: 69-70).

So Who is the Christ?

The search of liberation feminists for a new Christology has been fuelled by the history of women's exclusion and marginalization. The weight of ecclesial structures and fixed frameworks of interpretation have produced a longing for freedom and release and a desire to redo theology in a way which speaks to the lives and needs of women. And yet, the journey has been beset with problems and confusions which have not made the task either clear or easy. Unresolved questions about sin, about incarnation, redemption and eschatology, have compounded, rather than relieved, the issues that still need to be addressed. The most pressing questions are probably about women ourselves. The claims made about our power to mutuality, our identity as interconnecting healers are hardly substantiated in real lives. Guilt cannot simply be reallocated on to those who are not women. The truth is that women are as much oppressed by personal sin as are men, and that sin is not simply passivity or a resistance to developing the self. Women, as much as men, struggle with envy, selfishness, greed, mean-spiritedness, lack of love and a desire to wound. And even though the sins structured in our society unmistakably reflect the power of patriarchy, there is more to sin than sexism.

There is also more to Jesus than his healing activity in human mutuality. There is something vital about the way he both lived and died and in the reason for his death. For it says God is not only in 'our solidarity, our will to life and our lifeblood'. He is also in our brokenness, our suffering, and our dying. The divine paradox is that it is through the death of Christ that we can live life in all its abundance. God calls us, indeed, to be a redemptive body of love and to show compassion and service in a world which cries aloud for respect and healing. But the question remaining for liberation feminists is how we can ever become that redemptive body without first being redeemed ourselves, and how that is ever possible except through the grace of God.

The incarnation has at its heart a message full of hope and joy: of a God who comes to be one of us. The Christology of the New Testament presents us with the Christ who took on particular human form, but lived free from the sin that besets us all. That is why this Christ can lift us all out of our particularity, and both free us from and affirm our contexts. We can be lifted away from the limitations of all that confines us, and be given the possibility of a redemptive future.

Yet, rather than accept God in the spirit in which Godself is offered, we wrestle to own God as our possession. We guard our own need for inclusion, fiercely and tearfully, like a small child who is afraid of being left off the party list. But the incarnation of God as the baby in a cowshed does not give anyone a privileged 'stake' in God. Neither men nor women, Jews nor Gentiles, oppressed nor free, babies nor old people, are given preference, and God is no one's debtor. The fact that history is littered with those who have fought to sit on the right and the left hand of God does not mean that God heeds their wishes. Instead, as Mary prophesies, God is the one who topples the mighty from their seat and exalts the humble and meek. God-in-Christ includes each of us, and rebukes anyone who, through weakness, hatred, fear or egoism, want to exclude others from God's love.

It may be that liberation feminism has been bewitched by the very anthropomorphism which it warns against. For it needs to recognize that, though Christ is God-with-us in our humanity, pain, new life and our joy, God in Christ is not ultimately like us, any of us. There is no need to hold against the features of Christ's particularity some checklist, so that we can be assured of our inclusion in the mystery of divine love. For God does not incorporate within Godself our gender, time, language, ethnicity, region, skin-colour, lifestyle—nor confront us with any other which undermines our own. God does not need to be re-imagined in our image.

In reappraising the mistakes of the past and the limitations of the church in addressing the concerns and experiences of women, we may need to do some substantial work on areas of theology which have been wooden and unyielding. Yet I do not believe we also need to look for a re-gendered, newly constituted, Saviour to save women. Nor do we need to do the saving ourselves, either in acts of mutual service or in community—for we cannot. Guilt does not disappear because we deny its existence. If we can be saved from it at all it is only by God, and by virtue of the fact that although we have seen God in Christ, ultimately God is not like us; but in holiness and in truth is utterly and fundamentally other (West 1995: 184).

Veronica Brady

The famous proposition of Nietzsche's madman that God is dead (Kauf-mann 1981: 95) may be one Christians today need to take seriously since he claims that it is we who have killed him. This may be especially neces-sary for women for whom traditional images of God appear to condone and even to bless patriarchal attitudes, structures and values which oppress them and seem antithetical to the love, justice, compassion and promise of new life which the word 'God' is supposed to represent. Luce Irigaray expresses this sense of loss:

> We women, sexed according to our gender, lack a god to share, a word to share and become. Defined as the dark, often occult mother-substance of the word of men, we are in need of our subject, our substantive, our word, our predicate, our elementary sentence, our basic rhythm, our morpho-logical identity, our generic incarnation, our genealogy (quoted in Joy 1994: 126).

But our culture as a whole, not just those who call themselves Christians, suffers also. Not long after World War II, reflecting on the disaster it represented and looking for some possibility of a new beginning, Theodor Adorno, for instance, wrote:

> The only philosophy which can be responsibly practised in the face of despair is the attempt to contemplate all things as they would present themselves from the standpoint of redemption. Knowledge has no light but that shed on the world by redemption; all else is reconstruction, mere technique... The more passionately thought denies its conditionality...the more unconsciously and so calamitously it is delivered up to the world (1994: 247).

Adorno was a secular, indeed a Marxist, philosopher, not a theologian. But his experience of Nazism had brought him to the limits of thought, the point at which any theology worth the name begins. Irigaray highlights the ways in which for many women Christianity may seem far from the standpoint of redemption. For all too many, God, represented as male, blesses the patriarchal attitudes and values which not only oppress them but seem the antithesis of all that God is supposed to be. And my beginning has to be located here in this gap, in this anguish. Unquestionably the Christian tradition has been largely patriarchal and so for many women today the light of Christ does not reveal female/feminine cultural imagery and imaging but its absence. Women were, and often still are, seen as different, often as inferior, even, as in mediaeval times, as defective or 'misbegotten' human beings. Maleness is the norm. Thus in the standard Catholic encyclopaedia of theology, *Sacramentum Mundi* (Rahner *et al.* 1968), there is no entry for 'women': you pass from 'wisdom' to 'word of God'. Similarly the entries under 'women' in the reference edition to the NRSV of the Bible list texts which are nearly all misogynist.

So the question asked by Elisabeth Moltmann-Wendel,[1] whether Christ, a male, can be seen as a saviour for women, is an urgent one, and not just for women but for theology also since revelation tells us that in God there is no division just as there is no dimension.

> In Christ Jesus you are all children of God through faith. As many of you as were baptized into Christ have clothed yourselves with Christ. There is no longer Jew or Greek, there is no longer slave or free, there is no longer male and female, for all of you are one in Christ Jesus (Gal. 3.26-28).

Nor does this passage stand alone: the whole thrust of the life and work of Jesus was towards the liberation and unity of love. In their light the objection that the discomfiture many women Christians feel cannot be dismissed as merely fashionable, the result of merely secular thinking. The theological fact is that in Christ differences and divisions which have to do with power as domination vanish through our incorporation into the life of Christ and through him into the life of the Trinity, a ceaselessly generous exchange of love.

If the influence of merely secular thinking is strong, it is surely to be found amongst those who support patriarchal images of God and cling to notions of power as domination and exclusivity. The comment by one scholar, for instance, that 'such unity in Christ does not imply political equality in church or state' (Fitzmyer 1990: 787) suggests the hold that such divisions have, even on theologians. They may write about the end of

---

1.   I am referring not just to the positing of the question by Moltmann-Wendel's work in general (where she is, in any case, only one asking this among many), but to a specific address at an earlier symposium organized by the OTF held at Knox Theological Hall, Dunedin, in May 1991 (for the proceedings see Regan and Torrance 1993).

the law and liberation into the new life of Christ but seem to want to limit its implications.

This brings us to the central point I want to make; that the problem at issue is not, so to speak, on God's side but on ours. God remains God, abundant and full of mercy, in love with all that is made. But we are not always adequate to respond to this love. This issue is thus essentially hermeneutical, one of interpretation and response, of allowing divine reality to speak to, and to interrupt, the 'human, all too human'. By definition theology represents an attempt to speak the unspeakable, to bridge the gap between the sheer otherness of God and our human understanding; something that is impossible unless it is God who builds that bridge and crosses it, letting the mind be in us which was in Christ Jesus.

But how? How to crack the cultural mould which conditions us and let the newness, the otherness of God, break in? What is true elsewhere—that it is when we begin to be aware that an accepted paradigm no longer serves to explain our experience—is true theologically also. God can speak powerfully to our own woundedness.

If therefore the Christian God seems dead to many women we must reflect on what this might mean. As Paul Ricoeur says:

> The true question is to know, first of all, which god is dead; then who has killed him (if it is true this death is a murder); and finally, what sort of authority belongs to the announcement of his death (1974: 445).

Put simply, the god who is dead is an image, an image of human power, of a 'social system which supports and authenticates the predominance of men, brings about a concentration of power and privilege in the hands of men, and consequently, leads to the control and subordination of women' (Social Affairs Committee of the Assembly of Quebec Bishops 1989: 48) and thus to oppression and often violence against them. This is not the God who is revealed to us in Jesus, the embodiment of the all-encompassing love and kindness of God. He—and he is always a 'he'—may rather be a projection of the emotional, social, political and economic needs of those in power, and those who want to wield this power. Symbols, as Freud reminds us, are often the products of repression serving to discharge repressed or suppressed emotional energy (cf. Elder 1995: 349). Gender anxiety, essentially an anxiety about power, may therefore have more to do with patriarchal images of God than with theology. There is no theological reason why the many Scriptural images of God as feminine and Jesus' remarkably open, loving, and respectful attitude to women, might not now come into play in our thinking about God.

The first step towards this recovery of female/feminine imagery, however, is to reflect again on the conditions of any talk about God, on the tension which always exists between human understanding and divine revelation. As Gardiner reminds us, understanding generally, and theological understanding in particular, 'is not to be thought of so much as an action of subjectivity, but as the placing of oneself within a process of tradition in which past and present are constantly fused' (Jeanrond 1991: 65). Any theologian is a man/woman of their time, influenced by it and by the traditions of the past which weigh on this present. Yet these traditions are constantly interrupted by revelation. By definition human thinking is incomplete. We are not closed in on ourselves—or should not be—but open. As Heidegger puts it, 'as potentiality-for-Being...Dasein is not something present-at-hand which possesses its competence for something by way of an extra; it is primarily Being-possible' (Jeanrond 1991: 61).

What activates this Being-possible for us as Christians is encounter with the other/Other, in Scripture and in prayer. Moreover this encounter has a transformative power, enabling a 'real fusing of horizons', the irruption of revelation, 'which means, that as the historical horizon is projected, it is simultaneously removed' (Jeanrond 1991: 66). God's coming can thus be defined as interruption. Thus, in any text,

> the sense...is not behind the text, but in front of it. It is not something hidden, but something disclosed. What has to be understood is not the initial situation of discourse, but what points to a possible word (Jeanrond 1991: 73).

This is even more truly the case with any attempt to reflect on the question of who God might be for us. Our task as Christians is to grasp 'the world-propositions opened up by the reference of the text' (Jeanrond 1991), and, like Abraham, the pattern of faith, we must be prepared to leave our own place, our own presuppositions and go to the place God will show us—in this sense transgression is a mark of faith.

That is easily said, of course, but difficult in practice since we are all to a greater and lesser extent conditioned by the presuppositions of the culture we inhabit. As Heidegger points out:

> If...one likes to appeal to what 'stands there', then one finds that what 'stands there' in the first instance is nothing other than the obvious undiscussed assumption of the person who does the interpreting (Jeanrond 1991: 61).

Wittgenstein makes a similar point:

> One thinks that one is tracing the outline of a thing's nature over and over
> again, and one is merely tracing round the frame through which we look
> at it.
>
> A *picture* held us captive and we could not get outside it, for it lay in our
> language and language seemed to repeat it to us inexorably (1974: 114, 115,
> [p. 48e]).

This problem confronts feminist as well as other theologians. To take one instance, that of Elisabeth Schüssler Fiorenza; in her attempt to write women back into the history of early Christianity she challenges the traditional horizon of biblical scholarship which, she argues, has been 'sustained by an unconscious or conscious refusal to modify our androcentric grasp of reality and religion' (1983: xvii). The difficulty is, however, that in her first book, *In Memory of Her* (1983), at least it could be said that her method is merely a reversal of the one she criticizes, substituting a gynocentric grasp of reality and religion for an androcentric one, thus leaving intact the horizon of division and opposition. True, in her latest book, *Jesus: Miriam's Child, Sophia's Prophet* (1994b), she is aware of this problem, arguing that we need a different horizon which she finds in the notion of Sophia-Wisdom, and I would like to follow her in this. But the difficulty is a real one. It is not sufficient to replace masculine imagery and imaging with the feminine. We need also to rethink our notions of God.

The usual way has been to begin with women's experience, with a theology from below. In a sense, of course, this is inevitable. The person who theologizes is who she is and cannot escape her experience. But, for the Christian, existence is not one-dimensional but dialectical: God also acts upon us. We may need therefore to revive a theology from above, the apophatic tradition, which attempts to open out to the mystery of God and puts a premium upon listening, on letting God speak, on interrupting and expanding. Again, this is rhetorically satisfying and I suspect that few would disagree. But what actually does it mean?

In the first place, it means that we must see the cultural conditioning which makes the question of women and God such an urgent one today as itself relative. Although Nietzsche may be a surprising thinker to invoke, his attack on cultural conditioning is very much to the point:

> The 'true' world—an idea which is no longer good for anything, not even
> obligating—an idea which has become useless and superfluous—
> *consequently*, a refuted idea: let us abolish it! (Raschke 1982: 5).

This is a key text for the deconstructionist. But it is important for us also because it reminds us that what we call 'reality' is ultimately textual. For us the ultimate source, shape and goal of things is expressed in the Word made flesh who speaks in prayer and in Scripture, the book of books. This is an important point in my present argument because it reminds us that though being 'female' is a fact of biology, being 'feminine'—having qualities which are said to belong to women—is an imaginative construct, textual; something to which I will return later. At the moment, however, the point is that if we are to open ourselves out to the mystery of God and discover who God is for us as women we need to interrogate the common sense on which traditional theology relies, the metaphysics and epistemology which relies on instrumental reason that operates to order and to control what is perceived. Knowledge of the living God calls for a different attitude. Listening to the Word is a process of letting go, of depropriation rather than appropriation—and it may not be fanciful to see the Christ hymn in Philippians as the pattern (2.5-11). Now let us turn to the question of female imagery/imaging.

This position of depropriation rather than appropriation is rooted in the current dichotomy between 'masculine' and 'feminine'. In our culture the distinction is both oppositional and absolute. Female/feminine is what the male/masculine is not; a symbol of difference and exclusion. But as I remarked earlier, this opposition is a cultural construction. True, biologically men and women are different. But there are different ways of being human. Psychologically, as Jung insists, each of us possesses possibilities which are both 'masculine' and 'feminine', though in our culture men are taught to repress the feminine and women the masculine. Essentially therefore these qualities are complementary. Hélenè Cixous[2] makes this point. 'Masculine' and 'feminine', she argues, are not tied to biology but represent two different economies or ways of being in the world. The masculine she calls the 'economy of the proper' or, in another translation, the Empire of the Self-Same, rationally concerned with ordering and controlling and drawing distinctions with 'property, propriety and appropriation' (Moi 1987: 111). Traditional theologizing—as distinct from the apophatic tradition—has been practised within this economy. It has put a premium upon rational understanding, on fitting our discussions of God into the economy of thought as mental abstraction.

The feminine economy, however, according to Cixous, is less concerned with understanding and controlling and with rational categories. It refuses to draw boundaries or to make final pronouncements, ceaselessly giving

---

2.   A good general summary of her thought is in Moi 1987: 110-13.

itself away, attuned to the intuitive and the bodily, to the onward flow of existence through the whole of creation. It knows from within, as it were, by participation, responding to 'the resonance of fore-language' rather than attempting to analyse and dissect (Moi 1987: 112-13). This may sound exotic, but many contemporary women writers express a similar sense of reality. Anna Walwicz, for instance, in a prose poem 'Maps for the Future' begins 'The map of the world is felt from the inside' and ends 'Moving so fast that you become aware of the earth's surface being curved. Flying low but fast across the land mass. Make yourself feel like the world. As old but not as troubled' (Moi 1987: 112-13).

This is not gender specific, although in our culture it belongs on the margins, where most women find themselves. But the 'feminine' economy rejects oppositions, such as margin and centre. It is inclusive and concerned with verbs rather than nouns, the subjective rather than the objective, seeing all things contained within the mystery of what is. Its approach to God is therefore one of attentiveness. As Hildegarde of Bingen put it:

> And thus I remain hidden in every kind of reality as a fiery power. Everything burns because of me in such a way as our breath constantly moves us, like the wind-tossed flames in a fire…for I am life (quoted in Fox 1987: 10).

This kind of perception is sensuous and intuitive but it is not irrational —the 'rage against reason' characteristic of many contemporary feminists is not necessarily directed against reason itself, but at the way in which only one kind of reasoning, instrumental and objectifying, has come to dominate the traditionally rich and varied senses of the word (Lloyd 1993: 69). So Hildegarde hears God say:

> I am also reason, which bears within itself the breath of the resounding word, through which the whole of creation is made. I breathe life into everything so that nothing is mortal in respect of its species. For I am life (quoted in Fox 1987: 10).

This opens up a new mode of understanding, of opening out to the mystery which is God, one more in tune with the logic of redemption (to return to Adorno), a logic of giving and receiving, which, if we accept Cixous, is 'feminine' rather than 'masculine'.

The work of Jean Luc Marion and Emmanual Levinas is also helpful at this point. The title of Marion's book, *God Without Being*, indicates his concern to get away from the categories which have given us the God of the Philosophers, First Cause, Omnipotent, Almighty, Omniscient, and so on; terms which make God the first point on a continuum of human understanding and thus tend to confine him—it is always him—within the limits of our reason. For Marion also the problem is essentially hermeneutical. Theology prefers the image (which I would attribute to the economy of the proper, since it reduces what it describes to equivalence) to the symbol. But Jean Luc Marion argues that this is idolatrous because the image controls and limits what it presents: 'When the idol appears, the gaze has just stopped: the idol concretises that stop' (1995: 11). It 'presents itself to [our]…gaze in order that representation, and hence knowledge, can seize hold of it' (1995: 10). The conceptual knowledge on which theology generally relies is of this kind, offering a grasp of the divine that is limited and for that reason intelligible. In this sense, Marion says, it 'represents nothing, but presents a certain low-water mark of the divine, it resembles what the human gaze has experienced of the divine' (1995: 14) and it marks the 'death of God', in our perception at least.

The symbol or icon, however, is different. It 'is defined by an origin that is without original: an origin itself infinite, which pours itself out or gives itself this sign the infinite depth of the icon' (Marion 1995: 20). Levinas, to turn now to him, helps us to understand the implications of this point for the matter in hand. Writing from within the Jewish Talmudic tradition, he reminds us that in Scripture it is the living word of God which speaks, shining 'forth in a mode of thought that conducts its scrutiny by the secret light of hidden worlds. Suddenly, our world, embedded or lost in signs, is illuminated by an idea that comes to it from outside…revealing new possibilities' (1995: 492).

The language of Scripture is 'language [that] contains more than it contains… One can ask whether its meaning…is not already tearing at the text which contains it' (Levinas 1995: 492). This is traditional Talmudic wisdom. But it is not new—in fact, it is very old—in Christianity either. Think, for instance, of the passage from St Ephraem that still features in the prayer of the Church, which begins:

> Lord, who can grasp all the wealth of just one of our words? What we understand is much less than what we leave behind, like thirsty people who drink from a fountain. For your word, Lord, has many shades of meaning just as those who study it have many different points of view (Office of the Readings, Sunday of Week 6).

This takes us away from the dominant mode of thinking—the Man of Reason—and situates us in a mode which is open, dynamic and constantly crossing boundaries; the feminine economy of the gift. Philosophy—and by implication theology—is no longer what Levinas calls an egology, devoted to self-knowledge, but a matter of communion and communication, an approach much more in tune with Revelation. And this mode of knowledge is not gender specific, though in our culture women will probably feel more at home in it than men, conditioned as they have been to dominate and control and to suspect the symbolic as irrational. It makes our thinking about God personal rather than abstract; a point at which Levinas is again illuminating.

For Levinas, society, interpersonal communication, precedes impersonal structures of knowledge (Hand 1993: 6). Proper existence is not individualistic but relational, open to the other through whom we encounter the ultimate Other whose existence is supremely relational (Hand 1993: 34). Once more this is a deconstructive move. Traditional thought moves towards closure, enclosing even God in the categories of Being. But properly understood, God is otherwise than Being, or Being's other (which Marion also insists on). The point at which the God comes closest to us is in the absolute alterity revealed first of all in face-to-face relationships between human beings (Hand 1993: 7), a context which Marion calls 'Eucharistic', 'Where the Word in person, silently, speaks and blesses, speaks to the extent that he blesses' (1995: 151). (And this notion of God as blessing and abundance belongs to the Wisdom tradition, which it is well known, that feminist theologians such as Elisabeth Schüssler Fiorenza [1994b] and Elizabeth Johnson [1993] have also been exploring.) Marion too expands the notion of Wisdom. For him, the Eucharist, the table over which God/Sophia presides is where we are transformed:

> In fact, the Word, at the Eucharistic moment, does not disappear so much as the disciples, who, eating his body and drinking his blood, discover themselves assimilated to the one whom they assimilate and recognize inwardly (Marion 1995: 151).

This is maternal, feminine and creative, and takes us in the direction of the ultimate mystery of the Trinity, abundance, overflowing and ceaselessly loving generosity, which creates what it loves and lovingly returns to itself through creation. As far as any of our categories are adequate it may be that of Motherhood, as one of Julian of Norwich's 'Shewings' recognizes. Edited out of her work until very recently because it was seen as theologically suspect, it sets the mystery of Jesus the Christ within this Sophia tradition:

> Thus Jesus Christ, that Doeth good if against evil, is our very Mother. We have our being with him, for there the ground of Motherhood beginneth, with also the sweet keeping of love that endlessly followeth. As truly as

God is our Father, so truly is God our Mother. That showeth he in all and especially in those sweet words when he sayeth, 'I It Am'. That is to say, I am the might and goodness of Father God. 'I It Am', the wisdom and kindliness of Mother God. 'I It Am', the light and the face that is all blessed love. 'I It Am', that maketh thee to long. 'I It Am', the endless fulfilling of all true desires.[3]

Here imagery and imaging change from masculine to feminine, and maternal images of God such as Isa. 49.15, which compares God with a nursing mother, and Lk. 13.34, in which Jesus is the mother hen, take on a new and deeper significance, for women especially. So, too, does Luke's insistence on the role of Mary, bride of the very Spirit of God, made fertile by the glory of his presence—a woman's body is central to the mystery of God dwelling with us, the Word made flesh. Moving beyond the question how this great thing is to be accomplished in her, recognizing the presence which is absence coming to her, 'an apparition that un-makes, that disorganises the world' (Levinas 1995: 492), she is the pattern of faith as the opening of the self to the infinite. Her fertility is the answer to those sophisticates who see in faith only delusion, 'obligation to "an empty heaven"' (Levinas 1995: 500). The mystery she cannot see which nevertheless encloses her bears fruit in her body. This is no God who is a distant, imperial power but the living God beyond all human categories.

---

3.   Julian of Norwich, 'A Showing of Divine Love', in Reynolds 1994: 38.

GOD, PERSONHOOD AND PARTICULARITY: ON WHETHER THERE IS, OR SHOULD BE, A DISTINCTIVE MALE THEOLOGICAL PERSPECTIVE[*]

Alan J. Torrance

Introduction

It can now be considered a truism to comment, as Simone de Beauvoir argued in *The Second Sex* (1952) and, more recently, Luce Irigaray (1985, 1986, 1989, 1996), that Western culture and philosophy have identified maleness as the norm. The effect of our traditionally androcentric interpretations of humanity has been to make women invisible. They become a subset of a class of humanity which is defined with reference to the male norm and, in the English language, too often referred to by means of a male-gendered vocabulary. In recent years, however, women have sought to counter this by redetermining their own distinctive essence and identity with the knock-on effect that males have begun to find themselves stranded. Whereas women, we are told, are benefiting from this conscious engagement with questions of their identity and role-identification, men have found themselves overtaken in this process and some are left wondering how to conceive of their own identity in the face of an increasingly confident self-identification of women, much of which has been negative and critical of the nature of the male contribution to society and history.[1] In

*   I would like to express my gratitude to Keith Hyde for his helpful comments, suggestions and corrections.

1.   Male individualism and hierarchicalism have been accused of being responsible not only for war and violence in their various forms, but also for the rape of the world's resources and the threat of ecological catastrophe that hangs over us all. Patriarchal religion serves, quite simply, to undergird this. The obvious conclusion of this line of thought is that women stand to become the saviours of the world—that is, assuming that they are not entrenched in male-determined identities. In an article entitled 'Sisterstory: Women as Saviour', Enid Bennett argues that 'it is logical that women are the agents who can save the world' and realize 'the goal of a new heaven and earth' (1988: 48-49).

sum, the downside of the androcentric definition of the human norm has been a failure to take seriously the distinctiveness of males.[2]

It is suggested, therefore, that due to the failure of males to concern themselves with who they are, those of us who are male have no way of addressing the question of our identity. The implication is that the normification of maleness has meant the neutralization (or neuteralization) of male identity. Indeed, it has further been suggested that the new-found confidence in their identity on the part of women has sown the seeds of the marginalization of men in the next millennium.[3] It is now being asked whether this may explain in part the increasing failure of boys to achieve at school and the disproportionate number of women who

2.   As a somewhat forlorn male voice complained at the Society for the Study of Theology in Cambridge, 1996, 'Men are not aware of being a subset and therefore have nothing to celebrate. There is neither a plus-side nor a down-side to being around. We just wake up and that's it!'

3.   Recently, a men's movement has emerged in California in response to the perception that on television (and in popular soap operas in particular) men are invariably typecast by scriptwriters as dumb blondes—and it is now women who are invariably those who show initiative and intelligence and possess all the power. Men are increasingly given the role of sexual playthings with which powerful women decorate their soft-top Mercedes and swimming pools. Men's liberation is concerned about the role modelling which all this suggests.

In the mid-1990s in the United Kingdom an organization seeking 'rights for males' emerged in response to the fact that the only discriminatory laws remaining in operation were laws which discriminated against men. These were the divorce laws which prioritized women when it came to rights of access to children. It was assumed in the British legal system that where there was a parting of ways, the children should, under normal circumstances, be given into the care of the mother.

Recently, moreover, a BBC documentary interviewed a number of a growing class of lonely and bereft males in the UK who saw themselves as having been used by their girlfriends for the purposes of impregnation but where their intention throughout had been to become solo mothers—free of the hassle of having men around the home. The sorry bunch of males interviewed regarded themselves as having been seduced, used, cast off and deprived of access to their own offspring.

Recent statistics (resulting in further TV documentaries and newspaper articles) also suggest a marked reversal in the fortunes of women in the British educational system. Not only do they suggest that girls are doing considerably better at school in the subjects that matter, and that they are substantially more likely to gain access to, and excel in, tertiary institutions, but the indicators suggest that they are increasingly likely to hold the majority of influential positions in society by early next century. One should add that the gender imbalance in the education system was not something which worried male politicians in the past when it was girls who were being disadvantaged!

succeed in acquiring places at university and who become pregnant with the express intention of being solo parents—a privilege which is not an option for men. The supposition is that society needs to liberate males from self-oppressive attitudes and social attitudes that disadvantage boys and young men—that there needs to be, in short, a pedagogy of the oppressed male youth. All this begs the question: Is there anywhere that is the preserve of those males whom, in the *Timaeus*, Plato describes as the direct creations of the gods and who, if they fail to ascend to their original home in the heavens, return to earth as women or beasts? (Graham 1995: 13) Sooner than we think, perhaps, society may witness the triumph of the oppressed over the oppressor, and the male sex will begin to experience for itself the kinds of social repression and oppression that it has meted out to women for so long! Perhaps women may find themselves opting to utilize male pronouns of God out of a concern to identify with this marginalized underclass of unemployed, solo non-parents!

It may also be argued that the implication of all this will be that males should start drinking from their own wells—not the wells of an androcentric norm, but their own distinctively male (as opposed to female) wells—and begin an inner search for their true identities and spiritualities so that the consequent reconstructions of maleness generate new forms of maleness-affirming spiritualities and theologies to counter-balance the dignity and self-confident self-understanding of the opposite sex for the sake of an egalitarian (and inclusive?) church and society. Such a church or society would, naturally, be constituted by a balance of two self-fulfilled, self-realized, self-confident classes of polar opposites.[4]

Before, however, we leap into any such reactive project—a male theology of identity—let those of us who are male take cognizance of

---

4.   Some years ago in Wellington, New Zealand, the Conference of Churches of Australia and New Zealand (CCANZ) sponsored seminars with a session on male spirituality and theology of self-discovery. Similar issues are addressed in an essay by Frank Fletcher entitled 'Drink from the Wells of Oz: How an Australian Theologian Works at the Speciality of Foundations' (1988), in which he argues 'Foundations work at the discipline underlying all disciplines, taking possession of who I am subjectively and dynamically as a person: it takes quite a skill to take possession of oneself subjectively as a believing person, a follower of Jesus, in a particular historical culture' (p. 59). He goes on to consider the spirituality of Bondi Beach, the Australian pursuit of the physical, the sensual and hedonistic, and the 'turn to beach near nakedness' (p. 67). The American theologian, Tom F. Driver, devotes an entire opening chapter of a book on theology to a highly sensual contemplation of his body in the bath under the guise of pursuing a male spirituality (1977).

recent developments of feminist theologies—and, in particular, Elaine Graham's analysis and rejection of what she perceives as the reification of male–female differences, which conditioned the feminist writing of a couple of decades ago but which the contemporary debate seems now to be progressing far beyond. This poses questions vis-à-vis any reactive pseudo-theological search on the part of men for liberative male spiritualities.

Elaine Graham on the Reification of Sex Differences

In the opening chapter (entitled, 'What is Gender?') of her first—and profoundly important—book on gender, *Making the Difference: Gender, Personhood and Theology* (1995b), Elaine Graham articulates growing concern with the tendency to reify sex differences. Whereas this can be traced to the influence on Western culture of Greek philosophy, it has been compounded by two different kinds of research which have taken place since the 1930s. I shall briefly summarize the elements of her analysis pertinent to my discussion.

In the 1930s, research was conducted by scientists Terman and Miles (and others) to attempt to 'trace connections between biological sex and social and psychological behaviour by constructing indices of "masculinity and femininity"' (Graham 1995b: 17). Personality traits were distinguished as masculine and feminine and individuals were given a 'male-typical' or 'female-typical' rating. This sought to establish fixed or predetermined differences characteristic of males and females. Far from establishing such differences, however, it actually presupposed them. The effect of the research was to *reify* these presupposed male–female sex differences by confirming the popular assumption that gender differences (that is, behavioural differences between men and women) could be equated directly and straightforwardly with their biological sex (Graham 1995b: 18). Whereas masculine–feminine (M–F) or male-typical/female-typical testing seemed to offer support for the belief that there were innate and tangible qualities (personality traits, which are biologically grounded and contingent on our sex) the whole approach is now widely held to have been flawed. It simply was not possible, Graham argues, 'to construct a questionnaire that was able to discern fixed qualities independent of social contexts; nor were there stable unidimensional categories in which individuals displayed clearly bipolar groups of qualities' (cf. Graham 1995b; cf. also Deux 1987). By failing to take sufficient account of the cultural weighting of the research categories and techniques, the evidence from the biological sciences was mistakenly assumed to suggest that there were indeed natural propensities—albeit propensities which emerged in some kind of interaction with cultural factors. The consequence of this was an intensification of interest in the effects of sociological and environmental influences on gender development leading, in turn, to a proliferation within the social sciences of studies 'which examined how society produced expectations, stereotypes and conditionings which enforced sex roles' (Graham 1995b: 18). The syncretistic conclusion (which became widely adopted) was that society strengthened and contributed, in certain definable ways, to sex roles that were biologically determined. The result was that M–F testing in both the biological and the social sciences served to enforce 'clearly differentiated "male" and "female" spheres and behaviours' (Graham 1995b). However, as Graham points out, critics of this have since

> identified ways in which cultural representations of gender frequently exaggerated or reified gender difference, serving an ideological purpose in emphasising difference rather than similarity. In this way, popular and cultural aspects of gender helped to construct a perceived reality in which human experience and the natural order were axiomatically divided into two mutually exclusive and ontologically separate halves (Graham 1995b: 18).

The overall effect was, as I have suggested, to encourage (if not generate) a *fixity* in the definition of maleness and femaleness setting-in-concrete, as it were, a polarized interpretation of our sexual 'natures' through sociological and biological studies. Maleness and femaleness denoted a bio-cultural predetermination of our 'natures' leading ultimately to *polarized interpretations of sex-roles*. This is witnessed in contrasting ways. On the one hand, there are the health and sex education films of the postwar years which set forth what now appear to be staggeringly naive and dated portrayals of the roles of women and men differentiated in stereotypical ways. *But, on the other hand*, it is also witnessed in the reaction this generated—namely, the reactive playing up, in the face of the social oppression of women, supposedly distinctive and specific female strengths, that is, the specific (peace-loving, harmonious, relational...[5])

---

5.   See, for example, Elisabeth Moltmann-Wendel's utilization of the psychosocial analyses of Anne Wilson Schaef's book *Women's Reality* (1985). Moltmann-Wendel writes, '[f]or the self-understanding of men and as criterion with which they judge others...two things are decisive: the person and the work. For the self-understanding of women there is beyond this a third dimension: the relationship' (1993: 109). While acknowledging that this is a facet of our culture, the resulting methodological application of such generalizations suggests quasi-universal validity.

contribution which women are in a position to make to society over and against men and the associated toxic side-effects of testosterone (competitiveness, polarization, war...).

Both approaches, and much resulting recent theology, have operated on the basis of the self-same supposition of a *reified fixity of innate, polarized sex-roles with their attendant character-traits or personality definitions*. In this article I shall be suggesting that the suppositions that males and females have distinct, fixed, and predeterminable natures and personality traits, as these operate at a foundational level in pseudo-theologies of gender, are distortive, and neither do nor should constitute a basis for 'gender-specific theologies'. Moreover, such suppositions should, on no account, predetermine theological discussion of humanity per se let alone the nature and character of maleness. It should now be clear, therefore, why I am categorically refusing, in this article, to engage in any 'male' articulation of a 'male' theological perspective or 'male spirituality'. To do so would serve to reiterate this mistake. In short, recent 'feminist' thought serves to expose the worst forms of the (now dated) separatist, difference-reifying, feminist liberation theologies of a former decade.[6]

So what precisely was the underlying weakness of the kinds of research referred to above? First, as we have seen, M–F testing operated on the basis of flawed, question-begging questionnaires in an attempt to determine innate, tangible qualities belonging to the subjects' biological natures. Secondly, the subliminal ideological presuppositions underlying the research served to emphasize *difference* rather than *similarity*—the effect being to exaggerate gender difference. What both underlay and shaped such research (and was thereby confirmed by its conclusions) was the construction of a 'perceived reality in which human experience and the natural order were axiomatically divided into two mutually exclusive and ontologically separate halves' (Graham 1995b: 18).

The discovery that 'sex differences' were not as 'dichotomous and polarized as conventional wisdom supposed' but were subject to the powerful—perhaps decisive—influence upon individuals of culture, was perceived, Graham comments, to offer feminism some benefits. It was

---

6. I once asked a feminist colleague how she perceived the critical controls upon, and warrant for, her theological claims if the Bible ceased to have any authority for her. Her response was, 'That is a typically male question. Women are not, therefore, required to answer it'. Similarly, the emergence of woman church, if more than simply a means of exposing and opposing the exclusivist and androcentric nature of the traditional church, runs the risk of making this same mistake.

suggested that 'observable differences between men and women could not be attributed to the unmediated workings of "laws of nature" alone' (Graham 1995b). It was no longer possible for society to make easy, straightforward connections between biological sex and personality traits or characteristics, and it was no longer valid, therefore, to make easy assumptions as to strengths, weaknesses and abilities, on the basis of whether a person is 'biologically' male or female.

> This offered a means of refuting those 'naturalistic' arguments which rooted differences between women and men in the immutable logic of biological imperatives; instead, it could attribute the foundations of gender identity to social and cultural factors (Graham 1995b: 19).

Underlying and enforcing this was Stoller's distinction between 'sex' and 'gender' which emerged in 1968. One's sex is determined by a matrix of genetic, physiological and hormonal states and factors which determine whether one is 'male' or 'female'. Gender, by contrast, carries psychological and cultural, rather than biological, connotations. Whereas biological sex utilizes the terms 'male' and 'female', gender was denoted by the terms 'masculine' and 'feminine' and these last terms may be *quite independent of biological sex*. He continues, 'Gender is the amount of masculinity and femininity found in a person'. Nevertheless he still goes on to add 'obviously, while there are mixtures of both in many humans, the normal male has a preponderance of masculinity and the normal female a preponderance of femininity'.[7]

This, of course, raised problems! Is there a *normative* connection between being 'male' and being 'masculine' and being 'female' and being 'feminine'? And, if so, is this not itself simply an arbitrary construction determined and moulded by society—by customs and mores which are relative, which are in a process of flux and which may, indeed, invite critical revision or intentional transformation? Moreover, if one is not only biologically male but strongly 'masculine' in terms of what cultural trends associate with 'masculinity', is this good, bad, liberated, or the opposite? For example, did Margaret Thatcher represent a liberated woman or a surrogate male (by virtue of exhibiting 'masculine' tendencies), or does Madonna's utilization of her sexuality suggest a liberated appropriation of power or the selling of herself to male fantasization—and thus a compounding of culturally conditioned gender stereotypes? Clearly, debates as to whether Thatcher and Madonna were 'liberated women' or not are not

---

7.   Stoller, cited in Graham 1995b: 19, and Oakley 1972: 158-59.

easily resolvable. This is because morally evaluative pronouncements on what women and men *should* or *should not* be like involve the introduction of normative connections between being biologically female or male and specific gender roles. Personality differences, vocational commitments, and world-views, are identified with 'fixed' sex roles, the reification of which is usually considerably less than ideologically neutral whether it is men or women that are responsible for it.

Graham's Critique of the Androgyny Option

One potential resolution to this kind of dilemma, Graham argues, may be found if and when we play down the correlation between biological sex and gender and then define liberation in gender-neutral ways. This is illustrated by the appeal of the notion of androgyny in the early 1970s (cf. Graham 1995b: 19-22). Traditionally masculinity and femininity had been considered to be necessarily mutually exclusive and natural or innate. Repudiating any such connection and acknowledging gender to be a cultural construction led to the view that people of either biological sex could be analysed and classified on the basis of those qualities which had conventionally been considered to be gendered qualities, and their personality types defined accordingly. Shyness, tenderness, and so on, were conventionally deemed feminine qualities and assertiveness and independence masculine. As an example of this, Graham points to the Bem Sex Role inventory, by which Sandra Bem assessed individuals utilizing these three scales: masculine, feminine and neutral. Individuals with a neutral score which balanced feminine and masculine behaviours and obviated extremes were seen as 'androgynous'. This was assumed to be the ideal of liberated women and men. Why? Because, given that masculinity and femininity were cultural constructs, freedom from the extremes of these denoted the individual's liberation from social conditioning, that is, from culturally constructed gender roles—the extremes of which were either 'oppressed' (e.g. the shy reserve of the person lacking a sense of self-worth—feminine) or 'oppressive' (e.g. self-assertive aggressive attitudes—masculine).[8]

8.   I shall leave it to the reader to decide whether, on this model, Margaret Thatcher and Madonna should be counted liberated or not! Clearly, there are massive challenges in determining the extent of gender conditioning in both cases, how extreme this is, and whether it is less than liberative. Both exhibit supposedly masculine assertiveness but does this mean they are less than liberated? And does 'liberated'

So is androgyny, conceived along these lines, to be endorsed as the inclusive ideal? Is an egalitarian humanity to be conceived as an undifferentiated humanity (with respect to gender roles), one in which the culturally constructed differences which make us masculine and feminine cease to be identifiable in any way with sex and where, ultimately, 'masculine' and feminine' would ideally lose any association whatsoever with maleness and femaleness? Might not such an androgynous view, indeed, denote the specifically Christian way of the new humanity as defined by the one who breaks with traditional, masculine stereotypes and who is the one in whom there is neither male nor female? (cf. Gal. 3.28). Might not participants in the Body of Christ be conceived as constituting so culturally disestablished a community that gender roles cease to exist? Might it not be the case, indeed, that to be born again 'from above', to be recreated 'in Christ', is to be liberated from culturally constructed (and thus continually reconstructed) gender roles?

Not only is this the fundamental question for any theological engagement with gender debates; it is clearly central to any discussion of gender-specific approaches to theology. It is also one to which we shall give a (cautiously) negative answer. The risk which such an approach runs is that it can serve to compound a mind–body dualism, where our behaviours are conceived as being entirely separable from our biological conditioning and underlying sexual 'drives'. At the same time, to suggest that because certain biological drives *do* drive us they *ought* to drive us is, of course, to commit the naturalistic fallacy, that is, the unwarranted move from 'is' to 'ought'! To suggest that because we are 'in the flesh' we ought to be driven 'by the flesh' is to fail to perceive the extent to which the Gospel calls us to truer ways of bodily existence, and inspires these within us. This is the form of existence which Paul refers to as being 'in the Spirit', that is, oriented not simply by basic instinct but by appropriate and reverent forms of creaturely existence which are reconciled by the Spirit for participation in God's *koinonial* purposes—and where other persons are not to be conceived as mere objects of one's biological instincts.

This points us to the theological problem with androgyny conceived as an ethical goal. The androgyny ideal generates the view that the perfection of our natures is the transcendence and resulting neutralization of our bodiliness rather than the reconciling, redeeming and fulfilling of our irreducibly bodily behaviours. It therefore tends toward a dualistic outlook

mean freedom to operate advantageously within a sexist system or freedom from sexist systems in total?

and a dichotomization between our biological or physiological identities on the one hand, and our cultural or psychological personalities on the other. It is no coincidence that androgyny denotes the *Greek* vision of the perfect man—the one who transcends the lower drives and passions for higher drives and passions, namely, heavenly *eros* rather than bodily *eros*.[9] As Graham points out, the androgynous view that the sexed body is a prison which we should transcend amounts to 'a latter-day form of Gnosticism, in which sexuality, embodiment and physiology are denied in order to attain enlightenment'.[10]

Furthermore, androgyny compounds polarized qualities and thereby perpetuates the dualism. By defining itself (positively and negatively) in terms of, and with recourse to, reified gender stereotypes, the Bem approach effectively serves, rather than challenges, the reification of these stereotypes. Rather than undermining such easy distinctions, it relies upon them (Bem 1993). Later recanting this position, Bem wrote, 'androgyny can legitimately be said to reproduce precisely the gender polarization that it seeks to undercut, and to do so even in the most feminist of treatments' (Bem 1993, cited by Graham 1995b: 22).

Finally, the advocacy of androgyny as an ideal further implies that, by virtue of some kind of sophisticated, higher, and introverted act of mind over body, we can limit, condition, and alter our gender identities. To suggest we can—indeed should—by virtue of a process of self-liberation, become androgynous fails to take due cognizance of the depth of our gendered identities. It involves the supposition of a Cartesian ego constituted by pure, liberated thought which, more extreme than Descartes, does indeed indwell the body as a pilot in a ship[11] and which can not only steer the ship in a certain direction but can alter its orientation in fundamental ways. This would suggest that embodied experience becomes irrelevant in the 'generation of gendered personhood' (Graham 1995b: 22). Theologically understood this may be seen to exemplify the age-old connection between dualism and Pelagianism—both of which, of course,

---

9.   Cf. Plato's celebration of old age in the first book of the *Republic*: 'Old age has a great sense of calm and freedom; when the passions relax their hold…' (329c; cf. Lee 1955: 138), and then again in the *Phaedo* with its reference to the liberation of the mind from the body for the contemplation of higher things (84d-86b; cf. Tredennick 1969: 138).

10.   Graham 1995b: 21. It is interesting to note that Gnosticism has become so popular among contemporary feminist theologians.

11.   Descartes did not wish to support a dualism as radical as this.

characterized the Gnosticism with which the early church struggled. Salvation was the acquisition of the redemptive knowledge of our true, higher natures, and consequent self-liberation from the sinfulness of embodied existence for a higher order, supra-physical, soul-like existence.

A Theological Alternative to an Androgynous Ideal?

If the liberation of males from oppressive to inclusive roles is not to be found in the pursuit of the androgynous ideal, it is imperative that we neither return to the ratification of traditional stereotypes nor simply seek to counterbalance them—either by revising those listed, or by endorsing a complementary set of female stereotypes. What emerges constitutes nothing less than a fundamental challenge to theological anthropology. So how should theological anthropology proceed?

1. It must refuse to acknowledge biologically defined characteristics and differences as foundational. Consequently, it must reject any polarizing generic classification of men and women grounded in the linking of behaviours with biological sex. There are no theological grounds for the kind of potentially oppressive stereotyping which predetermines the roles for which people *may*, or more significantly *may not*, be suited in society.

2. It should also avoid two further tendencies: first, the tendency to endorse a dualistic dichotomization between biological drives and behaviours—the failure to recognize that we are physical, biological beings—and, secondly, an alternative tendency to construe whatever behaviours may be deemed to constitute the free and 'natural' expression of biological drives and appetites as good, or ethical, or as having 'spiritual' value.

3. In affirming human particularity (and thus difference) it must refuse to subsume particular persons under predetermined, generalistic categories of any kind—whether these involve either polarizing or anti-differentiating role specifications.

4. It must also recognize and affirm the irreducibly *relational* nature of our biological constitutions and sexed identities. However, it must do so in such a way that the matrices of relations also escape those kinds of reification and fixity which fail to recognize that personal particularity is irreducibly bound up with the particularity of personal relationships. Liberated and egalitarian personal relationships between women and men can take

diverse forms. A theology of communion recognizes the diversity, the specificity, and the uniqueness of relations.

5.   It must exhibit, both at the formal and the material level, that whereas *eros* is love of like for like, *agape*, as it is definitive of personhood, creatively bestows dignity not only on that which is like but on that which is radically 'other' and 'unlike'. *Eros* has, as its object, 'natures', *agape* persons (see my discussion in 2001).

6.   It must not endorse particularity and diversity such as to obscure the distinction between liberative and oppressive *forms* of relationship. Personal relations must protect the freedom and dignity of persons and serve their flourishing.

The Theological Revision of Western and/or Greek Approaches

In order to appreciate the extent of the need to reconstruct the way we should approach maleness theologically, it is necessary to consider, albeit briefly, the distortive influences on our thinking. The androgynous ideal constitutes, in many ways, the *reductio ad absurdum* of the Western tradition and its failure to escape its Greek philosophical heritage. The impetus for the Platonic philosophical mission was encapsulated in the Delphic oracle 'Know thyself!' As Kidd comments, 'introspection showed how man achieves his real personality—the perfectly efficient realization of his being (*arete*)—when the psyche is in control of the physical and the intellectual and moral part of the psyche is in control of the rest of it' (cf. *Meno* 88E; Kidd 1967). This view, expounded in Plato's *Meno* dialogue, focused on one central question: how can we discover that which is radically new? If we do not already know what we are looking for how can our inquiry succeed, for we will not recognize whether what we arrive at is what we have been looking for unless we already *know* what we are looking for. Alternatively, if we did not know what we were looking for, we would not have needed to look for it (Ryle 1967). The conclusion is simple. The sum of all knowledge is, and must be, immanent within us. The question for knowledge becomes a process of discovery or rather recovery of what we already know—what Plato portrays as a kind of remembering (*anamnesis*). This means that, for the Platonic tradition:

1.   self-knowledge constitutes the essential form of access to ultimate truth, truths and ideals;

2.   truth is a relation to eternal, unchanging, static truths/ideas which

undergird the flux of human experience, that is, the essential truths of human existence discovered by self-knowledge take the form of static, fixed essences; and

3. the self is conceived dualistically with absolute primacy being given to the mind. The bodily, which one can transcend by pure thought, is denigrated and, with it, all that belongs to our biological functioning.

These kinds of assumption had a profound impact upon the Augustinian tradition and it was from within this tradition that René Descartes emerged. Reiterating Augustine's insight that the self's own existence constitutes the grounds of epistemic certainty, he established the underlying agenda of Western thought by placing at the very centre of his philosophical system (at the roots of his 'tree of knowledge') the indubitable existence of the self conceived (dualistically) as a thinking thing—a *res cogitans*. This ratified Boethius's definition of the person as an individual substance with a rational nature. This language of 'natures', substantialist conceptions of the self, and the dualistic assertion of the primacy of thought over activity and relationality, have shaped the history of ideas.

What has been the effect of this in Western thought about selfhood and gender? First, the self has tended to be conceived in 'static' terms as a *thing* or *substance* with a *nature*. Second, access to the self's 'nature' of the self is conceived *introspectively*. Third, what this has served to generate is, of course, an inherently *dualistic* view of the self—it belongs to the very nature of the act of self-knowledge, conceived in these terms, that the analytic subject transcends the body. The body is bracketed out of the equation. What this has led to, finally, has been an individualistic or 'monadic' approach to *one's gendered nature*. The individual contemplates its own 'nature' and conceives of it as self-contained and fixed. And all this has been compounded still further by an additional legacy of Platonism (although it is generally associated with Locke), namely, an 'essentialist' view of language. The meaning of terms is interpreted to be the *essence* denoted by the term. Consequently, to use terms such as 'male' or 'masculine' suggests that there is an 'essence' (a form) which underlies —indeed constitutes—the meaning of that term.

Taken together, these facets of Western thought, deeply engrained within our tradition, have served to condition thinking about gender in an entirely predictable way. Human beings are individual things or substances with natures. Consequently, males have one kind of 'nature' and females another, that is, they have different essences as is implied by the different terms used. Our sex, therefore, is to be conceived in terms of a polarized, reified nature. The very meaningfulness of the terms 'male' and 'female' or 'masculine' and 'feminine' requires this. Finally, access to our natures is conceived introspectively and *ergo* individualistically! The recent flirtation with the concept of androgyny, with its additional inherent dualism, is an archetypical example of the outworking of these suppositions—and it is not surprising, therefore, that it was advocated by Plato himself! So-called 'gendered' theologies, which advocate that we operate from 'subjective experience', can only serve to further this tradition by supposing polarized models of gender identity and suggesting that the totality of truth (including theological truth) is to be conceived from a grounding in the self. This is compounded by the supposition that access to our identities is conceived introspectively, that is, by journeying into oneself in a process of self-discovery. (It is noteworthy here that the contemporary concept for 'birthing' can be traced directly to Plato's maieutic method.[12]) Religion, of course, is translated into the discovery of one's innate 'spirituality'. Elaine Graham's work, however, constitutes one example of a contemporary feminist who is determined to break with those forms of feminism that effectively repeated the mistakes of a largely male Western tradition, and hence is highly significant. For males, to attempt to emulate dated forms of feminist thinking by articulating a generalized and generalizing 'male' theology or spirituality would constitute the ultimate irony! It should be unambiguously clear, therefore, why I cannot endorse any such response to the emergence of 'feminist' theologies and spiritualities.

Toward an Ontology of Persons in Communion

A theological way forward from the 'stalemate' of monadic approaches to our gendered natures emerges in the thought of one of the most lively contemporary critics of the Greek dualist and monist (as also of the Augustinian and Cartesian) traditions, namely, John Zizioulas. His critique has not gone unnoticed by feminist thought—Catherine Mowry LaCugna, for example, expounds his thought enthusiastically and in some depth.

In an early article entitled 'On Human Capacity and Incapacity', Zizioulas exposes and repudiates the Western tendency to think about human being in terms of fixed essences or natures which have predetermined

---

12. 'Maieutic' comes from the Greek word *maieuesthai* meaning 'to be a midwife'—the essence of education is that the teacher constitutes a midwife, who facilitates the learner 'giving birth' to that knowledge immanent within them.

capacities (or, equally, incapacities). He argues instead for a relational view of the person as open-ended or open-structured, and which requires to be conceived in non-individualistic terms as having its *hypostasis* in *ekstasis*, that is, where it has its being in relation with others. In his later book, *Being as Communion*, he suggests that precisely such a discovery of the person constituted the most decisive breakthrough in patristic thought. The salvation of ontology from static models of substance was the emergence of the 'concept of the person with its absolute and onto-logical content'[13]—a philosophical landmark in the history of ideas. The precise nature of this 'revolution in Greek philosophy' in Christian Patristic thought took the form of 'the identification of the "hypostasis" with the "person"' (Graham 1995b: 36), allowing the admission of a relational term (*prosôpon*) into ontology, and drawing an ontological cate-gory (*hypostasis*) into the relational categories of existence. The culmination of this process was the identification of being and communion. 'To be and to be in relation become identical' (Graham 1995b: 88). It is no longer appropriate to conceive of the being of the person in non-relational terms.

Two central discoveries flow from this. First, 'The person is no longer an adjunct to a being, a category which we add to a concrete entity once we have first verified its ontological hypostasis. It is itself the hypostasis of the being'. And, second, '(e)ntities no longer trace their being to being itself—that is, being is not an absolute category in itself—but to the person, to precisely that which constitutes being, that is, enables entities to be entities' (Graham 1995b: 39). In short, rather than grounding the interpretation of the person in a static concept of being or substance or nature, patristic theology (obliged to reconceive reality in the light of the divine personhood) not only reconceived personhood as an ontological category but recognized it to be *the fundamental* ontological category.

Zizioulas highlights the contrast with the Western theological tradition by way of a play on the word 'substance'. Boethius had defined the person as an individual substance with a 'nature' of a particular kind. Zizioulas takes the Greek word *hypo-stasis*, which is a literal translation of the Latin *sub-stantia* and argues that a person is unique in having its *hypo-stasis* in *ek-stasis*. A person is a unique being in that it has its being relationally; in the fact that it stands out of itself. The very nature of a person, therefore, is precisely that it is *not* self-contained. Persons do not belong to a class of individual, circumscribable, 'things' or 'substances' with a fixed or deter-

13. 'The "revolutionary significance" of these in the development of Greek thought seems to have escaped the attention of the history of philosophy...' (Graham 1995b: 39).

minate nature. In short, the person is, at the most fundamental ontological level, *an irreducibly relational being.*

What does this mean? It means that at every level, it becomes profoundly inappropriate theologically to approach the question of gender in terms of polarized concepts of nature. The reification of natures and their interpretation in terms of fixity of gender identities is fundamentally flawed! It is only when we operate with an ontology of communion that we are liberated from the monist/dualist dilemma for dynamic and relational ways of conceiving of selfhood.

But where does this leave us on the question of the relationship between our biological sex and gender? Again, Zizioulas sheds some light here. At the heart of his understanding of persons is a repudiation of the view that personhood is defined by our biological constitution and results from some inevitable outworking of it. To put it simply, the analysis of our biology does not offer access to us as persons. This is again because personhood is an irreducibly *relational* concept and inconceivable in isolation from an event of *ekstasis* or love. But for precisely this same reason, Zizioulas is not a dualist either—the person is not to be identified with some additional 'soul' or 'spirit'; some spiritual substance which adopts a body. Rather, persons are biological beings and constituted as 'persons' in and through a creative event of communion initiated by and grounded in the divine *ekstasis.* His ontology of communion, therefore, is grounded in the triune communion of God and the ecclesial communion which derives from this. His is a radically *theological,* and *ergo ecclesiological,* anthropology.

What does this suggest vis-à-vis 'gender'? In emphasizing that a person is a *hypostasis* he emphasizes particularity, and by stressing the biological nature of this *hypostasis,* he emphasizes the irreducible bodiliness of persons. At the same time, we are not simply to be identified with biological 'natures' statically conceived. Our biological hypostases project toward that fulfilment which is conceived ecclesially as an event of communion. This suggests that a dichotomy between our biological sex and the form of our social relatedness (our gender) is no longer appropriate. Both require that they be reconstructed in 'ecclesial' terms—as integral to, and intrinsic to, God's purposes of communion. Consequently, our biological sexuality and complementarity are interpreted in precisely this light.

This does *not* mean that we start with our sexual identities from which we go on to produce a natural theology of (sexual) communion. Precisely the reverse. It is only in the light of our understanding of what communion is 'in truth' and what being human is 'in truth' that we can begin to interpret our bodiliness theologically, and thus our biological sex. It is for this reason that celibacy, for example, does not require to be seen as a betrayal of personhood—communion between embodied beings is not principally, let alone *exclusively*, defined in sexual terms. That persons come into being, however, as the result of an event of sexual communion can be interpreted, in the light of the Gospel, as divine endorsement of the fact that the 'becoming persons' of children takes place within a context of interpersonal love, covenant commitment and communion. At the same time, it emphasizes the fact that sexual 'union' when it is *not* conceived as an event of personal 'com-munion', depersonalizes precisely by 'reifying' or 'objectifying' persons—treating them as 'individual substances' (or even merely 'thinking things')!

Ecclesia or Androgyne as the Condition of Liberated Personhood?

We can now see the folly of androgyny that much more clearly. Androgyny, conceived as an ideal, is ultimately individualistic, perfectionist, and driven by the combination of a quasi-Pelagian belief in our capacity to create ourselves and a Platonic (dualistic?) concept of an ideal humanity. As Karl Barth commented, 'The androgyne or androgynous as the destiny of the human being is a boldly and freely invented fable on which, as on all such beings, we can decidedly turn our back'. Repudiating Plato's androgynous vision in the *Symposium*, he comments that the postulation of an 'original wholeness of humanity, its division into two, and the longing of the two halves for reunion' points to 'the undeniable temptation to seek to evade one's sex in the form of an aspiration to neutral humanity' (Barth 1961: 161). It is relevant also to note that Barth also repudiates (under the category of 'flight from one's own sex') Simone de Beauvoir's semi-androgynous vision of a liberated humanity. Although not explicitly endorsing the 'idealistic myth of the androgyne', it is plain, he argues, 'that she proclaims another new myth so much the more powerfully and unreservedly—that of the human individual who in the achievement of freedom overcomes his masculinity or her femininity, mastering it from a superior plane, so that sexuality is only a condition by which one is not finally conditioned, with which one can dispense and whose operation one can in any case control'.[14]

---

14. Earlier in his discussion Barth cites 'On ne naît pas femme, on le devient' (1961: 161).

Even in the masculine form presupposed by Simone de Beauvoir, is not this individual a product of wishful thinking rather than a reality? Is he not more a man-God or God-man than a real human figure? Man no doubt dreams of that radiant, victorious freedom from his conditioning... But he does not live in it (Barth 1961: 162).

That having been said, it should be added that Barth praises de Beauvoir's book highly for its devastating exposé of 'the way in which man has made and still makes himself master of woman, the presentation of the myth with which he invests her in this process and for this purpose, and the unmasking of this myth'—these are 'worthy of attention especially on the part of men and not least of Christian theologians'![15]

As to whether she should commend her ideal human, which she portrays as liberated from sexuality, to woman 'as one in the realisation of which she will achieve her own emancipation and humanity', Barth is clear. Her vision and that of the androgyne have, Barth writes,

the same basic *logos*—the freeing of humanity in the form of its emancipation...from sex. But in its execution, not to speak of its relationship to the divine command, this liberation can only end in the negation of the real human, and cannot, therefore, be a true *logos* (Barth 1961: 162).

Conclusion

A natural theology of gendered humanity is left with a predicament. In starting with self-knowledge, it is presented with a choice. On the one hand one may ratify and absolutize one's own sex and sexuality in their orientation toward the world making these, and the insights into human nature proffered by them, the critical control or criterion in one's theological and anthropological thinking. In many ways this characterizes our postmodern existence where truth, not least, moral truth, is 'the state of play' (so Cupitt) and 'god' is that to which one chooses to attach absolute value—whatever that may be. Alternatively, in the face of guilt and a realistic perception of the damaged, damaging, and dysfunctional nature of relations between the sexes, at the social as well as at the individual level, one can become a visionary in pursuit of an ideal world. The androgynous option would appear to be a cogent form of just this, the idealization and absolutization of a neutral humanity free from negative potential but, at

---

15. Barth 1961: 162. This constitutes a remarkable expression of sympathy toward feminist concerns and (written originally in 1951), expressed well before the emergence of 'feminist theology' as we know it!

the same time, defined, ultimately, *in negative terms*. The risk here is that we seek simply to negate the negatives and the perceived grounds of negativity—pursuing, through fear of sex, the vision of a world in which we might escape our sexual conditions; a Nirvana. Both of these approaches search the self in pursuit of ideals which they would universalize. To the extent that its devotees universalize from their own experience, they can only ultimately seek homogeneity by legislating from a base in their own particularity. Their mission (be it in relation to those of their own sex, or those of their own sexuality) can only be to clone their own selfhood, their orientations, and fears. Echoing Plato's *Meno*, this self-knowledge constitutes access to ultimate truth.

In reply we should reiterate Kierkegaard's question vis-à-vis the *Meno* and his consequent exposé of the radical incompatibility between the Christian Gospel and all forms of idealism, that is, with all attempts to deify self-knowledge of one form or another.

If the Situation is to be Different...

First, rather than allowing our theology of humanity to be driven by fear of our own biological conditioning or the dysfunctionality of human conditioning in general, and rather than making our own condition our own logos, or by postulating an ideal logos (an androgyne perhaps), the gospel recognizes one Logos and one Teacher who is not of illustrative or exemplary significance but of decisive significance; who does not point to some other ideal or set of ideals (gendered or otherwise) but is the truth in himself—the *counter-logos* with respect to all our *logoi*, as Bonhoeffer saw. This is that one Word who states in and through all he is: 'Do not be afraid. I am the First and the Last. I am the Living One'. This suggests that we neither prescind from (or abstract from) the fallen Adamic world to create a new 'Adamic ideal', nor retreat into the spiritual, supra-sexual, or meta-sexual, world of a neutralized humanity. Rather, we start by acknowledging the New Adam, the Second Adam, the truly human, as the one in whom we are brought, by the Spirit, to glimpse the *telos* of the created order *in toto*; a *telos*, purpose, end, and rationale, that is grounded in the very communion of the triune life.

Second, what emerges here is *not* a 'vision' of a new humanity, but the *event* of a new humanity with a reoriented apperception grounded in participation within a new humanity—a humanity in which the distinctions of sex, culture, background, and age, are neither annihilated nor superseded but, rather, affirmed; affirmed, that is, in such a way that they cease to constitute divisions. What transpires, therefore, is an event of communion which overwhelms and negates the fragmentation of humanity in a transforming and reconstituting event.[16]

Third, because such an event of communion is grounded in the Spirit, conceived as the *most concrete* reality (the *Ens concretissimum*), we are liberated from the vain pursuit of a spiritualized existence for radical embodiment. The biological, as also the spatio-temporal conditions of our existence in general, can now be seen to be the essential conditions of our being human in truth—conditions ultimately fulfilled in an event of communion grounded in the Spirit of God. In sum, bodily existence is perceived to be the essential created condition of our being 'in the spirit'!

In this way, the Gospel serves to endorse and to affirm our particularity. Our spatio-temporal bodiliness is seen to be the condition of our reality in communion with God rather than its negation, as idealism would have it. Paradoxically, it is our bodiliness which constitutes the means of participation in the divine. Just as it is the particularity of the incarnation, conceived as an *ephapax*—'once-for-all'—event, which identifies God as having his being in communion, so it is that same event, conceived as an event of communion, that delivers us from the need to escape our particularity.

Fourth, the event of the fulfilment of our biological, as of the other essential conditions of our humanity, is now conceived to be an event of reconciliation—reconciliation of our thinking, our apperceptions, and thus our orientation (our thinking, feeling and willing), so that we might be particular, bodily, biological persons *in truth*.

Fifth, personal, biological and gendered existence becomes existence before that Word of assurance, forgiveness, and commission uttered by the risen crucified Lord. As such it stems from the One in whom the law is fulfilled in an event of unconditional love—an event which is identical with the act and fact of his own life and death, resurrection and ascension. This Word is not normative in the sense of being norm-ridden, nor does it serve to impose legal grids on gendered humanity. Rather it liberates humanity by grace to unselfconscious love and unconditional acceptance of neighbour, of enemy, of spouse, of family, and, mediated through these, the acceptance of self. This means that every aspect of one's gender and biological orientation requires to be conceived in these terms.

16. Indeed, in and through the very recognition of the Logos we find ourselves already to be participants in an ecclesial event, for this event of participation in the Body of Christ is the condition, and not the result, of the perception of Christ and the creation of the new humanity.

Consequently, *sixth*, human being is defined without the specification or endorsement of personality traits conceived as 'male' or 'female'. To reiterate, there is no theological warrant for any reified set of male qualities which 'men' should exemplify. In the One Word we simply do not have a series of separate Words to and for each race or sex or culture. There is no separate series of gender requirements generically meted out to those of either sex! Nor is there any exclusive endorsement of sociocultural differences in the name of Christ (circumcision and so on). What this means is that there is infinite space for the celebration of difference and particularity without dichotomy and fragmentation.

Seventh, paralleling in some ways the contemporary reformulation of gender debates in terms of difference and the utilization of power, the Gospel commits us radically to reconceive both the definition and utilization of power in personal relations. As such it repudiates *quietist* or *isolationist* definitions of ecclesial existence by committing us, first, to the cultural disestablishment of the Gospel and, second, to the critique, revision and reconstruction of all forms of sociality and social participation.

At the same time—and finally—the Word from which and to which we are to live and move and have our being, and through which we are thereby given life anew, is the one whose purposes require to be conceived eschatologically. The one who is the first is also the last. The conditions of our humanity only ultimately find their goal, therefore, in the Eschaton when we will be oriented toward God and to one another as God is oriented toward us, and when we shall know even as we are known. Just as the Eschaton is present and yet not fully realized, so our humanity (as male and female) remains a humanity on the way to becoming human.

THE TRINITY AND GENDER IDENTITY

Miroslav Volf

'Out of a Rib of Man's God'

Not many would consider Friedrich Nietzsche a reliable guide on matters of gender. Some of his comments about women are simply silly while many others are downright misogynist. What wisdom on gender can we expect from a person who believed that 'woman's nature is a surface, a changeable, stormy film upon shallow waters'? Why pay attention at all to a person who insisted that whereas 'men should be trained for war' women should be trained 'for the recreation of the warrior', adding rather pompously that 'all else is folly'(1969: 91-92; 1974: 122-28). Yet Nietzsche would not be Nietzsche had he not written something profound even about things on which he was wrong. In a string of aphorisms at the beginning of *The Twilight of the Idols* he wrote, 'Man created woman—but what out of? Out of a rib of his God, his "ideal"…'(Nietzsche 1990: 33). The power of the aphorism rests on the inversion of the Genesis story about the creation of woman (Gen. 2.18-25): *man* created woman, not God, says Nietzsche; and it was from *God's rib* that woman was created, not man's.

The aphorism is more than just a clever and subversive play on words. In two important ways it anticipates some key feminist insights developed a century or so later. First, it underscores that what we mean by 'woman' is not simply a natural given, but a cultural construct whose primary agents are men. As Luce Irigaray puts it, 'more often than not…female identity still originates in man' (1996: 64). For instance, even such a seemingly stable biological given as a woman's body is partly defined and shaped by the expectations of men and the values of an androcentric culture. Second, the aphorism notes that the content of 'femininity' has something to do with man's god, with man's ideals. True, man has reserved his highest ideals for himself; woman was fashioned out of a rib of man's god rather than out of some more noble part. But it is precisely the high ideals of 'masculinity' that call forth the subordinate ideals of 'femininity'. Moira Gatens draws attention to an important mechanism in the construction of gender when she suggests that the ideal of 'the full, phallic, masculine body necessarily assumes its antithesis: the lacking, castrated feminine body, which is its complement' (1996: 38). On this, then, Nietzsche and the later feminists agree: men keep recreating women out of the ribs of their gods.

In the following I will explore the two themes addressed in Nietzsche's aphorism and explored by feminism—the construction of gender identity and the role played by God in this construction. My topic is God and gender, or more precisely, Trinity and gender identity. In one fundamental way I will diverge radically from Nietzsche, however. His inversion of the Genesis story rests on a figure of thought that owes much to Ludwig Feuerbach's theory of religion. God is nothing but an image fashioned out of human ideals; human beings are the creators and God is both their creature and the 'stuff' out of which they ought to recreate themselves. Unlike Nietzsche, I believe that Feuerbach's theory of religion is insightful on its fringes but mistaken at its center. Though we do keep projecting our interests and ideals onto God, God is not just our projection. Notice the consequences for the relation between God and gender if we discard the center of Feuerbach's theory. Since we have kept the 'fringes', we can still explore how men and women construct gender and what role their notions of divinity play in the process, say how a projected masculinity (or femininity) of God is employed to legitimize and stabilize a given cultural understanding of gender identity. But since the center of Feuerbach's theory no longer holds—since God is a reality apart from our projective activity—we will be unable to rest satisfied either with a phenomenological description or with a normative reconstruction of the function of religious symbols. If God is God rather than simply a patchwork of some social group's cultural ideals, and if human beings, their undeniable cultural creativity notwithstanding, are creatures of that God, then the decisive question will be *how the nature of God ought to inform the relations between men and women as well as their construction of 'femininity' and 'masculinity'*. This is the question on which I intend to concentrate.

As I have defined it, the topic suggests a clear and simple outline. I must explore the nature of God, in particular, the relations between the persons of the Trinity and then look into what such trinitarian explorations may mean for the construction of gender and for the relations between engendered persons. Prior to entering the world of the Trinity I need to inquire, however, into what significance the gender of God language may have for my topic.

But first a word of explanation. Throughout the text I will be using the traditional trinitarian names—the Father, the Son, and the Spirit. This linguistic practice may give rise to the objection that here again a male author is appealing to a male God to define who women should be. Since I do not know how to respond to the objection in a way that is both brief and adequate, I will simply state this: the following reflections on gender that I, an indisputably male author, offer by exploring an equally indisputably *non-male* God, are not a 'definition' but a suggestion—a suggestion that will, I hope, be judged in terms of its inherent plausibility, helpfulness, and attractiveness to both women and men rather than rejected (or accepted) simply on account of the gender of its author and of the divine names used. Those suspicious of such hopes are free to interpret the text as an exercise in the virtually non-existent discipline of 'masculinist theology'—a man addressing men on how properly to be men in relation to women.

Gender—Divine or Human?

It may seem that a good way to approach the relation between the Trinity and gender identity would be to concentrate on the gender of language about God. One would proceed something like this. The first step would be to question exclusively masculine metaphors for God on the grounds that they do not offer women a 'divine horizon' of development (cf. Irigaray 1986). The second step would be to highlight the femininity of one member of the Trinity—the Holy Spirit—as Elisabeth Moltmann-Wendel does in the *Weiblichkeit des Heiligen Geistes* (1995). Alternatively, if one were dissatisfied with dividing the Trinity into masculine and feminine members (Williams 1992)—say, on the grounds that this reduces the Spirit to 'a kind of girl Friday for the Father and the Son' as Amy Plantinga Pauw has suggested (1996: 49)—one could insist on the need to use feminine metaphors of all three persons of the Trinity and affirm the equivalence of feminine metaphors to male metaphors, as Elizabeth A. Johnson does in *She Who Is* (1993: 42-57). The third step would be to explore what the femininity and masculinity of individual members of the Trinity or the equivalence of feminine and masculine metaphors for all members of the Trinity may mean for the construction of women's and men's identity and difference. But would such an approach work?

Feminist theologians have made it abundantly clear how the gender of God language bears on the question of the *equality* of men and women. 'If God is male, then male is God', wrote Mary Daly bluntly, but correctly (1973: 19). Correspondingly, if the highest reality could be spoken of only in masculine metaphors, men would be more like God and therefore superior to women; similarly, if the feminine metaphors for God were intrinsically inappropriate or inferior to male metaphors, women would then be more unlike God and therefore inferior to men. As Johnson underscores, 'the equal dignity of women' demands that we be able to speak in feminine metaphors of God (1993: 211). My question here is, however, not the equality. The equality between men and women and the fundamental equivalence between masculine and feminine metaphors about God are rather my assumption; I take it for granted that men and women are '*equally* saved, *equally* Spirit-filled and *equally* sent', to borrow a phrase from Mary Stewart Van Leeuwen (1991: 36). My question is, rather, *gender identity and difference*. Does the gender of God language, which says much about whether men and women are inferior, superior or equal to one another, say anything about *what it means to be male or female*?

Most theologians would agree that God is beyond sexual distinctions. We use masculine or feminine metaphors for God not because God is male or/and female, but because God is 'personal' (Jewett and Shuster 1991: 44-45). There is no other way to speak of persons except in a gendered way. Since human beings, the only personal creatures we know, exist only in the duality of male and female, we must speak of a personal God by using masculine or/and feminine metaphors. This is a simple observation, but it has important consequences for our topic. If God is completely beyond sexual distinctions but our language of God is necessarily gendered, then all *specifically masculine or feminine* content of the language about God *stems exclusively from the creaturely realm*. The nature of God tells us nothing about what it means to live as male in distinction to female or as female in distinction to male. We can find in our notions of God only those things about femininity or masculinity that we ourselves have placed into these notions. Being gendered, language about God may shape how we understand femininity and masculinity, but it should not be used to legitimize a particular construction of femininity and masculinity. All employment of God language for construction of gender identity is illegitimate and ought to be resisted. Let me elaborate on these claims by looking briefly at Karl Barth's 'divine Father' and Luce Irigaray's 'divine woman'.

In his *Church Dogmatics* Karl Barth makes the famous argument that we do not come to know what it means for God to be the Father by observing human fathers, but the other way around: we know what it means for a man to be a father by observing God the Father (Barth 1975: 389). The anti-Feuerbachian thrust of the argument is correct. We should not proceed 'by analogy from below' and construct God in the image of human beings; we should proceed 'by analogy from above' and learn who human beings ought to be by considering who God is. Yet a good deal of Barth's own theologizing undermines this very insight (Janowski 1995). For Barth, God is the Father in the most original sense because he 'begets' the Son in eternity and because he 'begets' Jesus Christ in time. As he puts it, God is 'the first and true and indeed the only *man*' (1960b: 358). Human males image the maleness in God: they initiate, beget, lead and are superordinate (1960a: 287). The analogy goes from above—from God to human beings—but only after Barth has projected a patriarchal construction of masculinity onto God and tacitly declared it was there already from the beginning! Not exactly the most persuasive way to counter Feuerbach! For God to be the model of masculinity one must first project maleness onto God and then use the projection to legitimize certain allegedly specifically male characteristics and activities.

Since God is beyond sexual difference, there is nothing in God that can correspond to the *specifically fatherly* relation that a man has toward his progeny. A human father can in no way read off his responsibilities *as a father* from God the Father. What a father can learn from God are his responsibilities *as a human being* who happens to be a father and therefore has a special relationship to his daughters and sons as well as to their mother. One can learn from God the Father no more about what it means to be a human father than one can learn about what it means to be a human mother; inversely, one can learn from God the Mother no more about what it means to be a human mother than one can learn about what it means to be a human father. Whether we use masculine or feminine metaphors for God, God models our common humanity, not our gender specificity.

But what if we made a weaker argument than the one Barth made? The characteristics and roles of God, one could argue, correspond more to those of fathers and men than to those of mothers and women. Notice, however, that this is not an argument from *God's* fatherhood and *God's* maleness—from above; it is an argument from below, from characteristics of *human* fathers and *human* males. The argument must go something like this: God, as portrayed in the Scripture, is more like *what we know* fathers and men to be than *what we know* mothers and women to be. 'Fatherhood' and 'motherhood', 'femininity' and 'masculinity' are here all notions taken from creaturely realm and are therefore culturally conditioned and changing notions. Within the framework of this argument it is illicit to turn around and argue that since God is thus and thus (more like males as we know them), human beings as fathers or as men should be thus and thus. Again, God does not model gender identity.

A similar argument can be made from the other end, so to speak, from a critique of the demand for a female deity rather than from the critique of the assertion of the original divine masculinity. Unlike Karl Barth who tries to subvert Feuerbach's theory of religion, in *Divine Women* Luce Irigaray builds on it. Affirming the need of a 'projected' god, she notes that in the classical doctrine of the Trinity, which speaks of the Father, the Son, and the Spirit, woman is absent; mother does not appear and the relationship between mother and daughter is lacking. Hence, she argues, there is no 'horizon' in such a doctrine of the Trinity that beckons 'her' to become as a woman (Irigaray 1986, 1989). Instead, woman is suppressed by being absent from the 'masculine's transcendence' of 'a Law-making-God-the-Father, etc' (1996: 67).

The appropriate response to the objection is, I think, that in the doctrine of the Trinity expressed in *masculine* metaphors there is no 'horizon' beckoning 'him' to become *as a man* either (just as in the doctrine of the Trinity expressed in feminine metaphors there is no horizon beckoning 'her' to become *as a woman*). For such gender specific divine 'horizons' to exist, we would need female and male deities. And this is what Irigaray in fact offers. God for Irigaray, as Elizabeth Grosz puts it, is a projection of the subject 'onto a figure of perfection, an ego-ideal specific to that subject, a mode of self-completion without finality' (1993: 207). And since the subject is essentially gendered, the divine 'projection' must be gendered too. As the 'man' has constructed 'a unique masculine God'— the Father, the Son, and the Spirit—'to situate himself as a finite being in relation to the infinite', Irigaray argues, so also the woman needs a 'woman God', a 'feminine trinity: mother, daughter, spirit' which 'figures the perfection of *her* subjectivity' (1986: 3-6). Should we accept, however, Irigaray's offer of a gender-specific deity? Not if we are committed to the one God of the Christian tradition who is the God of both men *and* women.

The only way that the gender of God language can provide guidance for construction of gender identity is if we first ontologize gender in God, that is, if we take a particular understanding of femininity or masculinity, project it onto God, and then let that projection shape our social practice. Irigaray is able to avoid such ontologization only by a sleight of hand. She postulates a female God but claims that this God holds no other obligation and gives no other task to women except to help them 'become divine, become perfect' (1986: 9). The femininity of God is asserted in order to connect God with women, but God's femininity does no real work because it has no concrete content. There are good reasons for the vacuity of divine femininity. For if we were to give it concrete content, we could not avoid freezing a particular cultural construction of gender and then infusing it with divine powers and claims. The same holds true, of course, of the postulated divine masculinity which Irigaray affirms as a complement to divine femininity.

The ontologization of gender would ill serve both the notion of God and the understanding of gender. Nothing in God is specifically feminine; nothing in God is specifically masculine; therefore nothing in our notions of God entails duties or prerogatives specific to one gender; all duties and prerogatives entailed in our notions of God are duties and prerogatives of both genders. This, I think, is the significance of the fact that, as Phyllis Bird has shown, gender distinctions are unrelated to the image of God according to Genesis 1 (Bird 1981, 1991). Men and women share maleness and femaleness not with God but with animals. They image God in their common humanity. Hence we ought to resist every construction of the relation between God and femininity or masculinity that privileges one gender, say by claiming that men on account of their maleness represent God more adequately than women (LaCugna 1993) or by insisting that women, being by nature more relational, are closer to the divine as the power of connectedness and love.

If the content of gender identity has no transcendental grounding, no divine blueprint, in what is it rooted? The similarity with animals gives us a clue. For what human beings share with animals is the *sexed body*—a body that carries indelible marks of belonging to either male or female sex. True, sometimes the marks are mixed (Fausto-Sterling 1995). But bodily ambiguities are arguably the exceptions that prove the rule. Men's and women's gender identities are rooted in the specificity of their sexed bodies.

Notice that I speak of the sexed body as the *root* rather than the *content* of gender identity. This is because by stressing the importance of the sexed body I do not intend to discard the distinction between 'sex' as a biological category (genes, hormones, external and internal genitalia and so on) and 'gender' as a social one (for example, learned characteristics, personality traits, behavioral patterns), that has become so prominent in recent decades (Stoller 1968). The distinction is useful because it helps account for significant variation in the notions of 'masculinity' and 'femininity' in cultures over time and space as well as within the life span of individuals. These variations make plain that gender identity is not simply biologically given but also socially constructed; it is partly a result of interaction between men and women within a given culture. True, the patterns of interaction between engendered persons are historically sedimented and transmitted over generations; they are embodied in economic, political and cultural practices (Aronowitz 1995: esp. 315-18). So in a sense, gender identity is preset, and one grows into it. Yet as cultures and subcultures change, so does their understanding of gender and its embodiments in social practices. Though not arbitrary, gender identity is fluid, and it stands in a marked contrast to the stable difference of the sexed bodies.

The fluidity of gender by no means implies irrelevance of sex for the construction of gender, as some proponents of the sex–gender distinction suggest. To the contrary. The fluidity of gender is both constrained and made possible by the stability of the sexed body. Notice, first, the *constraints* of the sexed body on the formation of gender identity. Against much of the theory which operates with the distinction between 'sex' and 'gender', in *Imaginary Bodies* Moira Gatens has argued persuasively that bodies are not neutral and passive with respect to the construction of gender. While it is possible, for instance, for a man to be 'feminine', she argues that 'there must be qualitative difference between femininity "lived" by women and that "lived" by men' (1996: 9). It is the different bodies of a woman and a man, along with social valorization of male and female bodies, that makes that difference. A notion that cross gender identifications can make the differences inscribed in the body irrelevant is an illusion (Irigaray 1996: 61).

On the view that I am advocating here, the sexed body does not serve to *determine* the content of femininity and masculinity, such as, say, that 'the soft hand' of women would predetermine them for protective care or that their 'breasts' would indicate that motherhood is the fulfillment of woman's being (cf. Neuer 1990: 33). There is no way simply to read off the content of gender idenity from the sexed body; all such readings are specific cultural interpretations. The sexed body is the root of gender differences that are themselves always socially interpreted, negotiated and renegotiated. This in turn brings me to the positive contribution that the sexed body makes to gender fluidity.

Far from only placing constraints on the construction of gender identity, the stability of the sexed body also makes *fluidity* of gender identities possible. In *A Radical Jew* Daniel Boyarin has suggested that 'only a grouping which has some somatic referent can allow itself the possibility of reinventing its essence' (1994: 239). Without such a somatic referent a grouping would have either to insist on its unchangeable essence or be always threatened by disappearance. Applied to gender this means that men and women continue to exist in a duality as male and female through all the changes of their gender identity precisely because of the stability of their sexed bodies. It is because of the sexed bodies that we can speak of two genders at all and reflect on their changing identities.

If the fluidity of gender is both constrained and made possible by the sexed body, we must both assert that the differences between men and women are irreducible and refuse to spell out in advance what these differences are. While there are and always will be men and women, there is no 'essence' to their gender identity, no unchangeable 'femininity' and 'masculinity'. Instead, as Mary Stewart Van Leeuwen puts it in *Gender and Grace*, we are faced with 'constant invention and reinvention of gender roles' and gender identities (1991: 69). Such affirmation of both the irreducibility of genders and their undefinablity is, I think, capable of meeting adequately 'the challenge for critical studies of gender' as formulated by Elaine L. Graham: 'to reappraise the ontological and epistemological significance of the body, and the way in which morphological and biological characteristics can assist accounts of gendered experience without "enclosing us in our differences"' (1995a: 353).

My argument so far has been twofold: first, we should not seek to derive the content of gender identity by mirroring God, because any femininity or masculinity we may find in God was projected onto God; second, the content of gender identity is rooted in the sexed body ('nature') and forged by the history of social interaction between persons with such sexed bodies ('culture'). Given this biological and cultural grounding of gender identity, can reflection on God be of any help in discussion about construction of gender identity? I believe it can—provided we direct attention not to the one God but to the three persons of that one God and concentrate on the relations between the three persons and on the construction of their identity rather than on their 'gender'. So it is to the issue of the trinitarian identities that I now turn.

The critique of self-enclosed identities, carried out most consistently by postmodern thinkers, provides a good deal of the backdrop for my reflection here. Though I am not fully persuaded either by all postmodern arguments or by their proffered alternatives, I share their belief about the tendency of self-enclosed identities toward violence. The struggle for survival, recognition, and domination, in which people are inescapably involved, helps forge self-enclosed identities, and such self-enclosed identities perpetuate and heighten that same struggle. This holds true for relations between genders no less than for relations between cultures. To find peace, people with self-enclosed identities need to open themselves for one another and give themselves to one another, yet without loss of the self and domination of the other. I will explicate this thought by exploring the nature of the trinitarian identities and their implication for gender identities and relations.

Trinitarian Identities

Responding to Luce Irigaray's critique of what she calls masculine 'oppositional logic of the same' (1985, 1986, 1989)—a 'logic' that drives all remnants of non-identity out of the conceptual space occupied by a given identity—Serene Jones has hinted at the resources the doctrine of the Trinity provides for thinking about gender identity. 'God's very reality is radically multiple, radically relational, and infinitely active' (1993: 132), insists Jones by appealing to Karl Barth, and suggests that we should therefore not think in terms of 'pure identities' at the creaturely level either.

Jones's argument is a good one and deserves to be developed. The trinitarian thought of Karl Barth does not provide the best resource, however, for the development of a complex notion of identity that could serve as a viable alternative to the 'logic of the same'. Barth grounds the Trinity in the formal concept of a self-revealing God and understands the Triune God as an 'indissoluble Subject' and as 'the one God in threefold repetition' (see Barth 1975: 312 and 348-53). This model of the Trinity is 'structurally identical with that of the self-conscious Absolute' (Pannenberg 1991: 296), and God's threefold nature appears therefore in it not so much as a Trinity but as a 'holy tautology' (Moltmann 1981: 141). Barth's Trinity is much too close to the 'logic of the same' to offer an adequate alternative to that logic. Elsewhere in *Church Dogmatics*, in the discussion of the creation of human beings in the image of God, Barth does operate with a more 'social' understanding of the Trinity. Differentiation of humanity into male and female reflects the God in whose 'own being and sphere there is a counterpart; a genuine but harmonious self-encounter and self-discovery; a free co-existence and cooperation; and open confrontation and reciprocity' (Barth 1958: 185). This, I think, is a step in the right direction. Yet Barth uses precisely such a notion of the Trinity to ground subordination of women to men; the Father who begets the Son is the model for man's relation to woman (Janowski 1995: 28-34). I suggest therefore that we turn elsewhere for resources to develop a complex notion of gender identity. A cross-fertilization of the trinitarian thought of two rather diverse and in many respects opposing thinkers, Joseph Ratzinger and Jürgen Moltmann, would serve us better.

For Ratzinger the starting-point for the doctrine of the Trinity is the self-identity of God in revelation: 'God *is* as he *shows* himself [to be]; God does not show himself in a way in which he is not' (1970: 116-17). Having started with God's self-identity Ratzinger could have ended with the notion of the Trinity as a 'self-repetition' of the one divine subject, much like Barth did. But Ratzinger rightly resists the temptation to overburden the idea of divine 'self-revelation'. Though he starts with this idea, he *grounds* the doctrine of the Trinity in the phenomenon of a *dialogue* within God: because we can observe a dialogue within God, God must be triune. But how should we understand the 'partners' of the dialogue, termed in traditional trinitarian theology 'persons'? Following Augustine, Ratzinger defines person as 'relation', more precisely, as 'relatedness' (p. 131). But what is 'relatedness' and in what way could it define personhood? The best way to unpack his reinterpretation of the Augustinian notion of person as relation is to concentrate on the identity of the second person of the Trinity, the Son.

Commenting on Jesus' statement in John's Gospel, 'the Son can do nothing on his own...' (5.19, 30), Ratzinger writes, 'The Son as Son, and in so far as he is Son, does not proceed in any way from himself and so is completely one with the Father'; the Son has nothing of his own and therefore 'coincides with the Father, is "one" with him' (p. 134). Moreover, just as the Son is completely 'from the Father', so he is also completely 'for the others'—for humanity in need of redemption. The being of the Son is therefore being 'from' and being 'for'; and in this twofold way, his existence is 'complete openness' (p. 136). Summing up his argument Ratzinger writes,

> When it thus becomes clear that the being of Jesus as Christ is a completely
> open being, a being 'from' and 'towards', that nowhere clings to itself and
> nowhere stands on its own, then it is also clear at the same time that this
> being is pure relation (not substantiality) and, as pure relation, pure unity
> (Ratzinger 1970: 134).

Two interrelated aspects of 'complete openness' that defines the being
of the Son are important for my purposes here. First, complete openness
entails *complete self-giving*. The Son gives himself to the Father from
whom he receives his whole being; and he gives himself to humanity to
whom he mediates the Father. Second, the complete openness entails
complete presence of the other in the self. The Father is so much present in
the Son that the Son 'coincides with the Father' (p. 134); the Son nowhere
stands on his own; his 'I' is that of the Father. Consequently, what one
sees by looking at the Son is nothing but the Father. According to Ratzinger, it is because there is nothing of the Son's own to be seen that the
Johannine Jesus can say, 'Whoever has seen me has seen the Father'
(Jn 14.9).

Properly understood, the twin ideas of 'giving of the self to the other'
and of 'the presence of the other in the self' are both profound and significant. By suggesting that persons are never just themselves but harbor in
themselves others to whom they ought to give themselves in love, the two
ideas suggest a complex and dynamic understanding of identity that offers
a viable alternative to the 'logic of the same'. Ratzinger, however, squan-
ders his gains by insisting on the *complete* 'self-giving' and *complete*
'presence of the other' (Volf 1997: ch. 1). For one, he is unable to guard
the distinct identity of the Son. If the self of the Son consists in *complete*
self-giving who would then be doing the giving? How are the Son's
'coinciding' with the Father, and the Father's and the Son's 'coalescing'
into unity, different from the dissolution of the Son in the Father? The
Johannine Jesus, at any rate, provides no support for the claim that the Son
'nowhere stands on his own'. After the claim that 'the Son can do nothing
on his own', we read that the Son does what he 'sees' (5.19) and 'hears'
(5.30) the Father doing. Both 'seeing' and 'hearing' presuppose a self
which confronts the Father with *at least something* of his own. Second,
Ratzinger ends up with the most radical kind of hierarchy within the
Trinity. True, if the Son 'coincides' with the Father, then an equality of
sorts has been established between the Father and the Son. But the price of
this equality is, paradoxically, the most radical kind of inequality: the Son
is nothing, the Father is everything. To define the Father as 'the act of

begetting, of giving oneself, of streaming forth', as Ratzinger does, makes things only worse (1970: 132). If the Son is nothing and the Father everything, then the Father's giving of his own self amounts to his 'colonizing' of the Son's self. The Son is dissolved by being, so to say, pushed out of himself.

Instead of explicating a dialogue in God, Ratzinger silences the Son by making his whole being into the 'word of the Father'; a dialogue has mutated into a monologue because the Son is not a participant but a ventriloquist—and that not only in his mission in the world but also in his inner trinitarian relation to the Father. Is there a way to repair the damage Ratzinger has done to the notions of 'self-giving' and 'the presence of the other in the self' by the relentless radicality with which he has asserted them? Only if we can affirm self-giving without losing the self and hold onto the presence of the other in the self without slipping into inequality. Jürgen Moltmann can help us do both. He is the most notable representative of trinitarian thinking which both refuses to dissolve persons into relations and seeks to affirm their equality.

For Moltmann, the ground of the doctrine of the Trinity lies in the fact that 'the New Testament talks about God by proclaiming in narrative the relationships of the Father, the Son and the Spirit, which are relationships of fellowship and are open to the world' (1981: 64). In this 'narrative of God' we encounter the Father, the Son, and the Spirit as acting agents. The doctrine of the Trinity, which is nothing but the explication of 'the Trinitarian origin of the biblical story itself' (p. 64), must therefore conceive persons as 'subjects of the one, common divine substance, with consciousness and will' (p. 171). Though Moltmann underlines that divine persons are not self-enclosed individuals, but are determined in their particular personal identity by other persons, he refuses to reduce persons to relations. The concept of person as relation both 'dissolves the Trinitarian concept of person' and 'does away with the interpersonal concept of relation', he maintains (p. 173). To preserve both 'person' and 'relation' we must understand them in a reciprocal relationship: 'there are no persons without relations; but there are no relations without persons' (p. 172). Persons are not relations; persons stand in relations that shape their identity.

But are the relations between divine persons not asymmetrical, non-egalitarian, hierarchical? Is not the Father first, the Son second, the Spirit third? So it would seem, if the Father is the 'origin', if the Son is 'generated', and if the Spirit 'proceeds'. Moltmann has suggested, however, that we distinguish in the Trinity between the level of 'constitution' and the level of 'life'; the one level speaks about how persons are constituted and the other about how they relate to one another. At the level of the *constitution* of the divine persons, the Father is the 'first' because he is the source of the divinity. Without such a source, it would be impossible to distinguish between the three persons; they would collapse into one undifferentiated divine nature (so Zizioulas 1985: 45). At the level of *relations*, the Son not only 'comes from' and 'goes to' the Father, but the Father has 'given all things into his hands' and 'glorifies the Son' (Jn 13.3; 17.1). With respect to the immanent Trinity, these statements about the economic Trinity mean that in constituting the Son, the Father gives all divine power and all divine glory to the Son. As the source of divinity *the Father therefore constitutes the mutual relations between the persons as egalitarian rather than hierarchical*; all persons are equal in power and equal in glory. At the level of the life of the Trinity, the Father is not 'the First', but 'One among the Others' (Moltmann 1992: 308).

Now that we have 'secured' divine persons from the dual threat of dissolution and inequality, we can fruitfully return to the twin ideas of 'the giving of the self to the other' and 'the presence of the other in the self'. We have a notion of a self that can do the giving of itself and that can remain itself even after it has received the other. Now the 'self-giving' and 'mutual indwelling' of the trinitarian persons suggest the contours of a notion of identity not governed by the oppositional 'logic of the same'. The *self-giving* of the divine persons no longer entails a dissolution of the self (Ratzinger's Son). Instead, the self-giving is a way in which each divine person seeks the 'glory' of the others and makes space in itself for the others. The *indwelling* of the one divine person in the other no longer entails colonization of the other (Ratzinger's Father). Instead, the indwelling presupposes that the otherness of the other—the other's identity—has been preserved, not as self-enclosed and static 'pure identity' but as open and dynamic 'identity-with-non-identity'.

Since John of Damascus *perichoresis* has become the technical term for the idea of divine 'mutual indwelling' that results from 'self-giving'. Traditionally, *perichoresis* has been used mainly to explain divine unity (Prestige 1956: 298). John of Damascus writes, 'For…they are made one not so as to commingle, but so as to cleave to each other, and they have their being in each other without any coalescence or commingling' (*de fide* 1.8). Equally significant are the resources of *perichoresis* for thinking about identity (Plantinga Pauw 1993: esp. 14). For *perichoresis* suggests a dynamic identity in which 'non-identity' indwells the 'identity' and constitutes it by this indwelling. Father is the Father not only because he is distinct from the Son and the Spirit but also because through the power of self-giving the Son and the Spirit dwell in him. The same is true of the Son and of the Spirit.

Can such complex identity that rests on the twin notions of 'self-giving' and 'mutual indwelling' be brought from heaven down to the earth? In a sense, this 'bringing down' is the goal of the whole history of salvation: God came into the world so as to make human beings, created in the image of God, live with one another and with God in the kind of communion that divine persons live with one another. But what does human correspondence to God's 'self-giving' and 'mutual indwelling' mean concretely? I want to explore this issue by asking what a trinitarian understanding of relations between persons and their identity means for the question of gender identity.

Gender Identity

So far my argument about gender identity has consisted of two basic claims and one suggestion. I claimed that (1) the content of gender identity is rooted in the sexed body and negotiated in the social exchange between men and women within a given cultural context, and that (2) the portrayals of God in no way provide models of what it means to be male or female. I suggested, instead, that the relations between the trinitarian persons serve as a model for how the content of 'masculinity' and 'femininity' ought to be negotiated in the social process. Before I explore in what sense the relations between the divine persons can serve as a model, I need to attend to a possible objection.

It could be objected that my proposal is inadmissibly formal. I have formally rooted gender identity in the sexed body and in the interaction between men and women, and am about to suggest how this interaction should take place. The content of gender identity is underdetermined; anything seems to go. Granted that this content cannot stem from *who God is*, the objection could continue, should Christians not seek to determine it by listening to *what the Bible says*? Should we not analyze the biblical statements about men and women, try to reconstruct biblical 'manhood' and 'womanhood', and apply it in contemporary contexts? Without denying that we can learn much from men and women in the Bible, I propose that such an approach would be mistaken. Biblical 'womanhood' and 'manhood'—if there are such things at all, given the diversity of male and female characters and roles that we encounter in the Bible—are not divinely sanctioned models but culturally situated examples; they are accounts of the successes and failures of men and women to live out the demands of God on their lives within specific settings. This is not to say that the biblical construals of what men and women—of what men and women *as men and women*—should or should not do and be are wrong, but that they are of limited normative value in a different cultural context, since they are of necessity laden with specific cultural beliefs about gender identity and roles.

If neither the models of God nor the explicit statements of the Bible about femininity and masculinity are normative for the content of gender identities, what is? Does anything really go? My proposal is that we locate normativity in the formal features of identity as we encounter it in the identities and relations of divine persons. Instead of setting up ideals of femininity and masculinity, *we should root each in the sexed body and let the social construction of gender play itself out guided by the vision of the identity of and relations between divine persons*. What is normative is not some 'essence' of femininity and masculinity, but the procedures, modeled on the life of the Triune God, through which women and men in specific cultural settings should negotiate their mutual relations and their construc-tions of femininity and masculinity. A more stable definition of the content of gender identity would not only be unnecessary but harmful; it would inadmissibly freeze a particular cultural understanding of gender identity and seek to impose it inappropriately in changing situations. This proposal presupposes that, unlike Irigaray, we neither give up on the one God of both men and women nor slight (or is it outright reject?) the thought of a single humanity to which they both belong (Irigaray 1996: 35-43). It is precisely the one Triune God in whose image all human beings are created that holds the promise of peace between men and women with irreducible but changing gender identities.

In the remainder of this article I want to suggest how the construction and reconstruction of gender identity should go on if it is guided by the doctrine of the Trinity. I will proceed by reflecting theologically on three key biblical statements on gender. All three appear in implicitly or ex-plicitly subordinationist passages (Gen. 1 and 2; 1 Cor. 11.2-16; Eph. 5.21-33). I will simply disregard the subordinationism as culturally con-ditioned and interpret the statements from within the framework of an egalitarian understanding of the trinitarian relations and from the perspec-tive of the egalitarian thrust of such central biblical assertions as the one found in Gal. 3.28: 'There is no longer male and female; for all of you are one in Christ Jesus'.

'Male and Female'

In Genesis 1 we read: 'So God created humankind in his image, in the image of God he created them, male and female he created them' (v. 28). Human beings exist in an irreducible duality of male and female; there are no generic human beings, only male or female human beings. Genesis 2 suggests that the duality is rooted in their sexed bodies. Adam awakes from a deep sleep, sees Eve whom God has brought to him, and imme-diately recognizes—presumably, by seeing her body—both their profound unity and their undeniable difference: 'This at last is bone of my bones and flesh of my flesh; this one shall be called Woman, for out of Man this one was taken' (v. 23). Though the content of masculinity and femininity may vary from culture to culture and their boundaries may at times be blurry, the marks of maleness and femaleness are indelibly inscribed in human bodies, and gender difference is therefore an inalienable feature of human existence. This is the most basic lesson about femininity and masculinity that Genesis 1 and 2 teach.

Does not Gal. 3.28, however, contain a contrary lesson? Does it not delete the indelible and remove the inalienable? Does it not claim that the order of creation has been transcended in Christ, so that whereas in Genesis 1 humanity was created as 'male and female' in Galatians 3 there is 'no longer "male and female"'—a clear allusion to and denial of Genesis 1? Following in part Wayne A. Meeks (1973–74), Daniel Boyarin has suggested that Paul's ideal (which cannot be realized fully before the dawn of the eschaton) is 'a state of androgyny, a cancellation of gender and sexuality' (1994: 195). Paul is 'motivated by a Hellenistic desire for the One which among other things produced an ideal of a universal human essence, beyond difference and hierarchy' (p. 181), and he locates the unity of genders 'in the spirit' which is universal, in contrast to body, which is always particular (pp. 193, 197).

Boyarin's arugment does not persuade, however. The source of unity for Paul is not the abstract 'One' or 'the spirit', which erase particularity and difference, but the single and differentiated *body* of the crucified and resurrected Christ given for all (1 Cor. 10-12; cf. Eph. 4.11-18). Moreover, Paul does not operate anthropologically with a dualistic split between 'spirit' and 'body', which would make the erasure of bodily inscribed differences possible. Hence, just as the Hebrew Scripture knows of no primal androgyne, no sexually undifferentiated humanity from which 'male and female' have emerged (Gundry-Volf 1994a: 102-103; Trible 1978: 18), so also Paul's claim that in Christ there is 'no longer "male and female"' entails no eschatological denial of gender dimorphism. What has been erased in Christ is not the sexed body, but some important culturally coded norms attached to sexed bodies (such as the obligation to marry and procreate and the prohibition of women from performing certain functions in the church). The oneness in Christ is a community of people with sexed bodies and distinct gender identities, not some abstract unity of pure spirits or de-gendered 'persons'.

In the doctrine of the Trinity, I have noted, persons should not be reduced to relations. If such a reduction took place, one person would collapse into the other (the Son, for instance, into the Father) and ultimately all persons would disappear into a common undifferentiated divine nature. Analogously, the one gender should neither be transformed into another (say, femininity into masculinity) nor both melted into a new synthesis. The first option is rarely advocated, but it is lived out in most cultures, especially in public life; most cultures are to a large degree androcentric and women are excluded or pressured to conform either through outright discrimination and oppression or through a vague but persistent sense of homelessness in a world not constructed according to their measure. The second option was recently advocated by Rosemary Radford Ruether. Dissatisfied both with liberal monism (generic humanness as a front for dominance of masculinity) and the romantic binary split between genders (masculine men over against feminine women), she suggested 'a transformed synthesis' of femininity and masculinity. Coming from different sides, men and women need to make a journey into a common wholeness (Radford Ruether 1996: 251). Yet if we assume the permanence of gender differences (as I think we must), then the wholeness cannot be the same for both. Though both can become whole only together, the wholeness is specific to each. This in no way entails the affirmation of an unchangeable 'essence' of genders, but follows from the recognition of an *irreducible duality*, rooted in the sexed body, *of dynamically constructed gender*.

As we stress the irreducible duality and dynamic construction of gender identities, it is crucial not to lose sight of the fundamental equality between men and women. Endorsement of duality is always fraught with the danger of sliding into affirmation of inequality, especially since difference between men and women was in the past universally interpreted as superiority of one and inferiority of the other. Not surprisingly, those who strive to achieve equality sometimes seek refuge in sameness. As we reject sameness, we must both affirm equality between men and women and seek to change social practices in which the inferiority of women is embodied and through which it is perpetuated even when their equality to men is formally endorsed.

'Not Without'

Given the duality of genders, should the search for the wholeness of each take place independently of the other? At times, the identity of one gender, especially of women, is threatened. In such situations it is necessary to engage in 'boundary maintenance' and 'identity formation'. Protesting against the homelessness of women in modern culture, the circle of women around 'Libreria delle donne di Milano', for instance, has stressed the need of fostering women's identity by emphasizing 'symbolical order of mothers', 'feminine geneology', and 'feminine authority' as a way of putting women in the center (1989). Similarly, men increasingly feel the need to nurture their own masculinity. As Garrison Keillor notes in *The Book of Guys* (1994) in advanced industrial societies men are in trouble because whereas years ago 'manhood was an opportunity for achievement', now it is just 'a problem to overcome'. The 'guy trouble' stems from the decline of patriarchy—not 'of sexism, or misogyny, or even male dominance', as Barbara Ehrenreich (1995), who advocates the thesis about the decline of patriarchy, points out—and the consequent uncertainty of men about their roles as spouses and fathers.

Though turning inward and bolstering the identity of each gender can be important as a strategy, it is mistaken as a goal in and of itself. For one, more often than not an exclusive concern with one's own identity generates pernicious ideologies of superiority (though men, who in the past always and everywhere thought of themselves as superior, should not be bothered too much about the occasional rhetoric of female superiority). More importantly, the turn inward misses the very character of gender identities. We are neither masculine nor feminine 'from the start' (Irigaray 1985: 212); we are made so through relation to the other gender. Men's identity is not and cannot be only men's affair, just as women's identity is not and cannot be only women's affair. Gender identities are essentially related and therefore the specific wholeness of each can be achieved only through the relation to the other, a relation that neither neutralizes nor synthesizes the two, but negotiates the identity of each by readjusting it to the identity of the other.

Explicating the relationship between men and women 'in the Lord', Paul writes in 1 Cor. 11.11: 'Neither is woman without man nor man without woman'. Boyarin reads the passage in the same fashion as he reads Gal. 3.28: 'as a representation of an androgyny that exists on the level of the spirit' (1994: 194). On this reading, in the Lord 'woman is *not different* from man nor man from woman' (Kürzinger 1978: 270-75). Notice, however, the ground for the claim that neither gender is without the other that Paul gives in the following verse. It is not taken from the sphere of 'the pure spirit' but from *bodily creation*: 'For just as woman came from man so man comes through woman' (v. 12). As Judith Gundry-Volf (1997a) has shown, Paul has *two* readings of creation in 1 Corinthians 11: the one from the perspective of the patriarchal culture which finds hierarchy in creation (vv. 8-9), and the other from the perspective of the new life in Christ, which finds equality in creation (v. 12). Paul's second reading of creation, which underscores equality of genders, in no way erases the difference between genders, as Boyarin suggests. Since woman is 'from' man and man is 'through' woman, Paul argues, they are 'not without' each other (v. 12). The prepositions 'from' and 'through' both draw attention back to Genesis 2 and, in addition, suggest the ideas of begetting ('from') and birthing ('through'). 'In the Lord', the difference of the sexed bodies is not erased; to the contrary, this difference grounds interdependence of men and women.

The double negative expressing interdependence—'not without'—is significant. Let me try to explicate what it may mean for the construction of gender identity. Typically, gender is defined by employing 'oppositional logic'. In *Sacrificial Logics* Allison Weir has noted a failure even of feminist thought to 'theorize nonoppositional, nondominating relationships between identity and difference' (1996: 3). As is well known, Simone de Beauvoir in *The Second Sex* proceeds on the fundamental assumption 'that identity is necessarily a product of a subject-object opposition'; women will therefore be able to affirm their identity 'only through opposing themselves to an object/other' (1952: 4). But even those feminist thinkers who seek to subvert the formation of identity through the repression of difference, such as relational feminists (Nancy Chodorow) and post-structuralist feminists (Luce Irigaray), end up tacitly affirming oppositional logic, argues Weir. For they continue to operate with the idea that 'identity is necessarily based on subject-object opposition' and therefore entails 'the exclusion of the other by the self/same' (1996: 7). Weir rightly calls for alternative theories of identity 'which do not exclude but include difference and otherness' (pp. 7-8). I propose that the Pauline 'not without'—woman is 'not without' man and man is 'not without' woman—suggests precisely such a complex and dynamic understanding of gender identity that corresponds to the nature of identity that we have encountered in the doctrine of the Trinity.

In the Trinity, I have pointed out, distinct persons are internally constituted by the indwelling of other persons in them. The personal identity of each is unthinkable without the presence of others in each; such presence of others is part and parcel of the identity of each. A self-enclosed identity constituted in pure opposition to the other is unthinkable; the Father is the Father in no other way but in the dynamism of his relationship to the Son and the Spirit. Analogously, the Pauline 'not without' suggests that the identity of one gender cannot be thought 'without' the other. Men cannot be defined simply as what 'women are not'; women cannot be defined simply as 'what men are not'. Such oppositional 'logic of the same' would do violence to the identities of both men and women, which grow out of 'the necessary interconnectedness of our (social) images of ourselves' (Gatens 1996: 38). To be a woman means to be a human being of the female sex who is 'not without man'; to be a man means to be a human being of the male sex who is 'not without woman'. This holds true quite apart from whether men and women live in heterosexual relationships.[1]

Unlike the idea of 'neither-one-nor-the-other' which creates a neuter by erasing gender differences, and unlike the idea of 'both-the-one-and-the-other' which also creates a neuter by synthesizing gender differences, the idea of 'not-without-the-other' affirms gender differences while at the same time positing one gender identity as always internal to the other. The irreducible duality is preserved and made part of a complex identity in which each, in its own way, always already contains the other.

'He Gave Himself Up For Her'

The partial mutual internality of gender identities with the preservation of the dynamic specificity of each—these are the two aspects of the construction of gender identities that have emerged so far from the reflection on the nature of trinitarian identities in conjunction with some key biblical passages about men and women. Will they suffice as general guidelines for the construction of gender identities? Above all, will they work in a world of struggle, even outright violence between genders? The one gender seeks to colonize the other, and then pulls back leaving behind it scorched land; the one gender seeks to dominate the other, and projects disparaging

---

1.   As Caroline S. Vance has pointed out, though interwoven at many ponts, 'sexuality and gender are separate systems' (1995: 39).

images onto the other and manipulates the other; the person of one gender closes himself or herself off from the other, and maintains a forced purity which then mutates into aggression; most likely, persons of both genders do all these things, and a few more, all at the same time. Much like human relations in general, relations between genders all too often lack respect and love and are sometimes suffused with enmity.

No doubt, the twin strategies of pursuing the preservation of distinct gender identities and the construction of complex identities that include the other will help. For these strategies attend to some of the most important and interconnected causes of gender tensions—the threats to identity and the oppositional pursuit of identity. But why should we pursue these twin strategies, especially in the contexts of enmity? Why not insist on one's pure identity? Why not simply disregard the identity-needs of others? The answer will take us away from relations between gender identities to relations between engendered persons.

I have suggested that the life of the Trinity is characterized by self-giving love. The Son eternally gives himself to the Father by seeking to 'glorify' the Father and make space in himself for the Father. The same is, arguably, true of the Father and the Spirit. When the God of love enters the world of human enmity, the eternal self-giving of divine persons turns into the historical self-sacrifice of Jesus Christ for the salvation of those who are set on sacrificing others (see Volf 1996: ch. 3). Ephesians 5 takes the self-giving of Christ for humanity as the model for relations between engendered persons: 'Husbands, love your wives, just as Christ loved the church and gave himself up for her in order to make her holy' (vv. 25-26). The text addresses only husbands. The larger narrative of the Bible suggests, however, that the injunction applies to both men and women (though, given the underprivileged position of women in patriarchal societies, it is appropriately addressed here to the husbands).

'Self-giving' is a misused notion and needs careful nuancing if it is not to do more harm than good. It clearly has nothing to do with the loss of the self. To the contrary, both the text of Ephesians, and the doctrine of the Trinity which I use as the framework for reading the text, presuppose the affirmation of the self; in the Trinity, persons are more than relations, and in Ephesians one should love the other 'as' one loves oneself precisely because 'no one ever hates his own body' (5.29). But what does self-giving mean positively? First, it means abandoning self-absorption and moving toward the other in order to 'nourish' and 'tenderly care', in order to make 'without blemish' and clothe in 'splendor' (vv. 29, 27). Second, self-giving means the opening of the self for the other, letting the other find space in the self—so much so that love for the other, who remains the other and is not transformed into an inessential extension of the self, can be experienced as the love of the self (v. 28). In a beautiful phrase with which Irigaray closes *I Love to You*, in self-giving 'your retreat reveals my existence, as my withdrawal is dedicated to you' (1996: 150). In the twofold sense of seeking to make the other blossom and of creating space in the self for the other women and men should grow, as Jane Williams puts it, 'into the likeness of that great circle of God's self-giving love' (1992: 43).

In a world of enmity self-giving is the risky and hard work of love. There are no guarantees that self-giving will overcome enmity and that the evildoers will not try to invade the space that the self has made and crush those willing to give themselves for the good of others. We will have to resist such evil-doers without betraying the commitment to self-giving. But though self-giving has no assurance of success, it does have the promise of eternity because it reflects the character of the divine Trinity. It is on account of self-giving that divine persons exist in a perfect community in which each is itself only by being inhabited by the others. And it is through the power of self-giving that a new community of men and women will emerge, in which distinct but dynamic gender identities that are 'not without' the other will be fashioned and refashioned in peace.

Whose Rib?

In conclusion, let me return to Nietzsche's aphorism I quoted in the introduction. 'Man created woman—but what out of? Out of a rib of his God, his "ideal"...' said Nietzsche. Woman is man's creation, fashioned out of his ideals. This is exactly how Nietzsche wanted things to be. In *Thus Spoke Zarathustra* he writes that 'only he who is sufficiently a man will redeem the woman in woman' (1969: 189) and that for woman the world is perfect only 'when she obeys with all her love' (p. 91). Man is the creator, he is the redeemer, he is the commander; woman is the chaos that cries for the imposition of order, she is sinfulness that awaits redemption, she is irrationality that must receive a command. The construction of gender goes all in one direction: from the positivity of man's fullness toward the negativity of woman's lack.

As noted earlier, Nietzsche's aphorism inverts the Genesis account of the creation of woman. Did he get his misogyny from the Bible and Christian tradition? Is he only explicating a secularized version of a collusion between man and man's God to fashion woman as a deficient and subjugated being? Does not Nietzsche say bluntly and irreverently the same things about gender that many Christians say couched in a rhetoric of love and shielded by divine commands? The most radical atheist and the most pious fundamentalist seem to agree—against the women! But are these strange bedfellows right?

I have tried to show that at the very heart of the Christian tradition—in the doctrine of the Trinity and of the Cross—there are resources for thinking about gender identity that offer a radical alternative to Nietzsche-like misogyny. First, human beings exist in an irreducible duality of genders with equal dignity. Man is not a fullness and woman is not a lack; man does not command whereas woman obeys; they both command and both obey; they are both full and both lacking. Second, the construction of gender identities on the basis of sexed bodies goes both ways—from men to women and from women to men; in Nietzsche's terminology, each needs the other for its own 'creation' and 'redemption'. Third, the very identity of each gender may not be 'without the other'; the identity of each encompasses in its own way the identity of the other and both identities are fashioned and refashioned in relation to one another. Finally, all of this—the affirmation of the equal dignity of genders, the symmetry in construction of gender identities, and the presence of the other in the self—all of this is kept in motion by self-giving love. Though the goal of self-giving is the mutuality of perfect love, the road toward this goal in a world of enmity often leads through the narrow paths of one-sided giving of the self for the other. The model for the goal is the eternal embrace of divine persons; the model for the difficult road toward the goal is Christ's embrace of sinful humanity on the cross.

Nietzsche suggested that woman was created out of 'a rib of man's God, his ideal'. In contrast, I have tried to describe what the process of the mutual 'creation' of men and women would look like if we assume that they are to be 'created' out of a 'rib' of the Triune God and the 'wounded side' of the Crucified.

'CALL NO MAN FATHER!': THE TRINITY, PATRIARCHY AND GOD-TALK[*]

Alan J. Torrance

Introduction

One of the most important debates in the theological tradition concerns the problem of analogy. The question it raises is whether one can assume (and, if so, on what basis) continuity of meaning between human language used of the created contingent human context, on the one hand, and, on the other, of the divine context. Given that our language seems to derive its 'sense' from within the contextuality of the created order, the analogy debate raises the question as to whether we are entitled to use the *same* terms within the context of the transcendent, that is, the non-contingent, the uncreated. In short, the debate concerns the possibility of semantic continuity between the two realms and conceives of the question as an ontological or metaphysical one. Recently, however, developments in the philosophy of language, together with others in experimental psychology, sociology, educational theory, and feminist research, have exposed the extent to which the problem of continuity is not simply a metaphysical problem, but a moral one. Any supposed semantic continuity is pregnant with ethical ramifications! It is this question which I wish to consider in this chapter. This will lead us to a series of conclusions about the inter-relationship between the ethical and the ontological—issues which relate to the question of semantic continuity between the two realms.

The Connection between Language and Thought

It has been widely assumed within our Western tradition that we create or sustain pure concepts of theological realities in our minds and then attach names to these mental concepts. For example, we have a concept of God

* I would like to express my gratitude to Keith Hyde for his helpful comments, suggestions and corrections.

to which we then attach terms such as 'Father', 'Lord', 'King', and so on. What matters is the *pure concept* (our pure thinking about God) and not the names or words we happen to use—if their role is not neutrally denotative one can be reassured, it is believed, that in the context of referring, any metaphorical impropriety or extraneous associations that might attend the relevant term will simply fall away to the extent that they cease to apply to God. Thus descriptive terminology can be regarded as inherently neutral in the theological context. If the pure concept is not exclusive, then the *gender* of the name involved is irrelevant. Life, however, is not quite so simple!

As Wittgenstein and others have shown, language-use is a skill that we learn within linguistic communities. It is as we acquire linguistic skills—subliminally, unconsciously, and from an early age—that we learn to make distinctions and to interpret (and thus think about) the world in which we live. The rules of the language-games into which we are born, therefore, shape and influence the way in which we build up our world, define its contents, interpret relations between things, and explicate events. The world of our experience, therefore, is moulded, shaped, and conditioned by the language we are taught, the linguistic skills we acquire, and the distinctions intrinsic to this. To a substantial degree, therefore, *words (and the rules of use which constitute their meaning) shape the way we use concepts rather than vice-versa.* In short, the words we use impact on the way we process and think about reality—or, rather, they impact on the way we are incorporated into reality or, more accurately still, *are networked as part of reality!*[1]

What this implies is that we have a *prima facie* obligation to consider the ways in which language moulds and shapes this networking—that is, of course, to the extent that such consideration is possible.[2] At the very least, we need to consider the extent to which language threatens to distort our world-view. And the point to be made here is that gendered words applied to God *may* have a dysfunctional effect at the subliminal level by

1.   These insights are taken to their extreme in the 'postmodernist' emphasis on the reality-constituting character of language as expressed, for example, by Jacques Derrida. See, for example, his 1976. For a lucid exposition of Derrida's views see Llewelyn 1986. Theological parallels are to be found in Cupitt 1990.

2.   Given that language conditions our thinking at the level of our 'absolute presuppositions', to use R.G. Collingwood's language (see his 1948), the question needs to be asked how these might become the objects of assessment and critique—and thus 'relative presuppositions'.

conditioning us into thinking about God and ultimate Reality in very specific ways. That is, they may serve to shape our value systems by orienting our thinking toward the interests of a certain group. Such subliminal mis-orientation would corrupt a proper relatedness to God and humanity and distort or inhibit the 'proper function' of this whole networking process.[3]

As I have argued elsewhere (cf. A.J. Torrance 1996: 325), our use of language or what we might term our 'semantic participation'—*subliminal* participation in mind, thought, and word in the divine life—is responsible for the way in which our whole world-view is ordered and structured. It impacts on our systems of value-judgments and, therefore, on the ways we behave. What this suggests, therefore, is that there requires to be *a whole new level of questioning about the matter of the continuity* between talk about God and our relation to the human world. The question of continuity is not simply a metaphysical and philosophical one but a moral and ethical one! What I am suggesting, therefore, is that the traditional analogical debates relating to the question of continuity between the human and the divine concern not only matters of *epistemological* or *semantic* legitimacy but *ethical* legitimacy as well.

This poses a question with respect to the traditionally essentialistic presuppositions underlying god-talk, namely, the following: has not the assumption that our conceptual world possesses theological potential served to ratify the subliminal and potentially oppressive baggage that attends it? One of the major contributions of feminist thought over the last two decades has been its exposé of the potential of our language, and the concepts carried by it, to condition dysfunctional modes of thought leading to oppressive attitudes. Our theological terminology is, as it were, virus-laden and serves to corrupt our processing of theological realities! To the extent, moreover, that we assume the Cartesian concept of the detached, thinking, subject-self conceiving pure thoughts about God we fail to address the problem, and the relevant viruses continue their work unchallenged.[4]

---

3. 'Proper function' is borrowed from Alvin Plantinga's analysis of epistemic warrant (1993).

4. It fails, that is, to appreciate the extent to which we are integrated participative, semantic 'speaking-thinking' beings, as Wittgenstein shows: see his 1967 and 1969. The implication of this is that the proper functioning of the individual in relation to other individuals is contingent upon the 'proper functioning' of the semantic community as a whole.

Paul suggests that we are ἐχθροὺς τῇ διανοίᾳ ('alienated in our minds/conceptualities'; see Col. 1.21). What this suggests, therefore, is a need for the reconciliation or reschematization of our *noein* (transformation of our minds); literally a *metanoia*, for 'inclusive' participation in the all-inclusive humanity and mission of Christ. And, as I have argued elsewhere (A.J. Torrance 1996: ch. 5), this reconstruction of our speaking and thinking takes place within the context of the semantic community of the church, that is, within the Body, the New Humanity. Consequently, the ethical issues relating to the continuity question should not be interpreted as an imposition of feminist theology. Rather, these feminist criticisms serve to elucidate for us something of what is involved in being a semantically reconciled community, namely, the *ekklesia* in truth.

This is not, of course, to deny that the risks of god-talk have been appreciated more widely. They have! Until recently, however, fears have arisen primarily with respect to the 'focal' or explicit ramifications of claims made, for example, by German Christians or Afrikaner Calvinists or within other contexts of civil religion. To suggest that Jews or blacks or women occupy a lower ontological rung within divine orders of creation can clearly be interpreted as explicit warrant for non-egalitarian social policy. The social implications of explicit theological suggestions have long been appreciated. What feminism has served to highlight are the ethical ramifications of the *subliminal* dimension of our semantic participation in theological language games. Such participation serves to condition our orientation toward God and the world. Consequently, it stands to shape our value systems, our attitudes vis-à-vis gender and other social issues, and hence our behaviour from our earliest years. To use the word 'father' of God while simultaneously using it of male, gendered parents, for example, may serve to ratify and mould the subliminal associations of the term in such a way that these associations are transferred to other contexts of the word's usage. The same may clearly be said to apply to the words 'he' and 'himself' if they are to be used of God and humanity in uninterrupted continuity.

Precisely this concern was voiced in a paper written by three feminist theologians from the University of Otago entitled 'Sexism Ancient and Modern: Turning the Male World Upside Down', which draws on research conducted within the Department of Psychology of that same university (Bergin *et al.* 1990). Elizabeth Wilson and Sik Hung Ng conducted experiments which suggested that even when general terms were used to refer to men and women, if masculine *pronouns* were used people usually envisaged a male person. Consequently, when people heard the sentence, 'At university, a student can study whatever he wants', the majority pictured a male student (Wilson and Ng 1988). In the light of this, Bergin *et al.* argue that 'it seems fairly easy to deduce that when people hear "in these last days, he has spoken to us", some kind of male God is imagined' (1990: 164). In sum, if God is regularly referred to by the pronoun 'he', God will subliminally come to be conceived of as being 'male' in some sense.[5] And if we think about the ultimate authority in male terms, it is suggested, we may be subliminally led into thinking in ways which endorse male, authoritarian power structures, that is, we may be seduced into adopting an androcentric or patriarchal world-view to the detriment of community life where people ought to be conceived as having equal value and status and where people's roles should not be defined or confined by their sex any more than by their race or culture.

Thinking, Imaging and Imagining

If this suggests that we should be aware of the *subliminal* effects of the language we use, it is *a fortiori* the case that we should consider the psychological effects of any explicit imaging processes induced and encouraged by theological metaphors and practices. (The reason I am making the distinction here between subliminal semantic associations, on the one hand, and 'imaging' conceived as a psychological event, on the other, is due to the fact that meanings should not and must not be identified with psychological events.) That imaging has been perceived to be important is reflected in the church's age-old definition of its structures with reference to the maleness of Christ which, it has been assumed, must be 'imaged' in

---

5.   It is relevant to note that there is a highly significant non-parallelism here. In the case of the Otago study referred to, 'he' is being used of students, i.e. human beings, who are invariably gendered beings, whereas in the theological context the referent is 'God' who ought to be recognized by educated Christians to be beyond gender. The thrust of Wittgenstein's arguments, to which I refer above, is to suggest that meanings are *not* 'fixed' for all contexts. Consequently, a word does *not* carry identical psychological associations in all contexts of its use, as this argument assumes. The meaning and rules of use applying to the pronoun 'he' when used of God are clearly different from those that apply when the pronoun is used of the non-human. This applies as much to the English language as it does to the various other European languages (e.g. French and German) which use 'gendered' pronouns of non-human referents and where this clearly does *not* involve gender-projection on the part of the users. The French do not regard houses as female!

its ministry. I remember hearing a Catholic bishop offering justification to
the media for the exclusive ordination of males by arguing that the Roman
church only ordains males because it is integral to the priestly office that
the priesthood *image* Christ. This means, one would assume, that in
proclamation the content of that proclamation, that is the Word preached,
is somehow *intrinsically* related to the biological sex of the proclaimer—
what is proclaimed must be an appropriately 'imaged' Gospel. What is
implied by this is that if there is to be a *re-presenting* in the church of the
one in whom there is neither Jew nor Gentile, male and female (cf. Gal.
3.28), it is absolutely necessary that his maleness be 'imaged' by the one
who *re-presents* him. The femaleness of women can thus have no such
representative value. Observing that the traditional argument that the
Catholic church adopted against the ordination of women, which was an
argument from their subordinate status, has been dropped, Janet Martin
Soskice continues:

> The new argument is that women are equal but different, and different in
> such a way that they could not be priests. Women, in this new argument,
> still can't signify Christ... Jesus after all was a young man when he died yet
> an eighty year old priest is still judged able to signify Christ. Jesus was a
> Jew, yet a Chinese man can signify Christ. What then is so over-ridingly
> important about being a woman, that this feature out of all others makes
> some people un-Christlike in the one relevant sense? (1993: 118).[6]

It is not surprising, therefore, that there have been attempts to reverse
the transfer of value which attends the endorsement of exclusively male
imaging. One example was a painting on the theme of the Lord's Supper
commissioned by a group of women ministers in the Uniting Church in
Australia. Its concern was to re-image the Lord's Supper. The painting,
which hung for some months in North Paramatta Uniting Church College,
shows a group of 13 women (Jesus and the disciples) in ministerial garb
seated around a table on which we see a naked woman birthing her baby
with her blood flowing into a chalice. Around the side of the table is
written 'Take this cup...given for you'. As such it constitutes an explicit
attempt at reversing the value-transfer associated with male imaging over
the centuries by a process of female re-imaging. However, in this case the
contrast is so *focal* that it loses subliminal force with the effect that the

---

6.   She continues, '[t]he whole order of creation would be upset by ordaining a
woman, we are told. It would be like, well like ordaining a pigeon or a bunch of
bananas' (1993: 119).

contrasting message is likely to remain neutralized and the requisite subliminal transformation lost.

But what of the more subtle, tacit imaging that may go on in the church mediated by its God-talk—where imaging is endorsed in less explicit ways and at a deeper level by way of the similes, metaphors, analogies, and names used of God? Clearly, if God-talk involves the projection of human images on to God, all that is associated with these images stands to receive ratification as a result. The knock-on effect of this is predictable. The human origins of these images come to be conceived as 'types'—human fathers become 'types' of God!

The two questions which we must now ask, therefore, concern how we regard (1) the subliminal semantic associations which stem from our God-talk; and (2) the psychological events (the imaging) which attend our Christian language-games and our reiteration of biblical expressions, parables and similes. What is the potential here for biblically sourced and resourced proclamation to induce potentially oppressive imbalances in society? And what might be done to offset any potentially damaging or marginalizing effects? Or are we obliged to conclude that the Christian faith is so helplessly steeped in assumed but unethical forms of continuity between the human and the divine that it becomes, as Daphne Hampson (1996) argues, irredeemable? Two opposing types of response have resulted from these fears. First, there is the 'ostrich approach' where people choose to pretend that no problem exists and desperately hope that fashions will soon change and pressures ease. Second, there is the lock, stock and barrel rejection of the Christian tradition as intrinsically oppressive. Between these there have arisen radical, syncretistic attempts to define a new and constructive way forward. One response has been to adopt a twin-pronged approach and it is this which I should now like to consider. The first prong addresses the matter of the subliminal effects of our language-games generally and advocates semantic agnosticism or mysticism as the only means of escaping these. The second prong suggests we re-establish and reinvent the images we use or, at least, counterbalance traditional 'images' with new images in such a way that the offending anthropomorphisms of the old images are removed for the sake of a new-found theological and liturgical balance.

Just such a two-pronged tactic is advocated in the article to which I referred above. It argues:

[w]e may be at a period in our Christian history when an 'agnosticism' with regard to terms for God may be required. And then, throughout the time of silence, the old traditional images and the old untraditional images, the tested and the new, will together be able to lead us further into the Mystery who is God (Bergin *et al.* 1990: 170).[7]

Such an approach characterizes a broad band of feminist literature which seeks to wed an apophatic mysticism to an ethically inclusive theological agenda. Just such an approach was represented at the Minneapolis conference in 1993 on 'Reimagining God' where a number of feminist theologians set out to produce a plethora of new, diverse, and quite graphic images with recourse to which God, it was suggested, might be reimagined and reimaged.

Problems with this Solution

Several problems emerge here, however. First, the whole thrust of the feminist argument vis-à-vis the subliminal associations of our language rests on the view that language and thought are an integrally related unity. As every good Wittgensteinian knows, what cannot be said, cannot be thought! What this means is that agnosticism with regard to God-talk constitutes, in effect, agnosticism with respect to thought about God. The proposed solution is not, therefore, as theologically neutral as it appears. It amounts to an affirmation that *we have no warrant or impetus for God-talk that is sufficiently inclusive for us to be able to speak and ergo think about God in inclusive ways*. It is to assume that, as things stand, there is *no* divinely endorsed God-talk or, at least, no candidates for this which are ethically acceptable.

But if this really is the case, what grounds do we have for suggesting that a period of agnosticism will or can give rise to inclusive divine address and thus any appropriate 'images' of God at all? Any such suggestion cannot escape the inconsistency involved in assuming that withdrawal from God-talk will lead to a more inclusive and authentic series of theological claims. Where can we find any warrant for such an affirmation? Any such supposition itself involves and implies theological claims —and from where are these to come, if not from our irredeemably patriarchal Christian resources?

---

7.   I should add that I have drawn on the argumentation of this article (as a particularly insightful and lucid—if also highly problematic—source of feminist theological argumentation) at several points in this chapter.

Second, if old untraditional images, tested images, and new images are together going to lead us (apophatically) into the Mystery who is God, the question emerges: how do we distinguish between the Mystery that is God and our own subjective mystification, that is, our own speechlessness and thus 'thoughtlessness' vis-à-vis the Transcendent? And does this not risk theological projection of another and equally invalid form? In short, it is difficult to see how there can be any theological neutrality and, indeed, how we could conceivably opt out of our theological language-games conceived as the 'given' semantic rules of God-talk and continue to 'do and think' theology.

Third, there is an important qualitative distinction between absolutizing human mystery (or mystification), on the one hand, and affirming, in the tradition of the *Christian* mystics, a proper stress on the Mystery of God, on the other. And what it is *imperative* to appreciate here is that the former can in no sense lead to the religious endorsement of any ethical, moral or liberative agenda whatsoever. The second kind of approach (that is, a proper recognition of the Mystery of God), however, does and can. That is because to recognize God as Mystery is to recognize that God's actions and initiatives are grounded in God's own self and are thus neither calculable nor predictable nor predeterminable independently of, or in advance of, God and God's own initiative. Furthermore, to recognize God as Mystery is to recognize that God's being and purposes are only recognizable and affirmable in and through the concrete elevating and reconciling presence of God and not on the grounds of the furniture of the universe or creaturely supposition. To affirm God as Mystery is to affirm that God exists in God's own space and does not naturally inhabit ours. It is to affirm that any coinciding of the two is grounded in the space in which God freely determines to be and emphatically cannot, therefore, be grounded in our own creaturely imaginations or 'spiritual' capacities. To recognize God as Mystery is to recognize that we cannot 'divine' God! In sum, the enthusiasm for the mystical in much contemporary feminism, as in much liberal Protestantism and modernist Catholicism, reposes pre-cisely in a series of *a priori* determinations as to the way God can and cannot be and which, given the modification and adaptation of the Gospel to which this leads, may be argued, ironically, to be much too vocal at a point when a proper silence is what is required! As Bonhoeffer makes so clear in his lectures on Christology, silence before the Absolute means methodological silence before the anti-logos and thus the willingness to allow God's self-disclosure radically to revise all our prior predeterminations vis-à-vis what is and is not possible for God and his dealings with humanity.[8]

Fourth, if the way forward is the selection and creation of new images (perhaps in the tradition of the Minneapolis Conference), then we simply cannot avoid the obvious question: what is to serve as the objective warrant for (or, put negatively, the *critical control* upon) the selective process? How are we to conceive of the theological *impetus* for such a process? What is going to determine which images are appropriate to God and which not? Who is to say, for example, that Calvinistic metaphors of an absolute divine power or will are not to be controlling metaphors in the emergence of new images—God imaged as an omnipotent Rambo, perhaps! And who is to say that pantheistic images of radical divine helplessness and universal, infinitely impersonal process, are not to be preferred?

Clearly, the 'state of play' of our God-talk (and God-thought) cannot *itself* function as the criterion—as this would give rise to a regressive circularity. And, clearly, it cannot be the case that the emerging images themselves will 'lead us into the Mystery who is God' *off their own bat—* as seems to be implied in the article cited! Any such suggestion would imply a highly complex explanation including a whole variety of express claims about the nature of God and revelation—and we would then be required to ask where these came from.

One of the most common responses to this question is that it is 'experience' which constitutes both the warrant and the critical control here. But then again, as liberation and womanist theologians ask, 'Whose experience?'—that of the rich, the poor, women, men, the rulers, or the ruled, traditional Afrikaners or oppressed blacks, WCC committee members or solitary, voiceless and ecclesially marginalized male academics like myself?! What gives one person's experience any more or any less theological validity or veracity than anyone else's?[9] Furthermore, as every good Kantian and Wittgensteinian knows, experience is always *interpreted* experience, and moreover semantically conditioned experience. What I am asking, therefore, is whether there are controls on the semantic process that are anything other than arbitrary and which can usefully warrant the introduction of the term 'God' into liberated and liberative contemporary existence. What is left unclear is how the above

---

8. Cf. Bonhoeffer's 'Introduction' to his *Christology* (1978).
9. There is little that is more frustrating than the attitude of those who emphasize the role of 'experience' in theology and yet regard the experience of certain groups both within and outside the church as counting for nothing!

all-too-popular and widespread kinds of options can offer any kind of solution at all.

In short, it is difficult to see how the combination of semantic agnosticism with a reimagining or reimaging process does not lead to the arbitrary and uncontrolled creation of a god or gods who can no more affirm human beings (be they oppressed women or the victims of other forms of injustice) or endorse *ethical* principles than can some arbitrarily chosen and named 'cuddly toy' whom we determine to regard as transcendent and identity-affirming but which we know all along to be an hypostatized (semantic) construct or imaginative projection which is absent from our world in all the respects that might impinge on the existential struggles and dilemmas which characterize our lives.

The underlying problem here is one which is facing postmodernist theologies in general and is supremely illustrated by Lloyd Geering's lengthy book, *Tomorrow's God* (1994). Geering argues (following Rorty, Cupitt and others) that the world in which we live is essentially a product of our own making, and hence that it is we ourselves who supply its meaning. 'God' (in inverted commas), while being a central symbol of meaning, is entirely a human creation. The absurdity of this is then exposed in the exhortations to which Geering goes on to give voice, namely, that we must consciously create *new* meaning for our lives and that we must care for the earth, in addition to the observations he makes; namely, that new systems of meaning can only evolve out of our cultural past, and that the Christian tradition may lead towards a new world of meaning. Why 'absurd'? Because all these claims and imperatives *presuppose* a system of meaning—including the exhortation that we must consciously create new meanings for our lives.

The ethical dilemmas associated with such an approach are obvious. To affirm, for example, that child abuse is immoral and should be met with zero tolerance implies that there are grounds for this imperative. If the abuser asks 'Why not indulge my desires?' it is clearly inappropriate to respond, 'because we have decided to create a system of meaning within which child abuse, the annihilation of Jews and wearing tartan socks in public are ruled inadmissible'. In short, the potential abuser would be unlikely to feel the force of the imperative. If one were to reply that its force was tradition-specific and located exclusively within the community of one's contemporary postmodernist friends, the abuser could only interpret this as permissive encouragement!

To reiterate, Geering's argument that we create systems of meaning itself presupposes a system of meaning. And the system of meaning which underlies what he is advocating suggests that there *is* no real objective warrant, no ultimate reason, for valuing women or human beings whatsoever. In sum, reference to God and Humpty Dumpty's semantics in *Alice in Wonderland* become ethically synonymous and theology can have no more bearing on the oppression of women than Enid Blyton on the liberation of men.

Whereas Christian ethics has traditionally been grounded in the perception that women and men were created in the image of God, to reflect and to correspond to God's unconditional covenantal endorsement of humanity, we now find ourselves trying to reconcile two apparently inconsistent arguments. First, God has been oppressively created in the human image as a divine correspondent to an imaged *male* form and this should be rejected. Second, creating 'God' in our image is precisely what we should now be advocating! We are, moreover, justified in doing this to the extent that we elect to deem ourselves warranted in doing so. We ought simply to create whatever new systems of theological meaning that we find affirming of our identities—indigenous, female, male, and so on—and then adopt them!

This is nothing less than the *reductio ad absurdum* of the Western emphasis on the creativity of the human subject-self combined with a relativistic ethical pragmatism. The conclusion destroys any connection between the self and truth and value and must, therefore, be judged, (ironically, given its ethical pragmatism) to be normatively useless. The only potential ethical outcome of the universal acceptance of such thinking is social fragmentation into a mirage of non-identities.[10] The bankruptcy of such alternatives simply brings us back to our earlier question: can Christian theology offer a way forward that addresses the problems and handles the challenges raised by the profoundly valid feminist concerns I articulated at the start of this essay?

Is there a Genuinely Theological Alternative?

If Christian theologians are to argue that the Gospel offers ethical grounds and warrant, can it do so in such a way that the very form and, indeed,

---

10. As the etymology of the word 'identity' (from *is, ea, id* and *ens*) suggests, an 'identity' is something with particular being, that is, with specific, objective, given, ontological status.

existence of its God-talk is not itself ethically unacceptable? Space does not allow us to do any more than offer a series of theses:

(1) The central affirmation of the Christian faith is not the *inlibration* of the word (the divine word did not become a book) but the *incarnation* of the word (the divine word became a human being). Revelation is not of God's will or purposes or laws but of *God*, of God's being recognized as a once and for all being-in-becoming in Christ, a being-in-act. Revelation is an event of God's reconciling and reschematizing of our minds, our thought-forms, our apperceptions, our orientations and motivations (the μὴ συσχηματίζεσθε τῷ αἰῶνι τούτῳ, ἀλλὰ μεταμορφοῖσθε τῇ ἀνακαινώσει τοῦ νοός of Rom. 12.2) so that we might be brought into communion with God as persons and by the Spirit *in Christ*. Consequently, words only proclaim in so far as they witness to, bear testimony to, and serve the incarnation of the one self-disclosing word. To repudiate that is to repudiate the whole ground and grammar of the Christian Bible.[11]

The event of revelation, therefore, *is* the event of the creation of the new humanity in the second Adam, the one true image of God—the fulfilment of God's creative purposes in and through a communion of mind with God by the Spirit, for which the first Adam was created but which is realized in the last Adam. There is no separation, therefore, between God's revealing Godself to us and our being ἐν Χριστῷ. To be in Christ *is to be in the Word*; it is to be reconciled into epistemic and thus semantic communion with God.

(2) This does not mean that Jesus simply becomes some kind of Christic filter of our terms. It means that God-talk is to be regarded in *itself* as a form of participation in him. As such, this involves a semantic shift in the meanings of our terms, what Eberhard Jüngel has described as a commandeering of our language. There takes place what might be termed a process of semantic reconciliation.[12] Far from meaning that the explicit focal content of our terms must become *apparently* inclusive, it means something much more profound, namely, that the whole nature of our semantic participation in the language community, the *rhemata*, the speech-acts of the Body of Christ, *must* be inclusive if it is to be a participation in the one in whom there is neither Jew nor Gentile (Gal. 3.28).

That this was grasped by the early church is reflected in the remarkable account of the process of the claiming and redeeming of our language to

11. Cf. Watson 1994 and 1997. For an extended discussion see A.J. Torrance 1996.
12. Jüngel 1976: 12. See also the extremely important discussion of theological language by Karl Barth (1975: 339).

be found in Mt. 23.8-12. In that passage Jesus himself anticipates and
takes up precisely the feminist concerns about the ethical ramifications of
semantic continuity.[13] In this passage Jesus is concerned about oppressive
and hierarchical forms of teaching that burden and oppress their subjects
while serving vested interests. The Rabbis were securing and preserving
their status by the exclusive appropriation of the language of authority—
referring to themselves as 'Rabbis' or 'Teachers'. Jesus' response is simple
and radical. Such language is to be used of no one but the Christ. There is
only one who may be called 'Rabbi' and only one who may be called
'Teacher'.

Moreover, he does not stop with the language of 'Teacher' or 'Master'
but considers also the language of Fatherhood. Why? Because to use the
same conceptuality simultaneously in both the human and the divine
contexts would clearly have the effect of serving patriarchal or hierarchical oppression and undermining the inclusive egalitarianism he is advocating. What immediately becomes apparent is that there are two solutions
to the ethical dilemma of using the same term in both the divine and
human contexts. We can refuse to use terms of God which are simultaneously and selectively applied to humans, or we can stop applying to
humans terms which are 'claimed' for God. Much contemporary feminism
has opted for the former route. It has sought to undermine any apparent
divine endorsement of patriarchy (through the subliminal linkage of human and divine fatherhood) that might attend the utilization of the human
term 'father' with respect to God. Jesus, by contrast, can now be seen to
act out of a parallel concern in his concern for the inclusive egalitarianism
of the kingdom. This he does, however, by taking the alternative, second
route. Instead of suggesting that we continue to use the term 'father' in the
human context but cease using it of God, he proposes that the term should
be reserved exclusively for God and should no longer be used in the
human context. 'And do not call anyone on earth "Father", for you have
one Father and he is in heaven' (v. 9). Taken at its most literal this suggests that, at least within the Body, we are to regard ourselves and each
other as siblings under God, that is, as equal under God and in such a way
that our inter-relatedness as participants in the Body should be defined first
and foremost in terms of our sharing the one heavenly 'Father'.

In sum, Jesus' approach anticipates that of contemporary feminism
here—there should be no application of the same language both to God

---

13. It was my father, James B. Torrance, who drew my attention to the significance for
these issues of Mt. 23; see his 1996: 88-89. I discuss this same proposal in 1997: 119-20.

and humanity in such a way as to risk endorsing human hierarchies and the oppression that can attend these. All terminology with the potential to take on a hierarchical and oppressive function within the sinful human context is excluded from the community of faith and reserved exclusively for God and the one known as 'the Christ'. Far from taking the 'language-less' route or the re-imaging route which makes the human subject the control on God-talk—neither of which ultimately generates any endorsement of inclusivism—Jesus takes another route and for reasons that become clear!

We are now left with a further question. In reserving the term 'Father' for God, is Jesus suggesting that we should interpret God in hierarchical terms and project oppressive patriarchal interpretations of power and linear management on to God and the Christ? Quite the reverse! Peter, we discover, thought that divine authority did and should function in precisely this way and was consequently incensed and angry when Jesus suggested that, as the Messiah, he must suffer. Jesus' reaction is unambiguous. Peter is rebuked in the strongest possible terms. Indeed, Jesus suggests that the hierarchical views underlying his expectations are nothing less than demonic! (cf. Mk 8.33). Jesus then goes on to redefine the content and significance of those terms which he has reserved for God in more profoundly inclusive ways than anyone could have anticipated. What ensues is the radical reinterpretation by the incarnate Logos of the whole nature and character of God's reign and, simultaneously, the nature and role of the one for whom the words 'Rabbi' and 'Teacher' are reserved. The true teacher, the true Rabbi, takes the form of a servant and goes to the cross. In doing so, God's reign is redefined in terms of the self-giving love of the one who alone is to be called 'Father'. As I once heard Jürgen Moltmann comment, the whole story of Christ takes the patriarchy out of fatherhood. The patriarchal traditions of the Old Testament are thus transformed in their fulfilment and fulfilled in and through their radical transformation. The prophet is the Word made flesh. The teacher is the one come among us as Immanuel. The king is the suffering servant. The priest that slaughters the sacrificial offerings is the lamb slain for the world.

What we have is neither cultural religion nor anti-cultural religion; neither a divinization of indigenous religious God-talk nor an isolationist mysticism and repudiation of God-talk; neither fundamentalist identification of truth with verbal formulations nor the agnosticism of so-called postmodernist theologies. What we have, in the incarnation of the word, is cultural conversion, semantic reconciliation and cognitive reorientation and reschematization. And not one of these can happen without the other.

To perceive this the key metaphors in the Gospels need to recover their metaphorical force—we are given eyes to see, ears to hear, reborn from above, and so on. In sum, the New Creation in the Last Adam takes the form of nothing short of an all-embracing *metanoia* (semantic, cognitive, cultural, religious) constituting a new and radically inclusive humanity, a new creation created for the sake of God's all-inclusive purposes of communion.

Does this mean that 'father' can no longer be used of human beings? Only *per prius et posterius*, to use Aquinas's expression, acknowledging the priority of its new-found reference in God and the posteriority of any human application. This means that it can never be used 'properly' of human beings this side of the *eschaton*. Moreover, were it to be used *properly* of human beings in its commandeered form, it is now clear that it could no longer refer exclusively to male parents.

Images and Imaginings

So what do we say with regard to the whole question of imaging or re-imaging God? At one level, we must say that our thinking is attended by all sorts of psychological events, pictures, associations of ideas, and so on—some of these will be more appropriate, some less so, and some again, radically inappropriate. One response is to point to the fact that scientific thought, though brimming with metaphors, strives to be imageless—scientific advance would be frustrated if we set out to image or imagine in some visualistic manner relativity or electric fields or light waves despite the fact that when we first use these words there may be associated psychological imaging processes of one kind or another. As the scientist's work advances, these imagings or imaginings will be revised and fall away, becoming increasingly transparent or perhaps *translucent* so that the reality to which they point may increasingly come to be interpreted out of itself and in its own light.[14]

The means of this liberative process by which the mind is set free from imaging processes which can only eclipse God is not, however, a self-conscious attempt to think in image-free ways. To seek to remove associated and associative images from one's mind by an introspective or introverted act is clearly impossible and, theologically, could generate a

---

14. Cf. Martin Heidegger's analysis of phenomenology by way of analysis of the etymology of the Greek words *phos* (cf. p. 51) and *aletheia* (cf. pp. 56-57) in 1962: 51-57.

form of psychological 'works-righteousness'. Rather, liberation from the tyranny of imaging takes place in and through the reconciling of our attempts to image and imagine by the One who alone constitutes the true image of the Father—the single control on all our analogies, metaphors and similes.

In his book, *Gottes Sein ist im Werden* (*God's Being Is in Becoming*), Eberhard Jüngel discusses the difference between illustration and interpretation (1976: 12-13). In *interpretation* the intentional object of focus is that to which one is bearing witness. Interpretation is the attempt to allow it to show itself forth, to interpret itself on its own grounds. In *illustration* one seeks, by contrast, to focus away from the object to an image or a model or a simile—to view it in place of the reality imaged. For Jüngel, the whole Trinitarian dynamic of interpretation (what I am terming 'semantic participation') means a liberation from conscious imaging to an event of communion not with concepts, ideas, pictures, or even models, but with God in Christ and through the Spirit. Here the *informing* (and hence *re-forming*) of our minds is mediated by humble witness to the One who is the criterion and warrant for all our interpretative (as opposed to illustrative) devices, associative ideas, metaphors, liturgies and analogies.

Conclusion

At the beginning of my chapter I raised the question of semantic continuity between the divine and human contextualities. I suggested that the traditional problem of God-talk focused on the metaphysical issues concerning the continuity between the divine and the human, that is, the problem of analogy. I then distinguished this debate from a more recent series of concerns relating to the ethical problems associated with continuity, as highlighted by the so-called feminist debates. Now we see that there can be no dichotomy between these.

As Athanasius showed so long ago and with such clarity, non-mythological talk about God (*theologein* as opposed to *muthologein*), that is, God-talk which actually refers to God (*analogein*), finds its warrant in the incarnation of the word and the ecclesial presence of the Spirit who reconciles our minds to know and to recognize that word. God is all three. God is known as God in the word and by God, that is, through the Holy Spirit.[15] What clearly ensues from this is that the reconciliation of our

15. Cf. T.F. Torrance's discussion of Athanasius in 'The Logic and Analogic of Biblical and Theological Statements in the Greek Fathers' (1965: ch. 2).

minds, by the Spirit, in Christ, is inseparable from our participation in that semantic community, that speaking, language-using community, which is the body of Christ. Moreover, the speaking to be found here is not speaking for speaking's sake, for mere information's sake, so that we might eat of the tree of knowledge. Rather, it is speaking in, through and for an event of communion with and, indeed, within the triune life of God. This speaking is thus *for the sake of communion*—for the sake of participation in God's all-inclusive purposes.

What all this makes clear is that there is, and can be, *no dichotomy* between the philosophical or metaphysical issues and the ethical issues: both are simultaneously and identically addressed in an event of communion by grace. The ultimate and final warrant for God-talk is the personal, triune presence of God opened for us through the incarnate Christ who simultaneously constitutes the warrant and impetus for inclusive, ethical praxis—and that includes semantic praxis. So when Paul characterized participation in the body of Christ as ἀληθεύοντες...ἐν ἀγάπη, as 'being true in love' (Eph. 4.15a) or (following BAGD: 36) being truthful 'in such a way that the spirit of love is maintained', the implication is that we are *to be true in a manner which integrates all our acting, thinking, speaking and behaving*. Nowhere is the grammar of this communicated more succinctly than in John's Gospel where, in his great high priestly prayer, Jesus integrates the two continuity questions by addressing the nature of God-talk and also its ethical purpose: 'I have revealed you to those whom you gave me out of the world... I gave them the *rhemata* [i.e. speech/ language games] you gave me and they accepted them' (Jn 17.8). And as to the purpose of this Trinitarian, semantic participation: 'I have made you known to them, and will continue to make you known, in order that the *agape* with which you love me may be in them and that I myself may be in them' (Jn 17.26).

In Jesus' mission of a radical and all-inclusive communion, he created, grounded and 'schematized' semantic continuity between God and humanity providing *in himself* the condition for this (cf. Kierkegaard's *Philosophical Fragments*). He did this, moreover, in and through a profoundly inclusive and otherwise inconceivable event of communion—communion, that is, whose warrant reposes nowhere else than in that triune communion constitutive of the very being of God.

Intrinsic to this event of communion—to the extent that it includes and reconstitutes us—is to be found our participation in that radically inclusive, reschematized *rhemata* in and through which Jesus gives his disciples to participate within his body, and in and through which he defines its life in the world. Such a model is more radically and, indeed, semantically inclusive than could be warranted by any secular, modernist, postmodernist, or mystical feminist agenda, for every time we pray, 'Thy Kingdom come', we pray that we might be servants of the realization of this radically inclusive *rhemata* or speech.

BIBLIOGRAPHY

Adorno, T.
    1994   *Minima Moralia* (London: Verso).
Ammerman, Nancy Tatom
    1987   *Bible Believers: Fundamentalists in the Modern World* (New Brunswick: Rutgers University Press).
Ansell, Nicholas
    1994   *The Woman Will Overcome the Warrior* (New York: University of America Press).
Anson, John
    1974   'The Female Transvestite in Early Monasticism: The Origins and Development of a Motif', *Viator: Medieval and Renaissance Studies* 5: 1-22.
Aronowitz, Stanley
    1995   'My Masculinity', in Berger *et al.* 1995: 307-20.
Augustine
    1972   *Concerning the City of God Against the Pagans* (trans. H. Bettenson; Harmondsworth: Penguin Books).
Barclay, John M.G.
    1987   'Mirror-Reading a Polemical Letter: Galatians as a Test Case', *JSNT* 31: 73-93.
Barth, Karl
    1958   *Church Dogmatics. Part Three: The Doctrine of Creation, Volume One* (trans. G.W. Bromiley; Edinburgh: T. & T. Clark).
    1959   *From Rousseau to Ritschl* (trans. B. Cozens and H.H. Hartwell from 11 chapters of *Die Protestantische Theologie im 19. Jahrhundert*; London: SCM Press [German edn, 1952]).
    1960a   *Church Dogmatics. Part Three: The Doctrine of Creation, Volume Two* (trans. Harold Knight *et al.*; Edinburgh: T. & T. Clark).
    1960b   *Church Dogmatics. Part Three: The Doctrine of Creation, Volume Three* (trans. G.W. Bromiley and J. Ehrlich; Edinburgh: T. & T. Clark).
    1961   *Church Dogmatics. Part Three: The Doctrine of Creation, Volume Four* (ed. and trans. G.W. Bromiley and T.F. Torrance; Edinburgh: T. & T. Clark).
    1975   *Church Dogmatics. Part One: The Doctrine of the Word of God, Volume One* (rev. and trans. G.W. Bromiley and T.F. Torrance; Edinburgh: T. & T. Clark).
Baumann, H.
    1955   *Das doppelte Geschlecht* (Berlin: D. Reimer).
Beauvoir, Simone de
    1952   *The Second Sex* (trans. H.M. Parshley; New York: Vintage).

Bedale, S.
1954   'The Meaning of κεφαλή in the Pauline Epistles', *Journal of Theological Studies* 5: 211-15.
Bem, S. L.
1993   *The Lenses of Gender: Transforming the Debate on Sexual Identity* (London: Yale University Press).
Benhabib, Seyla
1992   *Situating the Self: Gender, Community and Postmodernism in Contemporary Ethics* (Cambridge: Polity Press).
Bennett, Enid
1988   'Sisterstory: Women as Saviour', in *With Heads Uncovered* (Auckland: Women in Ministry Network).
Berger, M., *et al.* (eds.)
1995   *Constructing Masculinity* (New York: Routledge).
Bergin, Helen, Judith McKinlay and Sarah Mitchell
1990   'Sexism Ancient and Modern: Turning the Male World Upside Down', *Pacifica* 3: 151-71.
Best, Ernest
1955   *One Body in Christ: A Study in the Relationship of the Church to Christ in the Epistles of the Apostle Paul* (London: SPCK).
Betz, Hans Dieter
1979   *Galatians: A Commentary on Paul's Letter to the Churches in Galatia* (Hermeneia; Philadelphia: Fortress Press).
1995   'Transferring a Ritual: Paul's Interpretation of Baptism in Romans 6', in T. Engberg-Pedersen (ed.), *Paul in his Hellenistic Context* (Minneapolis: Fortress Press): 84-118.
Bird, Phyllis A.
1981   'Male and Female He Created Them: Gen. 1.27b in the Context of the Priestly Account of Creation', *Harvard Theological Review* 74: 129-59.
1991   'Sexual Differentiation and Divine Image in the Genesis Creation Texts', in Kari Elisabeth Børresen (ed.), *Image of God and Gender Models in Judaeo-Christian Tradition* (Oslo: Solum Forlag): 11-34.
Birnbaum, Ellen
1996   *The Place of Judaism in Philo's Thought: Israel, Jews and Proselytes* (Atlanta: Scholars Press).
Bonhoeffer, Dietrich
1978   *Lectures on Christology* (trans. Edwin Robertson; London: Fount Paperbacks).
Bouttier, Michel
1976   'Complexio Oppositorum: Sur les formules de 1 Cor xii.13; Gal iii.26-28; Col iii.10.11', *NTS* 23: 1-19.
Boyarin, Daniel
1994   *A Radical Jew: Paul and the Politics of Identity* (Los Angeles: University of California).
Brock, Rita N.
1988   *Journeys by Heart: A Christology of Erotic Power* (New York: Crossroad).
Bruce, F.F.
1982   *Commentary on Galatians* (Grand Rapids: Eerdmans).

Buckley, Michael
    1987   *At the Origins of Modern Atheism* (New Haven, CT: Yale University Press).
Bullough, Vern, and Bonnie Bullough
    1993   *Cross Dressing, Sex and Gender* (Philadelphia: University of Pennsylvania
                Press).
Burton, Ernest de Witt
    1962   *A Critical and Exegetical Commentary on the Epistle to the Galatians* (ICC;
                Edinburgh: T. & T Clark).
Campbell, D.A.
    1992   *The Rhetoric of Righteousness in Romans 3.21-26* (JSNTSup, 65; Sheffield:
                JSOT Press).
    1996   'Unravelling Colossians 3.11b', *NTS* 42: 120-32.
    1997   'The Logic of Eschatology: The Implications of Paul's Gospel for Gender as
                Suggested by Galatians 3.28a in Context', paper presented to 'The Gospel
                and Gender', a conference held at King's College London, London (October,
                1997); and to the New Testament doctoral seminar, KCL (March, 1998).
    1998   'The ΔΙΑΘΗΚΗ from Durham: Professor Dunn's *The Theology of Paul the
                Apostle*', *JSNT* 72: 91-111.
Campbell, W.S.
    1991   *Paul's Gospel in an Inter-cultural Context: Jew and Gentile in the Letter to
                the Romans* (SIGC, 69; Frankfurt-am-Main: Lang).
Cartledge, Paul
    1993   *The Greeks: A Portrait of Self and Others* (Oxford: Oxford University Press).
Chanter, Tina
    1995   *Ethics of Eros: Irigaray's Rewriting of the Philosophers* (London: Routledge).
Christ, Carol P.
    1992   'Why Women Need to Goddess: Phenomenological, Psychological, and
                Political Reflections', in Christ and Plaskow 1992: 273-87.
Christ, Carol P., and Judith Plaskow (eds.)
    1992   *Womanspirit Rising: A Feminist Reader in Religion* (San Francisco: Harper):
                2-17 ('Introduction: Womanspirit Rising').
Clark, Elizabeth A.
    1986   'Ascetic Renunciation and Feminine Advancement: A Paradox of Late
                Ancient Christianity', in *Ascetic Piety and Women's Faith: Essays in Late
                Ancient Christianity* (New York: Edwin Mellen Press): 175-208.
Clark-King, Ellen
    2003   *Sacred Hearts: Feminist Theology Interrogated by the Voices of Working-
                Class Women* (Doctoral thesis, Lancaster University).
Coakley, Sarah
    1995   'Creaturehood before God: Male and Female', in R. Gill (ed.), *Readings in
                Modern Theology* (London: SPCK).
Collingwood, R.G.
    1948   *Essay on Metaphysics* (Oxford: Clarendon Press).
Conzelmann, Hans
    1975   *1 Corinthians: A Commentary on the First Epistle to the Corinthians* (Phila-
                delphia: Fortress Press).
Cope, Lamar
    1978   '1 Cor. 11.2-16: One Step Further', *JBL* 97: 435-36.

Cupitt, Don
    1990   *Creation Out of Nothing* (London: SCM Press).

Daly, Mary
    1973/1986 *Beyond God the Father: Towards a Philosophy of Women's Liberation* (London: Women's Press; Boston: Beacon Press).
    1990   *Gyn Ecology* (Boston: Beacon Press, 2nd edn).

Davies, Stevan
    1980   *The Revolt of the Widows: The Social World of the Apocryphal Acts* (Carbondale: Southern Illinois University).

Davies, W.D.
    1980   *Paul and Rabbinic Judaism* (Philadelphia: Fortress Press, 4th edn [1946]).

Deissmann, G.A.
    1912   *St Paul: A Study in Social and Religious History* (trans. L.R.M. Strachan; London: Hodder & Stoughton, 2nd edn).

Delcourt, Marie
    1958   *Hermaphrodite: Mythes et rites de la bisexualité dans l'antiquité classique* (MR, 36; Paris: Presses universitaire de France).
    1961   *Hermaphrodite: Myths and Rites of the Bisexual figure in Classical Antiquity* (trans. Jennifer Nicholson; London: Studio Books).

Derrida, Jacques
    1976   *Of Grammatology* (Baltimore, MD: The Johns Hopkins University Press).

Deux, K.
    1987   'Psychological Constructions of Masculinity and Femininity', in J.M. Reinisch, L.A. Rosenblum, and S.A. Sanders (eds.), *Masculinity/Femininity: Basic Perspectives* (Oxford: Oxford University Press): 289-303.

Downing, Gerald
    1997   'A Cynic Preparation for Paul's Gospel for Jew and Greek, Slave and Free, Male and Female', *NTS* 42: 454-62.

Driver, Tom F.
    1977   *Patterns of Grace: Human Experience as Word of God* (San Francisco: Harper & Row [repr. University Press of America, 1985]).

Dunn, J.D.G.
    1970   *Baptism in the Holy Spirit: A Re-examination of the New Testament Teaching on the Gift of the Spirit in Relation to Pentecostalism Today* (SBT Second Series, 15; London: SCM Press).
    1980   *Christology in the Making: An Inquiry into the Origins of the Doctrine of the Incarnation* (London: SCM Press).
    1993a   *The Theology of Paul's Letter to the Galatians: New Testament Theology* (Cambridge: Cambridge University Press).
    1993b   *The Epistle to the Galatians* (BNTC; London: A. & C. Black).
    1997   'Once More, ΠΙΣΤΙΣ ΧΡΙΣΤΟΥ', in D.M. Hay and E.E. Johnson (eds.), *Pauline Theology IV* (Atlanta: Scholars Press): 61-81.
    1998   *The Theology of Paul the Apostle* (Grand Rapids: Eerdmans; Edinburgh: T. & T. Clark).

Eckstein, Hans-Joachim
    1996   *Verheißung und Gesetz. Eine exegetische Untersuchung zu Galater 2,15–4,7* (WUNT, 86; Tübingen: Mohr–Siebeck).

Edwards, Felicity
    1995   'Spirituality, Consciousness and Gender Identification: A Neo-feminist
                Perspective', in King 1995: 177-91.
Ehrenreich, Barbara
    1995   'The Decline of Patriarchy', in Berger *et al.* 1995: 284-90.
Elder, C.
    1995   'The Freudian Critique of Religion: Remarks on its Meaning and Con-
                ditions', *JR* 75: 349.
Eliade, Mircea
    1965   *The Two and The One* (trans. J.M. Cohen; Chicago: University of Chicago
                Press).
Elliott, Neil
    1994   *Liberating Paul: The Justice of God and the Politics of the Apostle* (Mary-
                knoll, NY: Orbis).
Fausto-Sterling, Anne
    1995   'How to Build a Man', in Berger *et al.* 1995: 127-34.
Fee, Gordon
    1987   *The First Epistle to the Corinthians* (Grand Rapids: Eerdmans).
Fitzmyer, Joseph A.
    1957–58   'A Feature of Qumran Angelology and the Angels of 1 Cor. XI.10', *NTS* 4:
                48-58.
    1989   'Another Look at *KEPHALE* in 1 Corinthians 11.3', *NTS* 35: 503-10.
    1990   'Letter to the Galatians', in Raymond Brown, Joseph A. Fitzmyer and
                Roland E. Murphy (eds.), *The New Jerome Biblical Commentary* (London:
                Geoffrey Chapman): 787.
Fletcher, Frank
    1988   'Drink from the Wells of Oz: How an Australian Theologian Works at the
                Speciality of Foundations', in *Discovering an Australian Theology* (co-
                ordinated by Peter Malone; Homebush, NSW: St Paul Publications): 59-70.
Fox, M. (ed.)
    1987   *Hildegarde of Bingen's Book of Divine Works and Letters and Songs* (Santa
                Fe: Bean and Co.).
Fulkerson, Mary McClintock
    1994   *Changing the Subject: Women's Discourses and Feminist Theology*
                (Minneapolis: Fortress Press).
Galt, C. M.
    1931   'Veiled Ladies', *AJA* 35: 373-93.
Gatens, Moira
    1996   *Imaginary Bodies: Ethics, Power and Corporeality* (London: Routledge).
Geering, Lloyd
    1994   *Tomorrow's God: How We Create our Worlds* (Wellington: Bridget
                Williams).
Gill, David W.J.
    1990   'The Importance of Roman Portraiture for Head-Coverings in 1 Corinthians
                11.2-16', *TynBul* 41: 245-60.
Gilligan, Carol
    1982   *In a Different Voice* (Cambridge, MA: Harvard University Press).

Goldenberg, Naomi R.
1979   *The Changing of the Gods: Feminism and the End of Traditional Regions* (Boston: Beacon Press).

Goodenough, Erwin
1935   *By Light, Light: The Mystic Gospel of Hellenistic Judaism* (New Haven: Yale University Press).

Graham, Elaine L.
1995a   'Gender, Personhood and Theology', *SJT* 48: 341-58.
1995b   *Making the Difference: Gender, Personhood and Theology* (London: Mowbray).

Grant, Jacquelyn
1989   *White Women's Christ and Black Women's Jesus* (Atlanta: Scholars Press).

Grey, Mary
1989   *Redeeming the Dream: Feminism, Redemption and Christian Tradition* (London: SPCK).

Grosz, Elizabeth
1993   'Irigaray and the Divine', in C.W. Maggie Kim *et al.* (eds.), *Transfigurations: Theology and the French Feminists* (Minneapolis: Fortress Press): 199-214.

Grudem, W.
1985   'Does κεφαλή ['Head'] Mean "Source" or "Authority" in Greek Literature? A Survey of 2,336 Examples', *Trinity Journal* 6: 38-59.

Gundry-Volf, Judith
1994a   'Male and Female in Creation and New Creation: Interpretations of Gal. 3.28c in 1 Corinthians 7', in Moises Silva and Thomas E. Schmidt (eds.), *To Tell the Mystery: Essays on New Testament Eschatology. FS R.H. Gundry* (JSNTSup, 100; Sheffield: JSOT Press): 95-121.
1994b   'Celibate Pneumatics and Social Power: On the Motivations for Sexual Asceticism in Corinth', *Union Seminary Quarterly Rreview* 48: 105-26.
1996   'Controlling the Bodies: A Theological Profile of the Corinthian Sexual Ascetics', in R. Bieringer (ed.), *The Corinthian Correspondence* (BETL, 125; Leuven: Leuven University Press): 499-521.
1997a   'Gender, Identity and Creation in 1 Corinthians 11.2-16: A Study in Paul's Theological Method', in J. Ådna, Scott J. Hafemann and Otfried Hofius (eds.), *Evangelium–Schriftauslegung–Kirche: Festschrift für Peter Stuhlmacher* (Göttingen: Vandenhoeck & Ruprecht): 150-72.
1997b   'Paul on Women and Gender: A Comparison with Early Jewish Views', in Richard N. Longenecker (ed.), *The Road from Damascus: The Impact of Paul's Conversion on his Life, Thought and Ministry* (Grand Rapids: Eerdmans): 195-213.
1997c   'Christ and Gender: A Study of Difference and Equality in Gal 3,28', in C. Landmesser, H-J. Eckstein and H. Lichtenberger (eds.), *Jesus Christus als die Mitte der Schrift: Studien zur Hermeneutik des Evangeliums* (Berlin: W. de Gruyter): 439-77.

Gunton, Colin E.
1985   *Enlightenment and Alienation: An Essay towards Trinitarian Theology* (Basingstoke: Marshall, Morgan and Scott).

Hall, Stuart, David Held and Tony McGrew
    1992   *Modernity and its Futures* (Oxford: Polity Press, in association with the Open University).

Hampson, Daphne
    1990   *Theology and Feminism* (Oxford: Basil Blackwell).
    1996   *After Christianity* (London: SCM Press).

Hampton, S., and K. Llewellyn (eds.)
    1986   *Penguin Book of Australian Women's Poetry* (Ringwood: Penguin Books).

Hand, S. (ed.)
    1993   *The Levinas Reader* (Oxford: Basil Blackwell).

Harvey, Nicholas Peter
    1985   *Death's Gift: Chapters on Resurrection and Bereavement* (London: Epworth Press).
    1991   *The Morals of Jesus* (London: Darton, Longman & Todd).

Haward, Anne
    1990   *From Penelope to Poppaea: Women in Greek and Roman Society* (London: Macmillan).

Hays, Richard B.
    1983   *The Faith of Jesus Christ: An Investigation of the Narrative Substructure of Galatians 3.1-4.11* (SBLDS, 56; Chico, CA: Scholars Press).
    1997   'ΠΙΣΤΙΣ and Pauline Christology: What is at Stake?', in D.M. Hay and E.E. Johnson (eds.), *Pauline Theology IV* (Atlanta: Scholars Press): 35-60.

Heidegger, Martin
    1962   *Being and Time* (trans. John Macquarrie and Edwin Robinson; London: SCM Press).

Heine, Susanne
    1987   *Women and Early Christianity: Are the Feminist Scholars Right?* (London: SCM Press).

Héring, Jean
    1962   *The First Epistle of Saint Paul to the Corinthians* (London: Epworth).

Heyward, Carter
    1982   *The Redemption of God: A Theology of Mutual Relations* (Washington, DC: University of America Press).

Hofius, Otfried
    1989   *Paulusstudien* (WUNT, 51; Tübingen: Mohr–Siebeck).
    1994   'Glaube und Taufe nach dem Zeugnis des Neuen Testaments', *ZTK* 91: 134-56.

Hogan, Linda
    1995   *From Women's Experience to Feminist Theology* (Sheffield: Sheffield Academic Press).

Hooker, Morna D.
    1963–64   'Authority on her Head: An Examination of 1 Cor. XI.10', *NTS* 10: 410-16.

Irigaray, Luce
    1985   *This Sex Which Is Not One* (trans. C. Porter with C. Burke; Ithaca, NY: Cornell University Press).
    1986   *Divine Women* (trans. Stephen Muecke; Sydney: Local Consumption Publications).
    1989   'Equal to Whom?', *differences* 1: 59-76.

1996   *I Love to You: Sketch for a Felicity Within History* (trans. Alison Martin; New York: Routledge).

Isherwood, Lisa, and Dorothea McEwan
1993   *Introducing Feminist Theology* (Sheffield: Sheffield Academic Press).

Janowski, J. Christine
1995   'Zur paradigmatischen Bedeutung der Geschlechterdifferenz in K. Barths "Kirchlicher Dogmatik"', *Marburger Jahrbuch Theologie* 7: 13-60.

Jantzen, Grace
1996   'The Gendered Politics of Flourishing and Salvation', in U. Brummer and M. Sarot (eds.), *Happiness, Well Being, and the Meaning of Life* (Amsterdam: Pharos).

Jeanrond, W. (ed.)
1991   *Theological Hermeneutics: Development and Significance* (New York: Crossroad).

Jewett, Paul K., and Marguerite Shuster
1991   *God, Creation, and Revelation: A Neo-Evangelical Theology* (Grand Rapids: Eerdmans).

Jewett, R.
1979   'The Sexual Liberation of the Apostle Paul', *JAAR/Supp* 47.1: 55-87.

Johnson, Elizabeth A.
1993   *She Who Is: The Mystery of God in Feminist Theological Discourse* (New York: Crossroad).

Jones, Serene
1993   'This God Which Is Not One: Irigaray and Barth on the Divine', in C.W. Maggie Kim *et al.* (eds.), *Transfigurations: Theology and the French Feminists* (Minneapolis: Fortress Press): 109-41.

Joy, M.
1994   'Sainthood or Heresy: Contemporary Options for Women', in M. Joy and P. Magee (eds.), *Claiming our Rites: Studies in Religion by Australian Women Scholars* (Adelaide: Australian Association for the Study of Religion): 117-34.

Jüngel, Eberhard
1976   *The Doctrine of the Trinity: God's Being Is in Becoming* (trans. Horton Harris; Edinburgh: Scottish Academic Press).

Kahl, Brigitte
2000   'No Longer Male: Masculinity Struggles Behind Galatians 3.28?' *JSNT* 79: 37-49.

Käsemann, Ernst
1960   'Amt und Gemeinde im New Testament', in *idem, Exegetische Versuche und Besinnungen*, I (2 vols.; Göttingen: Vandenhoeck & Ruprecht, 2nd edn): 109-34.
1969   *Paulinische Perspektiven* (Tübingen: Mohr–Siebeck).

Kaufmann, W. (ed.)
1981   *The Portable Nietzsche* (Ringwood: Penguin Books).

Keillor, G.
1994   *The Book of Guys* (New York: Penguin Books).

Kidd, I.G.
1967   'Socrates', in Paul Edwards (ed.), *The Encyclopaedia of Philosophy* (New York: Collier-Macmillan), VII: 484.

Kierkegaard, Søren
  1967   *Philosophical Fragments* (ET David Swenson and Howard Hong; Princeton,
             NJ: Princeton University Press).
King, Ursula
  1995   *Religion and Gender* (Oxford: Basil Blackwell).
Kistemaker, Simon J.
  1993   *1 Corinthians* (Grand Rapids: Baker Books).
Knox, John
  1987   *Chapters in a Life of Paul* (London: SCM Press, rev. edn [1950]).
Kraemer, Ross
  1989   'Ecstasy and Possession: Women of Ancient Greece and the Cult of
             Dionysus', in Nancy Auer Falk and Rita Gross (eds.), *Unspoken Worlds:
             Women's Religious Lives* (Belmont, CA: Wadsworth): 45-55.
  1993   *Her Share of the Blessings: Women's Religions Among Pagans, Jews, and
             Christians in the Greco-Roman World* (Oxford: Oxford University Press).
Kroeger, Catherine Clark, Mary Evans and Elaine Storkey (eds.)
  1997   *New International Version Women's Bible* (London: Hodder & Stoughton).
Kroeger, Richard, and Catherine Kroeger
  1978   'An Inquiry into the Evidence of Maenadism in the Corinthian Congre-
             gation', in P.J. Achtemeier (ed.), *Society of Biblical Literature Seminar
             Papers 1978* (2 vols.; Missoula, MT: Scholars Press): II, 331-38.
Kürzinger, Josef
  1978   'Frau und Man nach 1 Kor 11,11f', *BZ* 22: 270-75.
LaCugna, Catherine Mowry
  1993   'God in Communion With Us: The Trinity', in Catherine Mowry LaCugna
             (ed.), *Freeing Theology: The Essentials of Theology in Feminist Perspective*
             (San Francisco: Harper): 83-114.
Lan, Kwok Pui
  1993   'Re-imagining Jesus' (paper presented at the Minneapolis Convention
             Centre, 5 November 1993).
Lee, Desmond (trans.)
  1955   *Plato: The Republic* (Harmondsworth: Penguin Classics).
Levinas, E.
  1995   'The Jewish Understanding of Scripture', *Cross Currents* 46: 492.
Libreria delle donne di Milano
  1989   *Wie Weibliche Freiheit Entsteht: Eine Politische Praxis* (trans. T. Sattler;
             Berlin: Orlanda Fraenverlag).
Liddell, H.G., R. Scott and H.S. Jones
  1968   *A Greek-English Lexicon* (Oxford: Clarendon Press, 9th edn with suppl.).
Lietzmann, H.
  1932   *An die Galater* (HNT, 10; Tübingen: Mohr–Siebeck, 3rd edn).
Lincoln, Andrew
  1990   *Ephesians* (WBC, 42; Dallas, TX: Word Books).
Litke, W.
  1995   'Beyond Creation: Galatians 3.28, Genesis and the Hermaphrodite Myth', *SR*
             24: 173-78.
Llewelyn, John
  1986   *Derrida on the Threshold of Sense* (Basingstoke: Macmillan).

Lloyd, G.
1993   'Maleness, Metaphor and the "Crisis" of Reason', in Louise Antony and
            Charlotte Witt (eds.), *A Mind of One's Own: Feminist Essays on Reason and
            Objectivity* (Oxford: Westview Press): 69-85.
Longenecker, Richard N.
1990   *Galatians* (WBC, 41; Dallas, TX: Word Books).
Luedemann, Gerd
1984   *Paul, Apostle to the Gentiles: Studies in Chronology* (trans. F.S. Jones;
            Philadelphia: Fortress Press [1980]).
1989   *Opposition to Paul in Jewish Christianity* (trans. M.E. Boring; Minneapolis:
            Fortress Press [1983]).
Lührmann, D.
1975   'Wo man nicht mehr Sklave oder Freier ist: Uberlegungen zur Struktur
            frühchristliche Gemeinden', *Wort und Dienst* 13: 53-83.
MacDonald. D.R.
1987   *There Is No Male and Female: The Fate of a Dominical Saying in Paul and
            Gnosticism* (Philadelphia: Fortress Press).
Marion, J.L.
1995   *God Without Being* (Chicago: Chicago University Press).
Martin, Dale
1998   'The Life and Times of Galatians 3.28: "No Male and Female" ' (un-
            published paper, delivered on 15 September 1998).
Martyn, J. Louis
1985   'Apocalyptic Antinomies in Paul's Letter to the Galatians', *NTS* 31: 410-24.
1997a   *Galatians* (London and New York: Doubleday).
1997b   *Theological Issues in the Letters of Paul* (Edinburgh: T. & T. Clark;
            Nashville: Abingdon Press).
McDonald, Celia
1998   'Feminist Proposals for Salvation without a Saviour' (unpublished paper
            presented at King's College London, London).
McNamara, Jo Ann
1983   *A New Song: Celibate Women in the First Three Christian Centuries* (New
            York: Haworth Press).
Meeks, Wayne
1973–74   'The Image of the Androgyne: Some Uses of a Symbol in Earliest
            Christianity', *Journal of the History of Religions* 13: 165-208.
Merode, Marie de
1978   'Une théologie primitive de la femme?', *RTL* 9: 176-89.
Moi, Toril
1987   *Sexual/Textual Politics: Feminist Literary Theory* (London: Methuen).
Moltmann, Jürgen
1981   *The Trinity and the Kingdom of God: The Doctrine of God* (trans. Margaret
            Kohl; San Fransisco: Harper Collins).
1992   *The Spirit of Life: A Universal Affirmation* (trans. Margaret Kohl; Minnea-
            polis: Fortress Press).
Moltmann-Wendel, Elisabeth
1991   'Is There a Feminist Theology of the Cross?', in Elisabeth Moltmann-Wendel
            and Jürgen Moltmann (eds.), *God: His and Hers* (London: SCM Press): 77-94.
1993   'Christ in Feminist Context', in Hilary Regan and Alan J. Torrance (eds.),

                Christ and Context (Edinburgh: T. & T. Clark): 105-16.
    1995   Die Weiblichkeit des Heiligen Geistes: Studien zur Feministischen Theologie
                (Gütersloh: Kaiser Verlag).
More, Hannah
    1990   Considerations on Religion and Public Education (Augustan Reprint Society
                262; Los Angeles: Wm Andrews Clark Memorial Library [Boston: n.p., 1794]).
Moule, C.F.D.
    1961   Worship in the New Testament (Richmond: John Knox Press).
Murphy-O'Connor, Jerome
    1976   'The Non-Pauline Character of 1 Corinthians 11.2-26?', JBL 95: 615-21.
    1980   'Sex and Logic in 1 Corinthians 11.2-16', CBQ 42: 482-500.
Mussner, F.
    1977   Der Galaterbrief (HTKNT, 9; Freiburg: Herder, 3rd edn).
Neuer, Werner
    1990   Man and Woman in Christian Perspective (trans. Gordon Wenham; London:
                Hodder & Stoughton).
Nietzsche, Friedrich
    1969   Thus Spoke Zarathustra: A Book for Everyone and No One (trans. and intro.
                R.J. Hollingdale; London: Penguin Books).
    1974   The Gay Science with a Prelude in Rhymes and an Appendix of Songs (trans.
                Walter Kaufmann; New York: Vintage Books).
    1990   Twilight of the Idols and the Anti-Christ (trans. R.J. Hollingdale; London:
                Penguin Books).
Oakley, A.
    1972   Sex, Gender, and Society (Aldershot: Gower).
O'Brien, Peter T.
    1982   Colossians, Philemon (WBC, 44; Waco, TX: Word Books).
O'Donovan, Oliver
    1986   Resurrection and the Moral Order: An Outline for Evangelical Ethics
                (Leicester: InterVarsity Press).
Oepke, A.
    1964a   'δύω' [k.t.l.], in TDNT, II, 318-21.
    1964b   'ἐν.', in TDNT, II, 537-43.
    1973   Der Brief des Paulus an die Galater (rev. J. Rohde; Berline: Evangelisches
                Verlaganstalt).
Oster, Richard E.
    1988   'When Men Wore Veils to Worship: The Historical Context of 1 Corinthians
                11.14', NTS 34: 481-505.
Padel, Ruth
    1993   'Women: Model for Possession by Greek Daemons', in Avril Cameron and
                Amélie Kuhrt (eds.), Images of Women in Antiquity (London: Routledge,
                rev. edn): 3-19.
Pannenberg, Wolfhart
    1991   Systematic Theology (trans. Geoffrey W. Bromiley; Grand Rapids: Eerdmans).
Park, Heon-Wook
    1988   Die Vorstellung vom Leib Christi bei Paulus (dissertation, University of
                Tübingen).
Paulsen, H.
    1979–80   'Einheit und Freiheit der Söhne Gottes–Gal. 3.26-27', ZNW 70–71: 74-95.

1980   'ἐνδύω κ.τ.λ', in *EWNT*, I: 1103-105.
Plant, Helen
1996   'The Interaction of Gender and Class in Anglican Evangelical Social and
            Political Thought, c. 1790–1820' (MA essay, Lancaster University).
Plantinga, Alvin
1993   *Warrant and Proper Function* (Oxford: Oxford University Press).
Plantinga Pauw, Amy
1993   'Personhood, Divine and Human', *Perspectives* 8: 12-14.
1996   'Who or What Is the Holy Spirit?', *The Christian Century* 113: 48-51.
Prestige, G.L.
1956   *God in Patristic Thought* (London: SPCK).
Radford Ruether, Rosemary
1974   *Faith and Fratricide: The Theological Roots of Anti-Semitism* (New York:
            Seabury).
1975   *New Woman New Earth: Sexist Ideologies and Human Liberation* (New
            York: Seabury).
1976   'Feminism and Christology', *Occasional Papers* (Board of Higher Education
            and Ministry of the United Methodist Church).
1981   *To Change the World: Christology and Cultural Criticism* (New York:
            Crossroad).
1983   *Sexism and God-Talk: Towards a Feminist Theology* (London: SCM Press;
            Boston: Beacon Press).
1985   'Theology as Critique and Emancipation from Sexism', in T.W. Jennings
            (ed.), *The Vocation of the Theologian* (Philadelphia: Fortress Press).
1996   'Christian Anthropology and Gender: A Tribute to Jürgen Moltmann', in
            Miroslav Volf *et al.* (eds.), *The Future of Theology: Essays in Honor of
            Jürgen Moltmann* (Grand Rapids: Eerdmans): 241-52.
Rahner, K. *et al.* (ed.)
1968   *Sacramentum Mundi: An Encyclopaedia of Theology* (London: Geoffrey
            Chapman).
Ramsey, Paul
1988   'Human Sexuality in the History of Redemption', *JRE* 16.1: 56-86.
Raschke, Carl
1982   'The Deconstruction of God', in Thomas Altizer *et al.* (eds.), *Deconstruction
            and Theology* (New York: Crossroad): 1-33.
Ratzinger, Joseph
1970   *Introduction to Christianity* (trans. J.R. Foster; New York: Herder and Herder).
Regan, H., and A.J. Torrance (eds.)
1993   *Christ and Context* (Edinburgh: T. & T. Clark).
Reynolds, Anne Marie (ed.)
1994   *Julian of Norwich's 'A Showing of Divine Love'* (London: Sheed & Ward).
Ricoeur, P.
1974   *The Conflict of Interpretations* (ed. Don Idhe; Evanston: Northwestern
            University Press).
Riesner, Rainer
1998   *Paul's Early Period: Chronology, Mission Strategy, Theology* (trans. D.
            Stott; Grand Rapids: Eerdmans, 1994).
Rouselle, Aline
1992   'Body Politics in Ancient Rome', in Pauline Schmitt Pantel (ed.), *A History*

of Women: From Ancient Goddesses to Christian Saints (Cambridge, MA: Belknap Press of Harvard University Press): 296-336.

Ryle, Gilbert
1967   'Plato', in Paul Edwards (ed.), *The Encyclopaedia of Philosophy* (New York: Collier-Macmillan), VI: 325.

Saiving, Valerie
1992   'The Human Situation: A Feminist View', in Christ and Plaskow 1992: 25-42 (repr. in *JR* 40 [1960]: 100-112).

Schaef, Anne Wilson
1985   *Women's Reality: An Emerging Female System in a White Male Society* (New York: Harper & Row).

Schlier, H.
1965   *Der Brief an die Galater* (KEK; Göttingen: Vandenhoeck & Ruprecht, 4th edn).

Schottroff, Luise
1993   *Let the Oppressed Go Free: Feminist Perspectives on the New Testament* (Louisville: Westminster/John Knox).

Schrage, W., and E. Gerstenberger
1981   *Woman and Man* (trans. Douglas W. Stott; Nashville: Abingdon Press).

Schüssler Fiorenza, Elisabeth
1983   *In Memory of Her: A Feminist Theological Reconstruction of Christian Origins* (New York: Crossroad; London: SCM Press).
1987   'Rhetorical Situation and Historical Reconstruction in 1 Corinthians', *NTS* 33: 386-403.
1993   *In Memory of Her: A Feminist Theological Reconstruction of Christian Origins* (New York: Crossroad; London: SCM Press, 10th anniversary edn [1983]).
1994a   'The Rhetoricity of Historical Knowledge: Pauline Discourse and its Contextualizations', in Lukas Bornkamm, Kelly Del Tredici and Angela Standhartinger (eds.), *Religious Propaganda and Missionary Competition in the New Testament World: Essays Honoring Dieter Georgi* (Leiden: E.J. Brill): 443-69.
1994b   *Jesus: Miriam's Child, Sophia's Prophet. Critical Issues in Feminist Christology* (London: SCM Press).

Schweizer, E., *et al.*
1971   'σάρξ κ.τ.λ.', in *TDNT*, VII: 98-151.

Scroggs, Robin
1972   'Paul and the Eschatological Woman', *JAAR* 40: 283-303.

Segal, Alan
1990   *Paul the Convert: The Apostolate and Apostasy of Saul the Pharisee* (New Haven: Yale University Press).

Smith, Jane I.
1987   'Islam', in Arvind Sharma (ed.), *Women in World Religions* (Albany, NY: State University of New York Press): 135-66.

Snodgrass, Klyne R.
1986   'Galatians 3.28: Conundrum or Solution?', in Alvera Mickelsen (ed.), *Women, Authority and the Bible* (Downers Grove, IL: InterVarsity Press): 161-81.

Social Affairs Committee of the Assembly of Quebec Bishops
1989   *A Heritage of Violence* (Montreal: n.p.).

Soskice, Janet Martin
  1993   'Response to Elisabeth Moltmann-Wendel's "Christ in Feminist Context"',
              in Hilary Regan and Alan J. Torrance (eds.), *Christ and Context* (Edinburgh:
              T. & T. Clark): 117-22.

Stauffer, E.
  1964   'εἷς', in *TDNT*, II, 434-42.

Stendahl, Krister
  1966   *The Bible and the Role of Women: A Case Study in Hermeneutics* (trans.
              Emilie T. Sander; Philadelphia: Fortress Press).

Stewart, James S.
  1935   *A Man in Christ: The Vital Elements of St. Paul's Religion* (London: Hodder
              & Stoughton).

Stoller, Robert J.
  1968   *Sex and Gender* (London: Hogarth Press).

Storkey, Elaine
  1985   *What's Right with Feminism?* (London: SPCK).
  1994   'Atonement and Feminism', *Anvil* 11: 227-33.
  1995   *The Search for Intimacy* (London: Hodder & Stoughton).
  2000   *Created or Constructed: The Great Gender Debate* (Carlisle: Paternoster
              Press).

Storkey, Elaine, and Margaret Hebblethwaite
  2000   *Conversations on Christian Feminism* (London: Harper-Collins).

Stowers, Stanley K.
  1994   *Rereading Romans: Justice, Jews, and Gentiles* (New Haven, CT: Yale
              University Press).

Tannehill, Robert C.
  1967   *Dying and Rising with Christ: A Study in Pauline Theology* (BZNW, 32;
              Berlin: Alfred Töppelmann).

Taylor, Charles
  1989   *Sources of the Self: The Making of Modern Identity* (Cambridge: Cambridge
              University Press).

Theissen, Gerd
  1974   'Soteriologische Symbolik in den paulinischen Schriften. Ein Strukturalis-
              tischer Beitrag', *KD* 20: 282-304.

Thesleff, Holger
  1965   *The Pythagoraean Texts of the Hellenistic Period* (Aabo: Aabo Akademi).

Thompson, Cynthia L.
  1988   'Hairstyles, Head-coverings, and St. Paul: Portraits from Roman Corinth',
              BA 51: 99-115.

Thurston, Bonnie
  1989   *The Widows: A Women's Ministry in the Early Church* (Minneapolis:
              Fortress Press).

Thyen, H.
  1978   ' "…nicht mehr männlich und weiblich…" Eine studie zu Galater 3.28', in F.
              Crüsemann and H. Thyen (eds.), *Als Mann und Frau geschaffen. Exegetische
              Studien zur Rolle der Frau* (Gelnhausen: Burkardthaus-Verlag): 107-201.

Torrance, Alan J.
  1996   *Persons in Communion: An Essay on Trinitarian Description and Human
              Participation* (Edinburgh: T. & T. Clark).

1997   'Theology and Political Correctness', in Lawrence Osborn and Andrew
            Walker (eds.), *Harmful Religion* (London: SPCK): 119-20.
2001   'Is Love the Essence of God?', in Kevin Vanhoozer (ed.), *Nothing Greater
            Nothing Better: Theological Essays on the Love of God* (Grand Rapids:
            Eerdmans): 114-37.

Torrance, James B.
1996   *Worship, Community and the Triune God of Grace* (Carlisle: Paternoster
            Press).

Torrance, T.F.
1965   *Theology in Reconstruction* (London: SCM Press).

Tredennick, H. (trans.)
1969   *Plato: The Phaedo* (Harmondsworth: Penguin Classics).

Trible, Phyllis
1978   *God and the Rhetoric of Sexuality* (Philadelphia: Fortress Press).

Trompf, G.W.
1980   'Attitudes towards Women in Paul and Paulinist Literature: 1 Cor. 11.3-16
            and its Context', *CBQ* 42: 196-215.

Van der Horst, P.W.
1972–73   'Observations on a Pauline Expression', *NTS* 19: 181-87.

Van Leeuwen, Mary Stewart
1991   *Gender and Grace: Love, Work, and Parenting in a Changing World*
            (Downers Grove, IL: InterVarsity Press).

Vance, Caroline S.
1995   'Social Construction Theory and Sexuality', in Berger *et al.* 1995: 37-48.

Vatican City, The
1976   *Declaration on the Question of the Admission of Women to the Ministerial
            Priesthood* (15 October 1976).

Vellacott, Philip (trans.)
1973   *Euripides, The Bacchae and Other Plays* (Harmondsworth: Penguin Books,
            rev. edn [*The Bacchae* 191-244]).

Volf, Miroslav
1996   *Exclusion and Embrace: A Theological Exploration of Identity, Otherness,
            and Reconciliation* (Nashville: Abingdon Press).
1997   *Trinity and Community: An Ecumenical Ecclesiology* (Grand Rapids:
            Eerdmans).

Völker, Walter
1938   *Fortschritt und Vollendung bei Philo von Alexandrien: Eine Studie zur
            Geschichte der Frömmigkeit* (Leipzig: J.C. Hinrichs).

Walker, William O.
1975   '1 Cor. 11.2-16 and Paul's Views Regarding Women', *JBL* 94: 94-110.

Watson, F.B.
1986   *Paul, Judaism and the Gentiles: A Sociological Approach* (SNTSM, 56;
            Cambridge: University Press).
1994   *Text, Church and World* (Edinburgh: T. & T. Clark).
1997   *Text and Truth* (Edinburgh: T. & T. Clark).

Weir, Allison
1996   *Sacrificial Logics: Feminist Theory and the Critique of Identity* (New York:
            Routledge).

West, Angela
1995   *Deadly Innocence: Feminist Theology and the Mythology of Sin* (London: Mowbray; New York: Cassell).

Whitford, Margaret
1991   *Luce Irigaray: Philosophy in the Feminine* (London: Routledge).

Wilberforce, William
1797   *A Practical View of the Prevailing Religious System of Professed Christians in the Higher and Middle Classes of this Country, Compared with Real Christianity* (London: Caddell and Davies).

Wilkinson, S., and Kitzinger, C. (eds.)
1993   *Heterosexuality: A Feminism and Psychology Reader* (London: Sage).

Williams, Delores
1993   'Re-imagining Jesus' (paper presented at the Minneapolis Convention Centre, 5 November 1993).

Williams, Jane
1992   'The Doctrine of the Trinity: A Way Forward for Feminists?', in Teresa Elwes (ed.), *Women's Voices: Essays in Contemporary Feminist Theology* (London: Marshall Pickering): 31-43.

Wilson, Elizabeth, and Sik Hung Ng
1988   'Sex Bias in Visual Images Evoked by Generics: A New Zealand Study', *Sex Roles* 18: 159-68.

Wilson, James Q.
1993   *The Moral Sense* (New York: The Free Press).

Winston, David
1985   *Logos and Mystical Theology in Philo of Alexandria* (Cincinnati: Hebrew Union College Press).

Wire, Antoinette Clark
1990   *The Corinthian Women Prophets: A Reconstruction through Paul's Rhetoric* (Minneapolis: Fortress Press).

Witherington, III, B.
1980–81   'Rite and Rights for Women—Galatians iii.28', *NTS* 27: 593-604.

Wittgenstein, Ludwig
1967/1974   *Philosophical Investigations* (trans. G.E. Anscombe; Oxford: Basil Blackwell).
1969   *On Certainty* (Oxford: Basil Blackwell).

Wolff, Christian
1982   *Der erste Brief des Paulus an die Korinther. Zweiter Teil: Auslegung der Kapitel 8-16* (ThHK, 7.2; Berlin: Evangelische Verlaganstalt).

Woodhead, Linda
1997   'Spiritualising the Sacred: A Critique of Feminist Theology', *Modern Theology* 13.2: 191-212.
1999   'Theology and the Fragmentation of the Self', *International Journal of Systematic Theology* 1.1: 53-72.

Wright, N.T.
1991   *The Climax of the Covenant* (Edinburgh: T. & T. Clark; Minneapolis: Fortress Press).

Zizioulas, J.
1985   *Being as Communion: Studies in Personhood and the Church* (London: Dartman, Longman & Todd).

INDEXES

INDEX OF REFERENCES

BIBLE

OTHER ANCIENT REFERENCES